Lecture Notes of the Institute for Computer Sciences, Social Informatics and Telecommunications Engineering

481

The LNICST series publishes ICST's conferences, symposia and workshops. It reports state-of-the-art results in areas related to the scope of the Institute.

LNICST reports state-of-the-art results in areas related to the scope of the Institute. The type of material published includes

- Proceedings (published in time for the respective event)
- Other edited monographs (such as project reports or invited volumes)

LNICST topics span the following areas:

- General Computer Science
- E-Economy
- E-Medicine
- Knowledge Management
- Multimedia
- Operations, Management and Policy
- Social Informatics
- Systems

Xiaolin Jiang
Editor

Machine Learning and Intelligent Communication

7th EAI International Conference, MLICOM 2022
Virtual Event, October 23–24, 2022
Proceedings

 Springer

Editor
Xiaolin Jiang
Jinhua Advanced Research Institute
Jinhua, China

ISSN 1867-8211 ISSN 1867-822X (electronic)
Lecture Notes of the Institute for Computer Sciences, Social Informatics
and Telecommunications Engineering
ISBN 978-3-031-30236-7 ISBN 978-3-031-30237-4 (eBook)
https://doi.org/10.1007/978-3-031-30237-4

This Springer imprint is published by the registered company Springer Nature Switzerland AG
The registered company address is: Gewerbestrasse 11, 6330 Cham, Switzerland

Preface

We are delighted to introduce the proceedings of the seventh edition of the 2022 European Alliance for Innovation (EAI) International Conference on Machine Learning and Intelligent Communications (MLICOM). This conference brought together researchers, developers and practitioners from around the world who are leveraging and developing machine learning and intelligent communications.

The technical program of MLICOM 2022 consisted of 16 full papers in oral presentation sessions in the main conference tracks. The conference tracks were: Track 1 – Applications of Neural Network & Deep Learning; Track 2 – Intelligent Massive MIMO Communications; Track 3 – Machine Learning Algorithms & Intelligent Networks.

Coordination with the Steering Committee Chairs, Imrich Chlamtac, Xin Liu and Xin-Lin Huang, was essential for the success of the conference. We sincerely appreciate their constant support and guidance. It was also a great pleasure to work with such an excellent organizing committee team who worked hard in organizing and supporting the conference. The Technical Program Committee, led by our TPC Co-Chairs, Mingyuan Ren, Tian Han, and Changchun Dong, completed the peer-review process of technical papers and made a high-quality technical program. We are also grateful to the Conference Managers, Ivana Bujdakova and Lucia Sedlárová, Kristian Mockovciak, Lucia Sladeckova, for their support and to all the authors who submitted their papers to the MLICOM2022 conference and workshops.

We strongly believe that the MLICOM conference provides a good forum for all researchers, developers and practitioners to discuss all science and technology aspects that are relevant to machine learning and intelligent communications. We also expect that future MLICOM conferences will be as successful and stimulating, as indicated by the contributions presented in this volume.

December 2022   Xiaolin Jiang

Organization

Steering Committee

Imrich Chlamtac   University of Trento, Italy
Xin Liu   Dalian University of Technology, China
Xin-Lin Huang   Tongji University, China

Organizing Committee

General Chair

Xiaolin Jiang   Jinhua Advanced Research Institute, China

General Co-chairs

Haibin Wu   Harbin University of Science and Technology,
      China
Xiaohua Qiu   Jinhua Polytechnic, China

TPC Chairs and Co-chairs

Changchun Dong   Jinhua Advanced Research Institute, China
Mingyuan Ren   Jinhua Advanced Research Institute, China
Tian Han   Jinhua Advanced Research Institute, China

Sponsorship and Exhibit Chairs

Jianguo Shen   Zhejiang Normal University, China
Jin Wang   Wuzhou University, China

Local Chairs

Xinmin Xu   Zhejiang University, China
Jianguo Shen   Zhejiang Normal University, China
Jinxian Zhao   Heilongjiang University of Science and
      Technology, China

Workshops Chairs

Weidang Lu	Zhejiang University of Technology, China
Ping Gong	Wuzhou University, China
Xinmin Xu	Zhejiang University, China
Aili Wang	Harbin University of Science and Technology, China
Tian Han	Jinhua Advanced Research Institute, China
Guanghua Yu	Heihe University, China

Publicity and Social Media Chairs

Chengyu Wu	ZheJiang Sci-Tech University, China
Huadong Sun	Harbin University of Commerce, China
Qingjiang Yang	Heilongjiang University of Science and Technology, China

Publications Chairs

Guanghua Yu	Heihe University, China
Xinmin Xu	Zhejiang University, China

Web Chairs

Xiaolong Chen	Jinhua Polytechnic, China
Fugang Liu	Heilongjiang University of Science and Technology, China
Ping Gong	Wuzhou University, China

Posters and PhD Track Chairs

Hui Guo	Wuzhou University, China
Guang Hua Yu	Heihe University, China

Panels Chair

Chengyu Wu	ZheJiang Sci-Tech University, China

Demos Chair

Qining Yang	Jinhua Central Hospital, China

Tutorials Chair

Weidang Lu   Zhejiang University of Technology, China

Technical Program Committee

Dong Changchun   Jinhua Advanced Research Institute, China
Han Tian   Jinhua Advanced Research Institute, China
Mingyuan Ren   Jinhua Advanced Research Institute, China
Qingjiang Yang   Heilongjiang University of Science and
                            Technology, China
Gong Ping   Wuzhou University, China
Liu Fugang   Heilongjiang University of Science and
                            Technology, China
Sun Huadong   Harbin University of Commerce, China
Wang Aili   Harbin University of Science and Technology,
                            China
Chunying Fang   Heilongjiang University of Science and
                            Technology, China
Bao Peng   Shenzhen Institute of Information Technology,
                            China
Wang Jin   WuZhou University, China
Zhao Fujun   Heilongjiang University of Science and
                            Technology, China
Yu GuangHua   HeiHe University, China
Mo ZhiYi   WuZhou University, China
Li Zhijun   WuZhou University, China
Zhang WenXiang   WuZhou University, China
Zhao JinXian   Heilongjiang University of Science and
                            Technology, China
Guo Hui   WuZhou University, China
Guo Tieliang   WuZhou University, China
Jinxian Zhao   Heilongjiang University of Science and
                            Technology, China

Contents

Secure and Reliable Transmission via Intelligent Reflecting Surface Integrated on Unmanned Aerial Vehicle

Yijie Luo[✉], Zhifeng Hou, and Yang Yang

Army Engineering University of PLA, Nanjing, China
yijieluo@sina.com

Abstract. Wireless communication environment becomes more and more complex especially when facing vicious eavesdroppers and external jammers. Intelligent reflecting surface (IRS) can provide secure or anti-jamming communication approaches via passively reflecting with low power consumption and high cost efficiency. Unmanned aerial vehicle (UAV) also can be used to cooperatively transmit useful signals of legitimate users with vicious attackers. Carrying IRS on UAV can add new cooperative strategies, such as trajectory or height of UAV, numbers of reflecting elements or phase shift of IRS, to improve secure and anti-jamming performance of legitimate users. Two cooperative transmission schemes assisted with UAV and IRS are proposed to confront passive eavesdroppers or smart jammers in this paper. The first kind of cooperation is to select UAV relay or IRS reflecting strategy to improve energy efficiency of system with passive eavesdroppers. The second kind of cooperation is to jointly optimize phase shifts of IRS and trajectory of UAV to enhance transmission capacity with smart jammers. Simulation results show that, with the help of the cooperation of UAV and IRS, secure and reliable communications can be realized and system performance can be improved compared with no cooperation scheme or only one kind of cooperation with UAV or IRS scheme.

Keywords: UAV · IRS · cooperative transmission · physical layer security · smart jammers

1 Introduction

The electromagnetic environment becomes more and more terrible as numbers of wireless communication devices increasing dramatically, while vicious eavesdroppers and external jammers make matters worse. To countermeasure external jammers or vicious eavesdroppers in civil and military communications, traditionally, appropriate design of transceivers, such as pre-coding or artificial noise generated in transmitters, interference avoidance or elimination used in receivers, or cooperative relay and friendly jamming introduced by intermediate nodes [1] were adopted. Although these technologies above are available for enhance anti-jamming or anti-eavesdropping performance of legitimate users, extra devices and energy are consumed. Therefore, it is necessary to search

X. Jiang (Ed.): MLICOM 2022, LNICST 481, pp. 1–12, 2023.
https://doi.org/10.1007/978-3-031-30237-4_1

some more economical approaches to guarantee secure and reliable communications of legitimate users in complicated electromagnetic environment.

Intelligent reflecting surfaces (IRSs) can realize programming or reconfiguration of wireless spectrum environment by modifying electromagnetic parameters via reflecting coefficients or phase shifts [2, 3]. On one hand, IRSs just reflect the received signals passively, don't need to add extra devices, consume huge forward energy or increase signal processing costs, since it can improve cost efficiency, spectrum efficiency and energy efficiency [4, 5]. On the other hand, as introduced with IRSs, a new degree of freedom of optimization strategies for wireless communication performance is increased. IRSs can modify their reflecting coefficients to enhance transmission rates or achievable security rates through magnifying useful signals of legitimate users and weakening vicious jamming signals, or reducing leakage of secrecy information in the wiretapping direction. In other words, as IRSs introduced, wireless spectrum environment become a new optimizable strategy to confront jammers or eavesdroppers. Usually, IRSs are always deployed on the outside surface of fixed buildings or on motionless aerial platforms. It makes adjustable strategies of IRSs being limited, and can't cope with serious effects on mobility of legitimate users and block of tall buildings.

Unmanned aerial vehicles (UAVs) can play the roles of aerial base stations, aerial users or relay nodes in the future mobile communication systems. They have been drawn extensive attentions since there exists distinct line of sight (LOS) communication links between UAVs and terrestrial users with lower deployment and hover costs, and they can adjust their position and trajectory flexibly [6–9]. Integrated IRSs on UAVs in the cellular networks on the next generation mobile communications can promote communication performance, since it can not only make IRSs configure spectrum environment more flexible, but also increase probabilities of LOS with obstacles.

2 Review of Secure Anti-jamming Cooperative Transmission with IRSs and UAVs

Based on the characteristic of wireless spectrum environment reconfiguration of IRSs, there are many works studying anti-eavesdropping and anti-jamming problems with the help of IRSs. Furthermore, concurrently considering flexible mobility of UAVs and wireless spectrum environment reconfiguration of IRSs, several works discuss secure and anti-jamming cooperative transmission on UAV-borne IRS systems. In this section, we will survey on the anti-eavesdropping and anti-jamming transmission technologies under IRS-only and integrated IRS to UAV scenarios.

2.1 Secure Anti-jamming Cooperative Transmission on IRS-Assisted Wireless Systems

There are a series of works [10–16] consider physical layer security problems with the help of IRSs. For instance, in [10], on the situation that one receiver and one eavesdropper were in the same direction and the eavesdropper was closer to the transmitter than the receiver, both beamforming of the transmitter and reflecting coefficients of IRS were optimized to maximize the minimum secrecy achievable rate. In [11], supposed that the global channel state information (CSI) can be acquired by the access point (AP) and IRS, the beamforming coefficients were designed to transmit or reflect the useful signals to maximize the secrecy achievable rate. It was reasonable to suppose that the CSI related with the eavesdropper was available, since the eavesdropper was the inner user but not be trusted by the legitimate receiver. In [12], phase shift of the IRS, beamforming of the transmitter and pre-code parameters were jointly optimized to reach a tradeoff between energy efficiency and secrecy performance of legitimate users.

While in practice, it is impossible for legitimate users to acquire eavesdropping related CSI easily. Therefore, there were another series of works considering robust and secure communications on IRS-aided wireless systems without perfect CSI. In [13], supposed that there were multiple eavesdroppers with multi-antenna and their wiretapping CSI couldn't be achieved perfectly, considering the robust and secure communication of an IRS-aided multiple-input-single-output (MISO) system. On the condition that the maximum information leakage was lower than a threshold, both artificial noise beamforming of the transmitter and phase offsets of IRS were optimized to maximize system sum rate. Authors in [14] also considered an IRS-assisted massive antenna system with the statistic CSI, to maximize the ergodic spectrum efficiency, proposed an optimal phase offsets scheme. In [15], with errors of statistic CSI, to minimize the transmission power, the variance matrix of the artificial noise, beamforming of the transmitter and phase offsets of IRS were jointly optimized, and a robust and secure wireless communication scheme with the assistance of IRS was designed. Then in [16], without CSI of the eavesdropper, the physical layer security performance of the MISO communication system was studied, the secrecy rate was enhanced in the way of minimizing transmission power of the transmitter and optimizing power beamfoming of other devices to interfere eavesdroppers.

Since most of anti-eavesdropping problems on IRS-assisted wireless communication systems were not convex problems induced by joint optimization of phase offsets design of IRSs and beamforming of transmitters, there were some numerical optimization technologies were used [17, 18]. In [17], secure transmission problem of a multiple antenna system with the assistant of IRSs was considered, the active beamforming and passive phase offsets were jointly optimized to maximize the secrecy achievable rate. Authors in [17] made this non-convex optimization problem into a convex problem via semi-definite programming (SDP) relaxing and solved it by CVX tool in Matlab. And in [18], IRS was applied on physical layer security, supposed that a system model with a transmitter with multiple antenna, an eavesdropper and a receiver with single antenna, secrecy achievable rate was optimized by phase offsets of IRS and beamforming of the transmitter. The minorization maximization (MM) and block coordinate descent (BCD) approaches were used to obtain the suboptimal solution of the non-convex problem.

There are lots of researches on IRSs at the present, but most of them focus on transmission rate or secrecy achievable rate improvement, there are few researches on confronting smart jammers. Smart jammers, which are a kind of jammers can destroy legitimate communication while can conceal its position and modify its jamming strategies dynamically. On this situation, it is difficult for legitimate users to countermeasure them. In [19] and [20], authors employed deep reinforcement learning algorithms to enable legitimate users to obtain fast or optimal communication strategies without any characteristic of smart jammers.

2.2 Secure Anti-jamming Cooperative Transmission on UAV-Borne IRS Systems

It is benefit to deploy IRSs on the UAV. Firstly, it is probable to decrease transmission with obstacles on UAV communications. By integrated IRSs, multiple LOS channels can be generated through reflecting signals passively, communication between UAV and terrestrial users is enhanced. Secondly, IRSs can work on the full duplex mode without any self-interference. Thirdly, deploying IRSs on the UAV, the air-to-ground link sustains much lower channel fading than the ground-to-ground link, it means that energy consumption can be decreased drastically. Besides, the mobility of UAV can enable IRSs to adjust its deployment, and dynamic environment can be fully used to bring communication performance improvement of legitimate users.

In this section, some works on cooperative transmission scheme where IRSs is deployed on UAV are given. In [21], a new method was proposed to enhance communication performance of mmWave network by integrating IRSs on the UAV, the Q learning and neural network-based approaches were used to modify reflecting coefficients of IRSs and location of UAV to maximize downlink capacity. Simulation results showed that, deploying IRSs on UAV, both the average transmission rate and LOS communication probability had a large promotion compared with still IRSs. In [22], power allocation of the base station and passive reflecting coefficients of IRS were jointly designed to fulfill communication requirement of legitimate users. However, when users move dynamically, the fixed deployment of IRSs can't play a perfect role for anti-jamming. Therefore, instead dynamic deployment of static deployment, fixing IRSs on UAV and planning UAV's trajectory can enhance the anti-jamming performance further. Then in [23], with the imperfect CSI of eavesdropping link, trajectory of UAV, passive reflecting beamforming and active transmission power of legitimate users were jointly designed to improve the physical layer security performance. Authors in [24] thought that it was effective to confront passive eavesdroppers and smart jammers via integrating IRSs on UAV through their cooperation. On one hand, part of reflecting cells of IRS can adjust their phase offsets to generate counteractive reflecting signals to minimize eavesdropping signals at special position. On the other hand, the distance can be shortened through the free mobility of UAVs, and reflecting signals can be superimposed to the source signals through adjusting phase offsets of other IRS cells, eventually improve signal-to-noise-ratio (SNR) of legitimate users. In [25], on the constraint of sum transmission power budget, the secrecy achievable rate was maximized via jointly optimizing beamforming weight of the transmitter, reflecting coefficients of IRS and position adjustment of IRS brought by the mobility of UAV.

Several cooperative methods of UAV and IRS were discussed in [26] and three modes were proposed, they were only UAV as for relay node, only IRS as for reflecting node, and both UAV and IRS working as help nodes. In the third mode, the number of reflecting elements of IRS and height of UAV were jointly optimized to maximize spectrum efficiency and energy efficiency. In [27], the deployment height and distance to the base station of IRS were adjusted to enlarge coverage of cellular networks and throughout of UAV users. Authors in [28] investigated that dynamic mobility of UAV and software-controlled IRS could be used to enhance security performance, and maximize the secrecy rate via jointly optimizing phase offsets of IRS and transmission power and position of UAV.

Because it is hard to find close expressions of optimization problems on IRS integrated UAV wireless system, machine learning methods are usually used. To enhance the secrecy achievable rate with smart jammers on an IRS-assisted communication system, authors in [22] designed a fuzzy win or learn fast-policy hill-climbing (WoLFCPHC) algorithm to meticulously design the transmission power of the base station and the reflecting coefficients of IRS. In [29], based on proximal policy optimization (PPO), a deep reinforcement learning framework was proposed to learn the activity randomness of internet of thing (IoT) devices, phase offsets of IRS and communication schedule were jointly optimized to minimize expected sum AoI (ESA). And in [30], a novel deep reinforcement learning enabled method was proposed to deploy UAV with IRS to promote downlink transmission performance in mmWave networks.

3   Cooperation Mechanism Designs and Numerical Results Discussion

We have mentioned that it was benefit for cooperative transmission with IRS-integrated UAV systems above. Therefore, we discuss the scheme that IRSs are deployed on the UAV, and furthermore they can cooperate with each other to improve secure and reliable communication performance of terrestrial mobile users. In this section, we introduce two cooperation mechanisms of UAV and IRS.

3.1   Cooperation Mode Design of IRS and UAV

The first one is cooperation mode design, such as relaying of UAV and reflecting of IRS. As shown in Fig. 1, considering that there is a base station, a terminal user, a passive eavesdropper and a UAV-carried IRS. There are two modes for communication enhancement, such as UAV relaying and IRS reflecting. On one hand, UAV relaying can obtain higher gains compared with IRS reflecting, while may bring the probability of being wiretapped. On the other hand, IRS reflecting only consumes lower power with passive reflecting elements to bring higher energy efficiency. Therefore, it is available to cooperate with UAV and IRS to forward the source signals to enhance security performance and energy efficiency simultaneously.

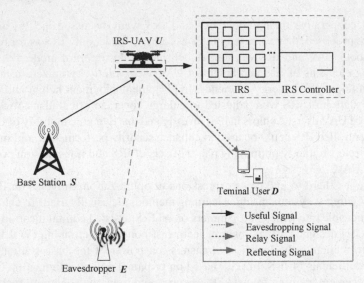

IRS-UAV U

IRS   IRS Controller

Base Station S

Teminal User D

→ Useful Signal
----▶ Eavesdropping Signal
- - -▶ Relay Signal
→ Reflecting Signal

Eavesdropper E

Fig. 1. System model of secure cooperative transmission with a passive eavesdropper on IRS-integrated UAV system

Specifically, through two cooperation mode design, such as UAV relaying and IRS reflecting, two joint strategies optimization, such as transmission power of UAV and numbers of IRS reflecting elements, energy efficiency of the system is maximized under the secrecy capacity constraint.

We set that the base station is located on the original point, the terminal user and the eavesdropper are located on coordinates with [1000, 0] and [2000, 0] respectively, and the height of UAV is 150 m for simulation. Suppose that the air-to-ground link suffers LOS pass-loss with a probability and Rician channel fading related to the urban environment, and the related wireless environment parameters are obtained by [31–33]. In Fig. 2 and 3, we can see that the energy efficiency first increase as transmission power of UAV and numbers of IRS reflecting elements, then decrease. Therefore, there exists an optimal transmission power of UAV and optimal number of IRS reflecting elements. As shown in Fig. 4, we can see that through jointly designing both of them, energy efficiency of system will be boosted enormously.

3.2   Cooperative Strategy Optimization of IRS and UAV

The second cooperative scheme is considering UAV as a carrying tool and IRS as the reflecting device, cooperating UAV and IRS in another way to realize secure and reliable communications for legitimate users. As shown in Fig. 5, we suppose there exists a smart jammer, a base station, a terminal user and an IRS carried on the UAV. We jointly optimize phase offsets of IRS and the trajectory of UAV to improve anti-jamming performance of terrestrial users. Since the attacking strategy of the smart jammer can't be obtained by legitimate users, we formulate the optimization problem as a Markov decision process and solve it via a 3-DQN multi-step learning algorithm in [34].

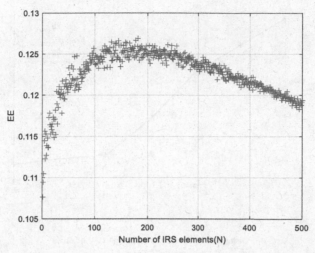

Fig. 2. Energy efficiency versus numbers of IRS elements with a passive eavesdropper

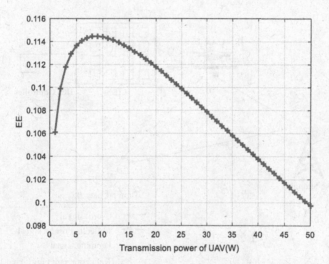

Fig. 3. Energy efficiency versus transmission power of UAV with a passive eavesdropper

As illustrated in Fig. 5, we consider that the base station and the terminal user are located on the original point and [1000, 1000], while there are three position sets of the smart jammer, such as [200, 500], [500, 500], and [800, 500], respectively. Depending [35], we suppose that our scenario meets the requirement of large-IRS far-field free space model. We compare the anti-jamming performance of joint optimization versus jamming

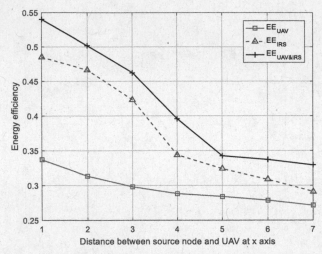

Fig. 4. Energy efficiency under different algorithms with a passive eavesdropper

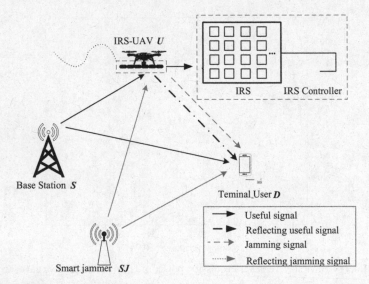

Fig. 5. System model of reliable cooperative transmission with a smart jammer on IRS-integrated UAV system

power and versus three different positions of the smart jammer in Fig. 6 and Fig. 7. In Fig. 6, we can see that the achievable rate under the algorithm we proposed outperforms the ones under other compared algorithms. It is verified that, by jointly designing phase shifts of IRS and trajectory of UAV, the performance for confronting smart jammers can be improved. And in Fig. 7, it is shown that whether the position of the smart jammer is, our proposed algorithm always has the best performance comparing to other strategies.

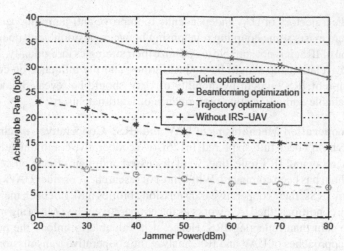

Fig. 6. Achievable rate under different algorithms versus jammer power of the smart jammer

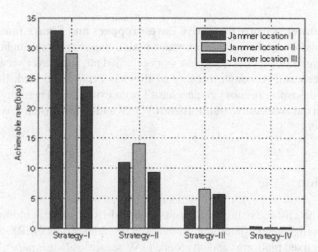

Fig. 7. Achievable rate under different algorithms versus position of the smart jammer

4 Future Research Directions

We have surveyed some works on IRS-assisted wireless system and IRS-integrated UAV communication system, and provide two cooperative schemes for IRS and UAV with passive eavesdroppers and smart jammers. We find that researches on anti-eavesdropping and anti-jamming problems with UAV and IRS are still in infancy, there are many open issues should be deeply studied.

Joint Optimization Designs of UAV and IRS: Some works have considered that mobility of IRS deployed on UAV, while the influence on strategy adjustment of IRS is rarely involved. Part of works mentioned that carrying IRS on UAV could increase adjustment flexibility of reflecting coefficients, and other works optimized phase offsets of IRS and the trajectory of UAV independently to improve anti-jamming performance. However, there exists some coupling relationship between position adjustment of UAV and deflection of IRS, it is not suitable to optimize their strategies individually. Therefore, their coupling relationship should be studied further, and the influence on cooperative communication of IRS brought by mobility of UAV should be revealed, and enhance secure and reliable communication performance of legitimate users.

Practical Cooperation Mechanisms of UAV and IRS: Cooperative mechanism of UAV and IRS hasn't been fully explored. In [26], two cooperative communication modes, such as UAV relay and IRS reflecting, were discussed and their effects on cellular network throughout has been compared. While most of researches consider UAVs as carriers used to deploy IRSs, their cooperative transmission abilities have not been mentioned. In fact, on some conditions, the UAV, works as the cooperative relay, can bring much more performance gain than reflecting IRS. Hence, it is valuable to unlock the potential of cooperative approaches of UAV and IRS, analyze the cooperative transmission effect on system capacity and physical layer security and jointly optimize cooperative strategies of UAV and IRS.

Intelligent Countermeasure for Active Eavesdroppers and Smart Jammers: At the present, most of works focused on transmission capacity or throughout improvement via integrated IRS on UAV, and few works studied physical layer security problem on the same scenario. Although mobility of IRS has been mentioned, flexibility and intelligence of eavesdroppers or jammers hasn't been expressed. Therefore, it is significant to research the cooperative transmission of UAV and IRS with active eavesdroppers or smart jammers.

5   Conclusion

We introduce the characteristics of UAV-assisted and IRS-assisted communication for anti-eavesdropping and anti-jamming, analyze the research results of IRS-assisted communications on fixed platforms and on mobile UAV scenarios in this paper. We also provide two use cases of secure and reliable cooperative communications on IRS-integrated UAV system for confronting passive eavesdroppers and smart jammers. Numerical results verify that cooperative mode design and cooperative strategy optimization can effectively enhance secure and reliable communication performance of legitimate users. Finally, open issues and conclusions are drawn.

References

1. Wei, Z., Masouros, C., Liu, F., Chatzinotas, S., Ottersten, B.: Energy- and cost-efficient physical layer security in the era of IoT: the role of interference. IEEE Commun. Mag. **58**(4), 81–87 (2020)
2. Wu, Q., Zhang, R.: Towards smart and reconfigurable environment: intelligent reflecting surface aided wireless network. IEEE Commun. Mag. **58**(1), 106–112 (2020)

3. Hu, S., Rusek, F., Edfors, O.: Beyond massive MIMO: the potential of positioning with large intelligent surfaces. IEEE Trans. Signal Process. **66**(7), 1761–1774 (2018)
4. Gong, S., et al.: Toward smart wireless communications via intelligent reflecting surfaces: acontemporary survey. IEEE Commun. Surveys & Tutorials **22**(4), 2283–2314 (2020)
5. Wu, Q., Zhang, R.: Weighted sum power maximization for intelligent reflecting surface aided SWIPT. IEEE Wirel. Commun. Lett. **9**(5), 586–590 (2020)
6. Gupta, L., Jain, R., Vaszkun, G.: Survey of important issues in UAV communication networks. IEEE Commun. Surv. Tutor. **18**(2), 1123–1152 (2016)
7. Motlagh, N.H., Taleb, T., Arouk, O.: Low-Altitude unmanned aerial vehicles-based internet of things services: comprehensive survey and future perspectives. IEEE Internet Things J. **3**(6), 899–922 (2016)
8. Hillman, J.L., Jones, S.D., Nichols, R. A., Wang, I.J.: Communications network architectures for the army future combat system and objective force. In: MILCOM 2002. Proceedings, Anaheim, CA, USA, vol. 2, pp. 1417–1421 (2002)
9. Matolak, D.W.: Unmanned aerial vehicles: communications challenges and future aerial networking. In: 2015 International Conference on Computing, Networking and Communications (ICNC), Garden Grove, CA, USA, pp. 567–572 (2015)
10. Chen, J., Liang, Y.-C., Pei, Y., Guo, H.: Intelligent reflecting surface: aprogrammable wireless environment for physical layer security. IEEE Access **7**, 82599–82612 (2019)
11. Cui, M., Zhang, G., Zhang, R.: Secure wireless communication via intelligent reflecting surface. IEEE Wirel. Commun. Lett. **8**(5), 1410–1414 (2019)
12. Wang, Q., Zhou, F., Hu, R.Q., Qian, Y.: Energy efficient robust beamforming and cooperative jamming design for IRS-assisted MISO networks. IEEE Trans. Wirel. Commun. **20**(4), 2592–2607 (2021)
13. Yu, X., Xu, D., Sun, Y., Ng, D.W.K., Schober, R.: Robust and secure wireless communications via intelligent reflecting surfaces. IEEE J. Sel. Areas Commun. **38**(11), 2637–2652 (2020)
14. Han, Y., Tang, W., Jin, S., Wen, C., Ma, X.: Large intelligent surface-assisted wireless communication exploiting statistical CSI. IEEE Trans. Veh. Technol. **68**(8), 8238–8242 (2019)
15. Hong, S., Pan, C., Ren, H., Wang, K., Chai, K.K., Nallanathan, A.: Robust transmission design for intelligent reflecting surface aided secure communication systems with imperfect cascaded CSI. IEEE Trans. Wirel. Commun. **20**(4), 2487–2501 (2021)
16. Wang, H.-M., Bai, J., Dong, L.: Intelligent reflecting surfaces assisted secure transmission without eavesdropper's CSI. IEEE Signal Process. Lett. **27**, 1300–1304 (2020)
17. Chu, Z., Hao, W., Xiao, P., Shi, J.: Intelligent reflecting surface aided multi-antenna secure transmission. IEEE Wirel. Commun. Lett. **9**(1), 108–112 (2020)
18. Yu, X., Xu, D., Schober, R..: Enabling secure wireless communications via intelligent reflecting surfaces. In: 2019 IEEE Global Communications Conference (GLOBECOM), Waikoloa, HI, USA, pp. 1–6 (2019)
19. Liu, S., et al.: Pattern-aware intelligent anti-jamming communication: a sequential deep reinforcement learning approach. IEEE Access **7**, 169204–169216 (2019)
20. Wu, Q., Zhang, R.: Beamforming optimization for wireless network aided by intelligent reflecting surface with discrete phase shifts. IEEE Trans. Commun. **68**(3), 1838–1851 (2020)
21. Zhang, Q., Saad, W., Bennis, M.: Reflections in the sky: millimeter wave communication with UAV-carried intelligent reflectors. In: 2019 IEEE Global Communications Conference (GLOBECOM), Waikoloa, HI, USA, pp. 1–6 (2019) •
22. Yang, H., et al.: Intelligent reflecting surface assisted anti-jamming communications: a fast reinforcement learning approach. IEEE Trans. Wirel. Commun. **20**(3), 1963–1974 (2021)
23. Li, S.-X., Duo, B., Renzo, M.-D., et al.: Robust secure UAV communications with the aid of reconfigurable intelligent surfaces (2020). https://arxiv.org/abs/2008.09404
24. Abdalla, A.-S., Rahman, T.-F., Marojevic, V.: UAVs with reconfigurable intelligent surfaces: applications, challenges, and opportunities (2020). arXiv:2012.04775v1

25. Nnamani, C.-O., Khandaker, M.-R., Sellathurai, M.: Joint beamforming and location optimization for secure data collection in wireless sensor networks with UAV-carried intelligent reflecting surface (2020). arXiv:2101.06565
26. Shafique, T.-Y., Tabassum, H., Hossain, E.: Optimization of wireless relaying with flexible UAV-borne reflecting surfaces. IEEE Trans. Commun. **69**(1), 309–325 (2021)
27. Ma, D., Ding, M., Hassan, M.: Enhancing cellular communications for UAVs via intelligent reflective surface. In: 2020 IEEE Wireless Communications and Networking Conference (WCNC), pp. 1–6 (2020)
28. Wang, W., Tian, H., Ni, W.-L., Hua, M.-H.: Intelligent reflecting surface aided secure UAV communications (2020). arXiv:2011.04339
29. Samir, M., Elhattab, M., Assi, C., Sharafeddine, S., Ghrayeb, A.: Optimizing age of information through aerial reconfigurable intelligent surfaces: a deep reinforcement learning approach. IEEE Trans. Veh. Technol. **70**(4), 3978–3983 (2021)
30. Zhang, Q., Saad, W., Bennis, M.: Distributional reinforcement learning for mmWave communications with intelligent reflectors on a UAV. In: GLOBECOM 2020 - 2020 IEEE Global Communications Conference, Taipei, Taiwan, pp. 1–6 (2020)
31. Al-Hourani, A., Kandeepan, S., Lardner, S.: Optimal LAP altitude for maximum coverage. IEEE Wirel. Commun. Lett. **3**(6), 569–572 (2014)
32. Al-Hourani, A., Gomez, K.: Modeling cellular-to-UAV path-loss for suburban environments. IEEE Wirel. Commun. Lett. **7**(1), 82–85 (2018)
33. Azari, M.M., Rosas, F., Chen, K., Pollin, S.: Ultra reliable UAV communication using altitude and cooperation diversity. IEEE Trans. Commun. **66**(1), 330–344 (2018)
34. Hou, Z.-F., Chen, J., Huang, Y.-Z., et al.: Joint trajectory and passive beamforming optimization in IRS-UAV enhanced anti-jamming communication networks. China Commun. Mag. **19**, 191–205 (2021). https://doi.org/10.23919/JCC.2021.00.001
35. Tang, W., Chen, M.-Z., Chen, X., et al.: Wireless communications with reconfigurable intelligent surface: path loss modeling and experimental measurement. IEEE Trans. Wirel. Commun. **20**(1), 421–439 (2021)

An Improved Dynamic Spectrum Access Algorithm Based on Reinforcement Learning

Chen Zhong[1] , Chutong Ye[2] , Chenyu Wu[2(✉)] , and Ao Zhan[2]

[1] School of Computer Science and Technology, Zhejiang Sci-Tech University,
Hangzhou 310018, People's Republic of China
[2] School of Information Science and Engineering, Zhejiang Sci-Tech University,
Hangzhou 310018, People's Republic of China
jerry916@zstu.edu.cn

Abstract. This paper proposes an improved dynamic spectrum access algorithm based on reinforcement Learning in cognitive radio networks. Q-learning algorithm is used as the core to update the optimal strategy for the established Markov decision process according to specific scenarios, and Q-table is updated iteratively to improve the learning rate. In order to verify the effectiveness of the proposed algorithm, we construct the mathematical model and the simulation environment. The simulation results validate the effectiveness of the proposed algorithm, which can effectively improve the system throughput under the condition that not affect primary users' communication. The proposed algorithm can quickly adjust the corresponding reward value and strategy in the iterative process of reinforcement learning training, so as to quickly converge to the optimal strategy, and the training results are consistent with the expected results.

Keywords: Dynamic spectrum access · Reinforcement learning · Q-Learning · Cognitive radio networks

1 Introduction

At a time when the number of mobile subscribers worldwide is growing, the available licensed spectrum is limited. In this regard, the new spectrum management scheme can not only meet the communication needs of the new generation of mobile communication technology with high bandwidth and low delay, but also solve the problem of scarce spectrum resources and the risks and even crises that spectrum management may face in the future [1]. Dynamic spectrum access in cognitive radio technology is the key entry point [2]. At the beginning of the

Supported by the Fundamental Research Funds of Zhejiang Sci-Tech University under grant 2021Q029.

21st century, the theory of dynamic spectrum access has been perfected after more than ten years of research, and the traditional dynamic spectrum access technology model has gradually taken shape [5]. At present, dynamic spectrum access technology based on reinforcement learning theory is the main direction to solve the current resource limitation problem, and it is also the inevitable trend of future spectrum allocation strategy, which is also the significance of this paper [3,4].

In [6,7], the authors combined Deep Q-Network (DQN) with dynamic spectrum access technology and verified that the system throughput and the network utilization were significantly improved. For the combination of reinforcement learning theory and traditional single-agent learning, domestic researchers put forward a new multi-agent distributed learning and centralized strategy theory [8–10]. Based on the DQN algorithm, the optimization of the algorithm and the improvement of the strategy by domestic researchers have further improved the communication effect of dynamic spectrum access [11–14].

This paper mainly studied the design and implementation of dynamic spectrum access algorithm based on reinforcement learning. By setting up training environment and adjusting training strategy and return, the q-table corresponding to channel state of single cognitive user in random spectrum environment close to the real environment was obtained, and the q-table obtained by training was taken as the core of the system. A dynamic spectrum access system algorithm based on Q-learning is constructed.

1.1   Dynamic Spectrum Access Technology

Dynamic spectrum access technology does not apply to primary users who are authorized to use a fixed frequency band by the spectrum resource management party, but to secondary users who are not authorized to use this frequency band, which is also called unauthorized users. After resource allocation, the users who can legally preferentially use this frequency band are called the authorized users of this frequency band, namely primary users (PUs). Unauthorized users who are not authorized are usually called cognitive users (CUs) or secondary users (SUs). cognitive users can carry out unauthorized communication when the authorized frequency band produces spectrum holes. Therefore, the biggest challenge faced by dynamic spectrum access technology is how to reduce the interference caused by unauthorized communication to the original authorized frequency band of primary users when the cognitive user accesses the unauthorized frequency band.

As shown in Fig. 1, after each cycle, the secondary system senses the environment and captures the corresponding frequency band information to learn about the current environment status and use these parameters to select and plan access policies. The basic principle of machine learning is that the agent obtains the current environmental information in the external environment, makes judgments and decisions according to the obtained information, and stores the environmental information and decisions in the knowledge base for updating, so as to achieve the effect of interacting with the environment, feeding back to the knowledge base and making decisions.

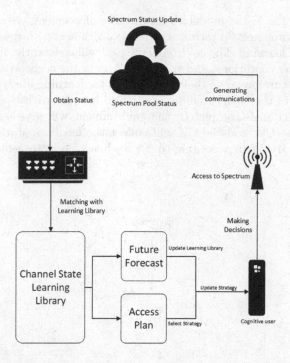

Fig. 1. Dynamic spectrum access System concept diagram.

1.2   Reinforcement Learning

As the most widely used and important branch of machine learning, reinforcement learning is inspired by psychology. Its main content is to focus on how CUs take different strategies and take different actions in different environments according to different environmental states, so as to obtain the highest possible returns.

Reinforcement learning was first born in psychology, and in principle, it is an algorithm evolved according to the adaptability of humans or other animals to the environment. In reinforcement learning theory, an interaction between an CU and the environment will generally affect the current environment, and this influence is the feedback obtained by the CU. How to judge whether the interaction is appropriate requires judgment based on the feedback of the environment, which is the common "reward". Generally speaking, the reward value representing the feedback is positive or negative, and the greater the absolute value of the reward, the greater the impact of the interaction. After multiple interactions with the environment, the rewards obtained from each interaction will be recorded in the learning module of the CU, which will be continuously updated, accumulated and optimized. Finally, after completing a certain degree of learning, the reward values of interactions under different environmental states will be formed in the learning module. In theory, the higher the reward value, the higher the probability of choosing an action in such an environmental state, so as to select the optimal and avoid mistakes [15].

As shown in Fig. 2, the model structure of reinforcement learning is divided into CU and environment in terms of objects, which are the largest components of reinforcement learning. The environment itself will constantly update its state with time or other conditions, and the CU will make the decision with the greatest theoretical return based on the experience in the learning library according to the observation of the environmental state, and interact with the environment. After the interaction is completed, the environment will give feedback to the interaction of the CU, and the CU will collect the feedback status and update the learning library again according to the feedback, so as to achieve a learning cycle.

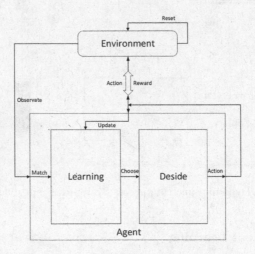

Fig. 2. Structure diagram of reinforcement learning model.

According to the above, reinforcement learning is essentially a process of multiple interactions to achieve the learning effect. In a single reinforcement learning process, there are five steps to complete an interaction:

- Step 1: According to the current environment, obtain the environmental state of the current CU, and extract various parameters required by this reinforcement learning from the obtained state.
- Step 2: The state parameters obtained in step 1 are combined into a set, which is consistent with the state set type set in the learning library. The state set is matched with the states in the learning library to select the strategy for this state, which contains the actions to be carried out by the CU in the current state.
- Step 3: After selecting the actions to interact with the environment according to the strategy, the CU starts to interact with the environment. For the environment, if an CU performs an action, it will have an impact on the environment, that is, the result and feedback under the action will be generated. At this point, the environment status, the environment feedback, will be updated.

- Step 4: After the environment status and feedback are updated, the ai obtains the environment status and feedback again. If there is an interaction with the environment, the feedback is extracted and recorded, and if there is no interaction with the environment, only the updated environment state is retrieved.
- Step 5: Update the feedback to the learning library in the form of rewards, that is, give a "positive" and "negative" feedback result to the interaction. The reward update after each interaction makes the environment-action strategy in the learning library constantly updated, so that the standard can be referred to when the environment state is obtained next time, so as to achieve the learning effect.

In addition, after introducing the basic principle of reinforcement learning, the classification of reinforcement learning is also the key content of reinforcement learning. For reinforcement learning, it can be divided into reinforcement learning with model and reinforcement learning without model from the perspective of environment model. The biggest difference between the two is whether an CU needs to interact with the environment to explore the environment state.

Generally speaking, model-free reinforcement learning is more widely used at present. Compared with model-free reinforcement learning, modeling reinforcement learning has the advantages of higher generalization ability and stronger sampling efficiency. Once the environment model is established, the CU can even break away from the actual model to some extent and train in the environment model, and then put into the actual scene after learning. Common Model reinforcement learning algorithms include World Model, Alpha Zero and so on. Model free of intensive study, although from the learning efficiency will be slightly lower than there are models of reinforcement learning, but it has the best performance steps, namely when the strategy and the environment interaction gradually achieve convergence condition, no model than reinforcement learning with a model of reinforcement learning as a result, the strategic choice, more outstanding, especially the application in the actual situation, Model-free reinforcement learning performs better in avoiding compounding problems. Under the classification of model-free reinforcement learning, it can also be divided into two categories, namely, reinforcement learning based on value optimization and reinforcement learning based on strategy optimization. For the difference of the two, reinforcement learning based on value optimization is usually applied to discrete environment, according to the value of every action is updated, learning, and determine the next action, and reinforcement learning based on strategy optimization is often applied to the continuous action space, and the state after discretization, action dimension higher environment, in this premise, to reduce the learning cost, Figuring out the probability of the next action to choose the best strategy is reinforcement learning based on strategy optimization. Generally speaking, the more common value-based reinforcement Learning includes Q-learning, SARSA, DQN, etc., while the strategy-based reinforcement Learning includes PPO and TRPO. The detailed classification of reinforcement learning is shown in Fig. 3.

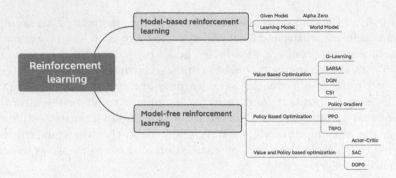

Fig. 3. Types of reinforcement learning algorithms.

2 Dynamic Spectrum Access Algorithm Based on Reinforcement Learning

2.1 Reinforcement Learning Algorithm

The main principle of reinforcement learning is to keep trying in the process of interaction with the environment, and then conduct the next interaction according to the reward, so as to form the learning of the environment. Model-free reinforcement learning can also be divided into value optimization based reinforcement learning and strategy optimization based reinforcement learning. The more common algorithms in model-free reinforcement Learning based on value optimization include Q-learning, DQN and SARSA(State-Action-Reward-State-Action). Among them, Q-learning is the most classical and earliest model, and it has good effectiveness and coverage while being less difficult to implement.

The purpose of Q-learning is to obtain more suitable solutions to the problems corresponding to different models established by Markov decision process under different environmental conditions. In markov decision making, the environment models are discretized in time, and the states are discretized into finite dimensional tuples. Generally speaking, Markov decision process model is expressed as M, and expressed as $M = (S, A, T, R,)$, where the components of M are also called "quintuples", which are:

- S: $S = \{S_1, S_2, S_3, \cdots, S_n\}$ represents the set of environment states.
- A: $A = \{A_1, A_2, A_3, \cdots, A_n\}$ represents the action set that CU can select.
- R: R represents the reward obtained by the CU after executing the action.
- T: $T : S \times A \to [0, 1]$ represents the state transition probability between the environment and the CU.
- π: π represents the result and is usually expressed as the optimal policy.

Compared with Markov decision process model, the most important thing of Q-learning is the addition of Q-table, that is, Q Table. Generally, in Q-learning algorithm, the interaction results of state S and action A are expressed and stored in the form of matrix. The interaction result, i.e., reward R, is the performance and reward degree of each action under different finite discrete states. For each state, the return values of different actions are calculated and then become a new quantization standard, namely Q-value, which is stored in Q-Table. The Q-value calculation formula is as follows:

$$\pi Q'(S_t, a) = (1 - \alpha) * Q(S_t, a) + \alpha * [R + \gamma * Q_{\max}(S_{t+1},)] \tag{1}$$

In addition to the quintuple described above, there are several key parameters in Formula (1), which are:

- α: Learning rate of Q-learning, that is, the updating degree of Q-value after each Learning.
- γ: discount factor, which takes into account expected future return in addition to current return after performing an action.

In addition, parameters such as greed rate θ and limit index also play a key role. Under the influence of greed rate θ, the action selection of an CU will not only cover the most current situation, but also cover the overall action as far as possible in different environments, so as to find the optimal solution among all solutions and avoid falling into local optimum [16].

According to the characteristics of Q-learning, the selection of actions and strategies in Q-learning is based on values, namely Q-value, which is stored in a list named Q-table. A Q-table generally has multiple dimensions, and each dimension divides states in a discrete form. In this paper, Q-table has a total of four dimensions, including state three dimension and action one dimension. The state three dimensions are the internal influencing factors of frequency band: bandwidth and signal to noise ratio, and the external influencing factors: interference rate. One dimension of action is the corresponding effect of two actions "communication" and "non-communication" made by the CU, and the communication and non-communication are directly regarded as the action set of the CU.

For the primary user in the unauthorized frequency band, the interference rate should be as low as possible. As shown in Table 1, when the interference rate is higher than 40%, the reward obtained by CU is negative and positively correlated with the interference rate. If the CU chooses to stop communication knowing that the interference rate of the unauthorized frequency band is greater than 40%, the reward obtained will not become 0. When the interference rate is lower than 40%, the CU chooses to communicate with the unauthorized frequency band to obtain the reward and the interference rate is negatively correlated. If the interference rate is lower than 40%, the reward of the CU ending the communication with the unauthorized frequency band will be smaller than the reward of generating the communication.

Table 1. CU performs the main rules of action reward.

Interference rate of unauthorized frequency band (%)	Communication reward	Non-communication reward
0–40	Positive	Negative
40–100	Negative	Zero

Meanwhile, the q-value update rule is optimized. After optimization, the updated q-value of the action will be updated not only in the action in the environment state, but also in the action selected by the initial environment Value. That is, since the interference rate and noise ratio in the training environment are affected by the previous state, and in the system, access is only determined by the initial Value of the system state before access, q-value will be updated in the initial value and present value positions.

2.2 Dynamic Spectrum Access Algorithm

As shown in Fig. 4, the whole dynamic spectrum access structure is divided into two parts: dynamic spectrum access module and the corresponding reinforcement learning module. The reinforcement Learning module contains the learning environment required by reinforcement Learning, the core algorithm Q-learning and the corresponding Q-table. Dynamic spectrum access module includes DSA algorithm and DSA environment. The DSA environment includes authorized frequency band status and unauthorized frequency band status. The CU obtains the status of authorized frequency band and unauthorized frequency band, and according to the Learning results of Q-learning, accesses the unauthorized frequency band for communication on the premise of not affecting the primary user as much as possible.

In the system, we assume that the communication quality is low when the interference rate of authorized frequency band exceeds 70% and the SNR is less than 16 dB; the communication quality is extremely low and the communication is considered invalid when the interference rate exceeds 85% and the SNR is less than 10 dB. When the communication quality is low, if the status of the authorized frequency band is not ideal, and the status of the unauthorized frequency band does not meet the accessibility requirements, the CU will not forcibly access the unauthorized frequency band, and will continue to use the authorized frequency band for communication.

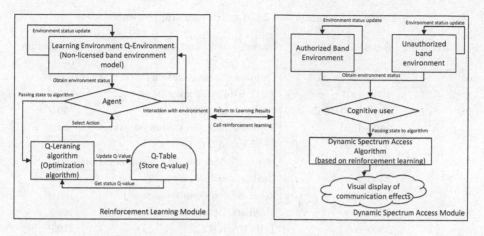

Fig. 4. Environment model parameter structure.

3   Simulation Analysis and Results

3.1   Simulation Environment Setting

To simplify the channel, the main elements included in the environment model will be set as interference rate, noise ratio and channel bandwidth, as well as the parameters used to reflect the communication quality: average interference rate, SNR and communication throughput.

The authorized band environment is based on the realistic domestic three major operators mobile, Unicom or telecom civil wireless communication operator bands, and the static spectrum allocation strategy is used, and the band environment parameters are shown in Table 2.

Table 2. Authorized band environmental parameters.

Authorized Band No	Band (MHz)	Authorized band name	Bandwidth
0	1745–1765/1840–1860	China Unicom FDD-LTE	42.5
1	2575–2635	China Mobile 4G TD-LTE	45.0
2	1765–1780/1860–1875	China Telecom FDD-LTE	40.0

The unlicensed band environment is based on a realistic domestic unlicensed wireless communication frequency bands selected from ten bands with different bandwidths, and the band environment parameters are shown in Table 3.

The initial interference rate is set as a Gaussian distributed random number with mean 0.5 and variance 0.17, and the mean interference rate at a later moment is a Gaussian distributed random with the same variance of 0.17 as the interference rate at the previous moment, and is re-randomized when it is greater than 1 or less than 0. The noise rate is set to a Gaussian-distributed

Table 3. Unauthorized band environmental parameters.

Unauthorized Band No.	Band (MHz)	Unauthorized band name	Bandwidth
0	885–890/930–935	Railroad Communication	10.0
1	1400–1427	Earth Satellite Exploration	27.0
2	1965–1980/2155–2170	Unallocated FDD	30.0
3	1626–1660	Maritime Satellite Communication	34.0
4	2655–2690	Unallocated TD-LTE	35.0
5	1660–1710	Meteorological satellite communication	50.0
6	2400–2483.5	Unallocated ISM	83.5
7	2025–2110	Fixed station communication I	85.0
8	2200–2300	Fixed station communication II	100.0
9	3400–3600	TDD BAND42	110.0

random number with a mean value of the median of the communication quality midpoint and a variance of 0.08 at each moment.

For non-authorized frequency band, set the initial interference rate for the mean value of 0.3, variance of 0.08 Gaussian distribution of random numbers, the latter moment interference rate mean value of the previous moment interference rate variance of the same 0.08 Gaussian distribution of random, re-random in greater than 1 or less than 0. The noise rate as above, but set its mean value at each moment for through wireless communication standard signal-to-noise ratio communication quality median, variance of 0.02 Gaussian-distributed random number.

3.2 Analysis of Simulation Results

In the simulation, DSA represents the proposed dynamic spectrum access system for communication based on reinforcement learning, while Tradition represents the communication via traditional static spectrum allocation.

As shown in Fig. 5(a), the communication interference rates are all lower than 70%, which is in line with the expected communication interference rate target. The large jump in the interference rate in the communication is because when the interference rate of the authorized band is high, if the interference rate is higher than 70% at the next moment, the band will be selected from the unauthorized band for communication. As shown in Fig. 5(b), the average signal-to-noise ratio of this system gradually converges to 19.26 dB, which indicates a relatively excellent communication quality according to the Chinese mobile communication signal-to-noise ratio standard. As shown in Fig. 5(c), the communication throughput of this system gradually stabilizes at 400 bps, and as shown in Fig. 5(d), there is no invalid communication time in the communication process, which ensures the continuity of communication.

Figure 6 gives the performance comparison between DSA and Tradition. As shown in Fig. 6(a), it can be seen that the average interference rate using tra-

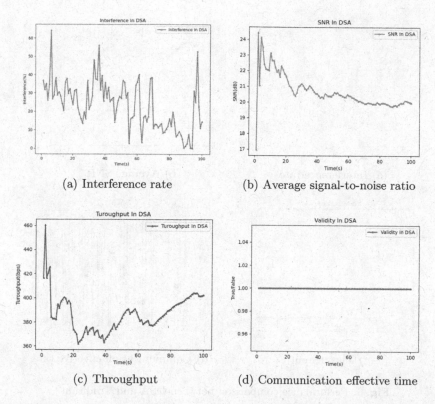

(a) Interference rate

(b) Average signal-to-noise ratio

(c) Throughput

(d) Communication effective time

Fig. 5. Performance of the proposed DSA algorithm based on reinforcement learning

ditional static spectrum allocation communication is 47.159%, while the average interference rate of dynamic spectrum access algorithm communication is 23.275%, which proves the effectiveness of the algorithm in improving the interference rate. Figure 6(b) shows the signal-to-noise ratio comparison graph. According to the domestic mobile communication standard, 12.8 dB signal-to-noise ratio is near the midpoint of communication quality, and 19.9 dB signal-to-noise ratio has been the midpoint of good communication quality. It can be seen from the graph that the signal-to-noise ratio of this system has been greatly improved compared with the traditional method, which proves that the algorithm can effectively improve the signal-to-noise ratio. As shown in Fig. 6(c), it can be seen that since the CU can access to the unauthorized band for communication when the quality of the authorized band is not satisfactory, it effectively improves the communication throughput of the algorithm, which is almost 2–3 times of the traditional method. As can be seen from Fig. 6(d), during the communication process, there is no invalid communication under this system, while the communication efficiency under the static spectrum allocation strategy is only 58%, so the proposed DSA algorithm can effectively improve the communication continuity.

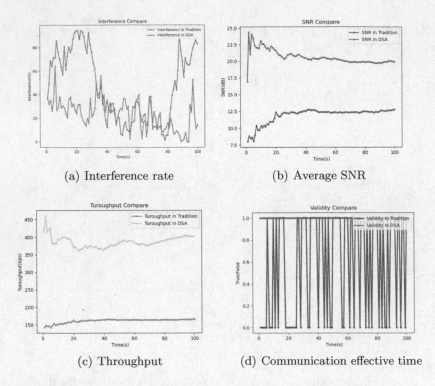

(a) Interference rate

(b) Average SNR

(c) Throughput

(d) Communication effective time

Fig. 6. Performance comparison between DSA and Tradition

4   Conclusion

Aiming at the classical dynamic spectrum access technology algorithm based on Q-learning algorithm, this paper realizes and optimizes the original algorithm, and builds a simulation system environment model on the premise that the default hardware can obtain the real frequency state, and verifies the effectiveness of the system algorithm in the form of simulation. The overall system effect is about 90% similar to the expected effect, and the communication quality is tested, including interference rate, signal-to-noise ratio, etc., and the effectiveness of the algorithm is verified. Finally, the communication effect is visually compared with that of the traditional static spectrum allocation algorithm, which implies that the proposed DSA algorithm can quickly adjust the corresponding reward value and strategy in the iterative process of reinforcement learning training, and also achieve better performance.

References

1. Li, C., Jian, S.: Research on dynamic spectrum allocation in high mobile wireless communication network. Comput. Integr. Manuf. Syst. **37**(10): 124–127+146 (2020)
2. Song, T., Zhang, D., Chen, Z., Hang, X.: Spectrum allocation of cognitive wireless sensor network based on residual energy. Chin. J. Sens. Actuators **32**(12), 1875–1880 (2019)
3. Mekuria, F., Mfupe, L.: Spectrum sharing for unlicensed 5G networks. In: IEEE Wireless Communications and Networking Conference (WCNC), pp. 1–5 (2019)
4. Oyewobi, S.S., Hancke, G.P., Abu-Mahfouz, A.M., et al.: An effective spectrum handoff based on reinforcement learning for target channel selection in the industrial Internet of Things. Sensors **19**(6), 1395–1416 (2019)
5. Hu, F., Chen, B., Zhu, K.: Full spectrum sharing in cognitive radio networks toward 5G: a survey. IEEE Access **6**, 15754–15776 (2018)
6. Nguyen, H.Q., Nguyen, B.T., Dong, T.Q., et al.: Deep Q-learning with multiband sensing for dynamic spectrum access. In: Proceedings of International Symposium on Dynamic Spectrum Access Networks, pp. 1–5. IEEE, Seoul (2018)
7. Han, Z., Lei, T., Lu, Z., et al.: Artificial intelligence-based handoff management for dense WLAN: a deep reinforcement learning approach. IEEE Access **7**, 31688–31701 (2019)
8. Zhang, L., Liang, Y., et al.: 6G visions: mobile ultra-broadband, super internet-of-things, and artificial intelligence. China Commun. **16**(8), 1–14 (2019)
9. Luong, N.C., Hoang, D.T., Gong, S., et al.: Applications of deep reinforcement learning in communications and networking: a survey. IEEE Commun. Surv. Tutorials **21**(4), 3133–3174 (2019)
10. Karmakar, R., Chattopadhyay, S., Chakraborty, S.: Dynamic link adaptation in IEEE 802.11AC: a distributed learning based approach. In: IEEE 41st Conference on Local Computer Networks (LCN), pp. 87–94. IEEE, Dubai (2016)
11. Xiao-hua, W.: Dynamic spectrum access technology for cognitive wireless communication. Inf. Technol. **44**(11), 137–141 (2020)
12. Zhou, X., Chen, Y., Zhang, Y., He, P.: Multi-channel access dynamic spectrum allocation under hybrid spectrum sharing mode. Commun. Technol. **54**(11), 2518–2526 (2021)
13. Le, T., Tao, L., Zhang, Yu., Pengzhi, Q.: Dynamic spectrum allocation method based on multi-agent reinforcement learning. J. Terahertz Sci. Electron. Inf. Technol. **19**(04), 573–580 (2021)
14. Zhang, Y., Zhou, Y.: Dynamic spectrum access algorithm based on Q-learning. Natural Science Journal of Hainan University (2018)
15. Liu, Q., et al.: A survey on deep reinforcement learning. Chin. J. Comput. **41**(01), 1–27 (2018)
16. Bin, M., Haibo, C., Chao, Z.: Network selection algorithm based on improved deep Q-learning. J. Electron. Inf. Technol. **44**(1), 346–353 (2022). https://doi.org/10.11999/JEIT200930

Inception Resnet V2-ECANet Based on Gramian Angular Field Image for Specific Emitter Identification

Zibo Ma[1] , Chengyu Wu[1](✉) , Chen Zhong[2] , and Ao Zhan[1]

[1] School of Information Science and Engineering, Zhejiang Sci-Tech University, Hangzhou 310018, People's Republic of China
jerry916@zstu.edu.cn
[2] School of Computer Science and Technology, Zhejiang Sci-Tech University, Hangzhou 310018, People's Republic of China

Abstract. In this paper, we seek to efficiently and accurately identify the specific emitter with the DroneRF dataset. Firstly, we convert one-dimensional data to a Gramian Angular Field (GAF) image showing a spatial correlation, and add three kinds of noise to the original GAF image to prevent overfitting. Secondly, we propose an Inception-Resnet-V2 model based on the attention mechanism ECANet, which can improve the training effect obviously. Finally, we verify the validation and accuracy of the proposed model with GAF in the experimental results. Test accuracy of Inception Resnet V2-ECANet reaches 99.5% by using the same training set of five networks through 10-fold cross-validation.

Keywords: Specific Emitter Identification · Gramian Angular Field · Convolutional Neural Network · Inception Resnet V2-ECANet

1 Introduction

Specific emitter identification (SEI) is an essential research content in the field of electromagnetic spectrum confrontation [1], and is widely used in military applications in electronic reconnaissance, intelligence, communication confrontation, and other fields [2]. SEI is to compare the radio frequency fingerprint (RFF) in the signals received by the receiver to detect and identify the radiation source.

In [3], CNN is utilized to classify the Radio Frequency (RF) signals transmitted during the real-time communication session between the UAV and its controller. In [4], the authors use Discrete Fourier Transform (DFT) to extract features from the low-frequency RF signal of UAV to flight controller communication in the dataset, utilize the XGBoost model, and use 10-fold cross-validation

Supported by the Fundamental Research Funds of Zhejiang Sci-Tech University under grant 2021Q029.

X. Jiang (Ed.): MLICOM 2022, LNICST 481, pp. 26–38, 2023.
https://doi.org/10.1007/978-3-031-30237-4_3

to evaluate the model. The average accuracy of UAV detection, UAV type identification, and UAV flight mode identification is 99.96%, 90.73%, and 70.09%, respectively. The RF signal is subjected to discrete DFT as the input of the network in [5]. The intrinsic feature maps of RF signals are gathered from three different types of UAVs through the deep convolution layer. In [6], two Fully Connected Neural Networks (FCNNs) and two CNNs were mentioned and trained. In [7], the authors propose using high-performance CNN to detect and classify UAVs effectively. In [8], an integrated learning method for improving UAV identification and detection is proposed, which is composed of KNN and XGBoost learning methods. In [9], the authors prove the effectiveness of the selection of compressed sensing technology and multi-channel random demodulation for data sampling. Multi-stage DL UAV identification and detection method are proposed based on the difference in communication signals between UAV and controller in unusual situations. Two neural network structures (DNN and CNN) are constructed by the DL algorithm and are evaluated and verified by 10-the fold cross-validation method. The accuracy of detecting UAVs, and identifying UAV types and their flight modes is above 99%.

In [10], the author introduces a DL model of a multi-channel one-dimensional convolutional neural network (1-DCNN). This model consists of two parts, one is a feature extractor for learning features from the original data, and the other is Multilayer Perceptron (MLP) which performs a classification function through the features learned in the first part. On this basis, the RF signal is transformed into the frequency band of the spectrum for network training. The performance of the 1-DCNN proposes in the literature is significantly better than that of the DNN technology for UAV type and state identification introduced in [11]. The average accuracy of the first model for the two classifications is 100%. The second model for the four classifications is 94.6%, and the last model for every class is 87.4%.

In [12], the VGG16 neural network is used to evaluate the classification results of UAVs by Logistic Regression (LR), Support Vector Machine (SVM), and random forest. The results demonstrate that the network input for higher power spectrum density (PSD) image classification accuracy is higher. The accuracy rate of UAV detection is 100%. UAV types classification is 88.6%, and ten categories containing flight modes are 87.3%. In [13], the author regards UAV detection as an image classification problem. PSD, Spectrogram, Histogram, and Raw IQ constellation diagram are available in network input to CNN ResNet50 for feature extraction and classification. The results are verified by cross-validation and independent dataset, and the accuracy of the input PSD diagram in 10 classifications exceeds 91%.

In summary, the current research on the detection of UAVs and the identification of UAV types is better. So the contemporary task requires an in-depth study of the UAV flight pattern classification tasks. In [4, 7–9, 11–13] all carry out similar tasks for UAV flight modes. To identify the different flight modes of the three UAVs more accurately based on the theories and methods in the above literature, the CNN model for effectively identifying the different flight modes of the three

UAVs is obtained by changing the input form of the network model, expanding the dataset, and training multiple neural networks for multiple verifications.

In this paper, we explore extracting the spatial correlation with CNN for the input data firstly, and convert each one-dimensional signal data to a GAF image, by adding three kinds of noise to the GAF image to prevent overfitting. Then, we propose an improved Inception-Resnet-V2 network with three ECANet attention mechanisms to optimize the network performance. Finally, we study the proposed network with VGG16, Resnet18, Resnet50, Inception-Resnet-V2, and Inception Resnet V2-ECANet. The results demonstrate that the proposed network can achieve higher accuracy than others.

2   The Network Structure Formation

The designed network structure is given in Fig. 1, which is composed of data pre-processing, improved Inception Resnet V2-ECANet model, 10-fold cross-entropy verification, and classification.

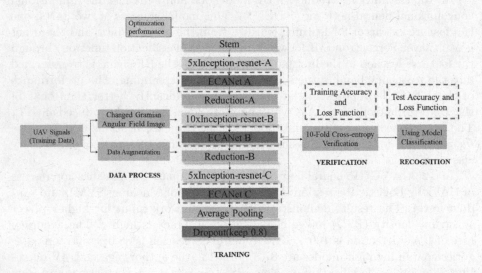

Fig. 1. Overall Structure

The spatial connection of images is based on the correlation between pixels. The local pixel correlation is accurate, while the far pixel correlation is weak. The image of GAF is the calculation of eccentric covariance between features, which expresses the correlation between data features and reflects the tightness between data. It is reasonable to convert the one-dimensional signal data into the GAF image as the input of the CNN, which avoids the complex process and effectively extracts the corresponding features from a large number of data. The increase in depth is not hard to cause over-fitting due to the insufficient training data, which makes the model unable to complete sufficient training. To ensure that the training data is vast and the sample of each type of data is balanced through data enhancement, the quality and quantity of the original data are improved without a substantial increase in the dataset.

In order to better fit the characteristic network layer, it is necessary to be deep enough to ensure the reasonable use of calculation effective and reasonable training time. The deeper the network is, the more intricate features will be learned through a nonlinear expression. This network is improved based on the Inception Resnet V2 network. In addition, under the current constraints of computer computing resources, an attention mechanism is absolutely a necessary means to improve the effectiveness. ECANet is an improvement attention mechanism. The original Inception-Resnet-V2 is improved by adding the ECANet module.

2.1   GAF Image

GAF image is the visualization of the Gram matrix which is regarded as an eccentric covariance matrix between features. Then Gram calculates the correlation between two features to upgrade the classification accuracy of the model [14]. The main process of conversion is to convert a one-dimensional signal sequence into a polar coordinate representation and generate a GAF matrix with trigonometric function.

Step 1: First of all, the dimension reduction of Piecewise Aggregation Approximation (PAA) piecewise aggregation approximation is needed. PAA always satisfies the lower bound condition. The formula is shown as (1), (2), (3), and the sequence length n is used to aggregate the time series by taking the average value of point M.

$$\bar{x}_i = \frac{M}{n} \sum_{j=n/M(i-1)+1}^{(n/M)i} x_j \tag{1}$$

$$\bar{y}_i = \frac{M}{n} \sum_{j=n/M(i-1)+1}^{(n/M)i} y_j \tag{2}$$

$$D_{PAA}(\bar{X}, \bar{Y}) \equiv \sqrt{\frac{n}{M}} \sqrt{\sum_{i=1}^{M} (\bar{x}_i - \bar{y}_i)} \tag{3}$$

Step 2: Normalization is carried out to reduce the signal value between $[-1, 1]$ or $[0, 1]$, and the formula is as follows:

$$\tilde{x}_{-1}^i = \frac{x_i - \max(X) + (x_i - \min(X))}{\max(X) - \min(X)} \tag{4}$$

Or

$$\tilde{x}_0^i = \frac{x_i - \min(X)}{\max(X) - \min(X)} \tag{5}$$

Step 3: Use the timestamp N as the radius, the scaling value in Step 2 is used as the angle chord to generate the polar coordinates to provide the angle to get the new time series X. The formula is as follows :

$$\phi = \arccos(\tilde{x}_i), -1 \leq \tilde{x}_i \leq 1, \tilde{x}_i \in \tilde{X} \tag{6}$$

$$r = \frac{t_i}{N} \tag{7}$$

t is a timestamp that is a constant factor to adjust the polar coordinates.

Step 4: Generate GASF and calculate the value of each pixel. The formula is as following:

$$GASF = \cos(\phi_i + \phi_j) \tag{8}$$

After the above four steps, a total of 22700 grid GAF graphs can be obtained. In Fig. 2, GAF images of ten signals in the dataset are shown. One signal for each type is viewed as a display.

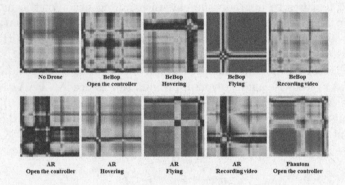

Fig. 2. Representation of each type of UAV signal converted to a GAF

2.2   Noise Adding for GAF Images

Based on prior experience, a network with deeper layers is needed to extract subtle features. However, the small amount of original data is not difficult to cause over-fitting, so it is necessary to carry out data enhancement and expansion to increase the number and diversity of training samples. By using the image processing method, more data images are generated on the limited data images to reinforce the generalization ability of the model. The method is to add random noise, Gaussian noise, and salt and pepper noise to 22700 images converted from one-dimensional data to two-dimensional images. As showm in Fig. 3.

Random noise is generated by the accumulation of a large number of random fluctuations generated randomly in time. The excessive number of noise points

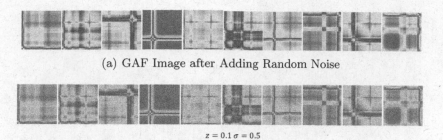

(a) GAF Image after Adding Random Noise

$z = 0.1\,\sigma = 0.5$

(b) GAF Image after Adding Gaussian Noise with Mean of 0.1 and Variance of 0.5

$SNR = 0.8$

(c) GAF Image Adding Salt And Pepper Noise With SNR=0.8

Fig. 3. Three noises are added to each signal for data enhancement.

will lead to a larger gap between the original image and the image after adding noise. As shown in Fig. 3(a).

The probability density of Gaussian noise obeys Gaussian distribution. The probability density expression is:

$$P(z) = \frac{1}{\sqrt{2\pi}\sigma} e^{-(z-\bar{z})^2/2\sigma^2} \tag{9}$$

where σ is the standard deviation of z, and $\bar{z}$ is the mean. The brightness of the image is determined by the mean value. The larger the variance, the more dispersed the data, and the more noise, as shown in Fig. 3(b).

Salt and pepper noise in the image of random black-white pixels is a kind of noise caused by signal pulse intensity. Signal-to-noise ratio SNR needs to be specified, followed by random access to each pixel position to be added noise, and finally, the pixel value is specified as 255 or 0, as shown in Fig. 3(c).

2.3 The Improved Inception Resnet V2-ECANet

The improved inception Resnet V2-ECANet consists of three parts, namely the Resnet [15]module, Inception [16], and ECANet [17], one of the three attention mechanisms. The main principle is to upgrade the Inception-Resnet-V2 [18]network and add the ECANet module of attention mechanism after three Inception Resnet modules in the Inception-Resnet-V2 network.

As shown in Fig. 4, the input size of the Stem module in the main structure is 3×3 in the Inception-Resnet-V2. Three convolutions, maximum pooling, two convolutions, and final stacking are required after input. Replacing stems with convolutive pooled sequential connection is intended to design deeper networks.

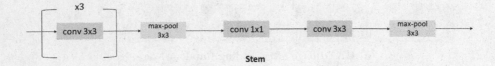

Fig. 4. Stem Module in Main Structure

Three Inception-Resnet blocks in the backbone structure are the most important. The module structure is given in Fig. 5. The Inception-resnet module introduces ResNet layers in the Inception module. The different structure helps to accelerate convergence and prevent gradient dispersion. The Inception module solves the use and pooling operation of the network self-determined filter. The module uses $1 \times n$ and $n \times 1$ instead of $n \times n$ convolution to reduce the amount of calculation.

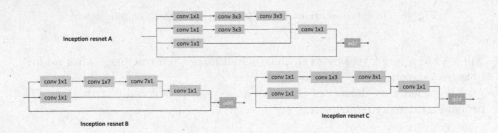

Fig. 5. Inception-resnet module in Main Structure

ECANet module is inserted after each Inception-Resnet module, as showed in Fig. 6. ECANet is an improvement of SENet [19]. ECANet utilizes the satisfactory cross-channel capability of convolution.

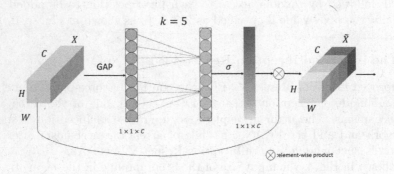

Fig. 6. ECANet Network Structure

The convolution kernel k of 1D convolution is called the coverage rate of cross-channel interaction, which is extremely significant for the number of channels to be considered in the weight calculation of the attention mechanism. When the model is implemented, select the convolution kernel size k. The coverage of a cross-channel interaction is proportional to the number of filters C. There exists a mapping φ between k and C.

$$C = \phi(k) \tag{10}$$

$\varphi(k)$ can be regarded as a linear function, then

$$\phi(k) = r * k - b \tag{11}$$

C is usually $2 \wedge n$, let $n = r * k - b$, then

$$C = \phi(k) = 2^{(r*k-b)} \tag{12}$$

$$k = \psi(C) = \left| \frac{\log_2(C)}{r} + \frac{b}{r} \right|_{odd} \tag{13}$$

where $= \frac{\log_2(C)}{r} + \frac{b}{r}$, $|t|_{odd}$ denotes the nearest odd number to t and $r = 2, b = 1$.

There are also two Reduction modules in the main structure, as shown in Fig. 7. The convolution structure of the observable module is used many times. One of the reasons can be reduced dimension operation. The second reason is that after adding nonlinear incentives, the expression ability of the network is enhanced. On the premise of keeping the scale of the feature map unchanged, the nonlinear characteristics are greatly increased. It can increase the overall network depth and extract more detailed features.

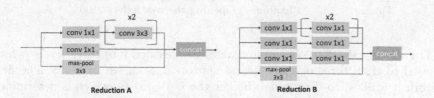

Fig. 7. Reduction Module in Main Structure

In addition, the core structure of the network is more complex, with more parameters. The global average pooling layer greatly reduces the network parameters and prevents overfitting. The Dropout layer is also designed to prevent overfitting.

This shows that since ECANet does not change the dimensions of input and output after increasing. ECANet is inserted after each module. However, in order not to increase network complexity as much as possible, attention mechanism is introduced to optimize network performance only after three important Inception-Resnet modules in the network structure.

3   Experiment

The model of training and testing DL methods needs an appropriate dataset. In [20], an open-source DroneRF dataset generated in the laboratory is constructed from three brands of UAV (AR, Bepop, Phantom), collected four flight modes: opening and connecting to the controller, automatic hovering, no video recording flight, and video recording flight signal respectively, and collected the radio frequency background signal without UAV, as shown in Table 1. The DroneRF dataset has taken advantage of by many papers and has a high use value. The dataset is stored in Comma Separated Values (CSV) format to facilitate loading. The network calculation loss is large, so it is necessary to train in a configured GPU environment. In the experimental setting, we utilize Tensorflow 2.5 with GPU RTX3060Ti in Ubuntu 18.04.

Table 1. The specific content of the DroneRF dataset.

UAV Detection	UAV Type	UAV Flight Mode	Segments
No Drone	No Drone	No Drone	4100
Drone	Bebob	Opening the controller	2100
Drone	Bebob	Hovering	2100
Drone	Bebob	Flying	2100
Drone	Bebob	Recording video	2100
Drone	AR	Opening the controller	2100
Drone	AR	Hovering	2100
Drone	AR	Flying	2100
Drone	AR	Recording video	1800
Drone	Phantom	Opening the controller	2100

The RF signals of UAVs in the dataset are divided into three levels, which are used to train three different neural networks, as shown in Fig. 8. The first network is utilized to determine whether the UAV exists, which is determined as a binary classification problem. The second network is used to determine the type of UAV, which is determined by four classification problems. The third network is used to identify the UAV flight mode and determine the appropriate class of problems. Given the high accuracy of the two and four classifications in the existing research results, that is, the full text mainly discusses the ten categories.

This experiment verifies the performance of Resnet18, Resnet50, Inception V3, Inception-Resnet-V2, and Inception Resnet V2-ECANet by a Tenfold cross validation. The cross-entropy loss function is as follows:

$$Loss = -\sum\nolimits_{i=1}^{10} y_i \times \log_2(\hat{y}_i) \tag{14}$$

In (14), y_i represents the type i probability of the true label, and $\hat{y}_i$ represents the type i probability predicted by the model.

The flight pattern classification ability of the five networks in the dataset is 20 epochs of the same iteration and the same dataset are applied. The test accuracy is 96.76%, 94.26%, 51.84%, 99.4% and 99.5%, respectively. As shown in Fig. 9, clearly illustrates the specific training accuracy and test accuracy of each network for 20 epochs, and its training loss function and test loss function. It is observed from Fig. 9 that the proposed Inception Resnet V2-ECANet network and Inception-Resnet-V2 have reached stability after 20 training epochs. Inception Resnet V2-ECANet has reached 99.5% accuracy and remained stable after the fourth training epoch, while Inception-Resnet-V2 has reached 99.4% and remained stable after the eighth training epoch.

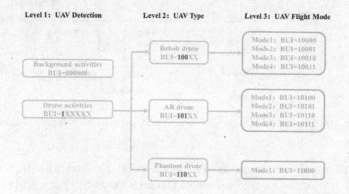

Fig. 8. Signal Distribution for Three Classifications

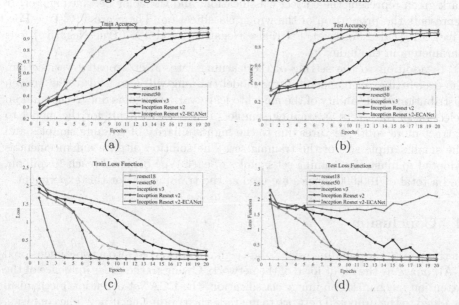

Fig. 9. Accuracy and Loss performance of the proposed network compared with others.

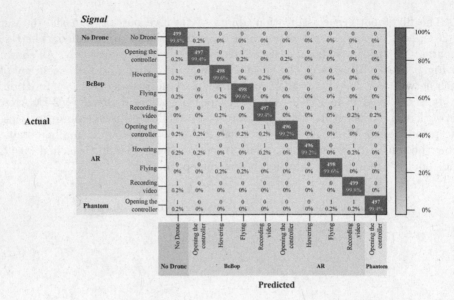

Fig. 10. Confusion Matrix of Prediction Model. (Color figure online)

Figure 10 represents a confusion matrix used to discriminate UAV flight modes. The row of the matrix represents the prediction category, and the column of the matrix represents the actual category. The cells showing the diagonal of dark green represent the correct classification, and the color becomes lighter. It represents the proportion of the wrong classification. There are TP (True Positive), FP (False Positive), FN (False Negative), and TN (True Negative) four parameters in the index.

In addition to the setting of the learning rate, after repeated verification, the over-fitting phenomenon in the model training will also lead to the uneven distribution of the ability of the model to learn various signals due to the random selection of data sets as training samples. It will be difficult for the model to extract more subtle features due to the high similarity of training samples and the small sample size of the training set. The solution of data enhancement is adopted to make the training set samples of each type of signal reach 10 million, and a total of 100,000 images are used as the training set for this experiment.

4   Conclusion

In this paper, the one-dimensional data signal is converted into a two-dimensional GAF image as the input form of the network. Owing to the great influence of the attention mechanism on image classification, the ECANet attention mechanism is added to the proposed network to upgrade the training accuracy. The confusion matrix shows that the proposed inception Resnet V2-ECANet network model with a complex structure has the best prediction effect. The trained Inception

Resnet V2-ECANet network effectively classifies the nine RF signals and RF scene signals of UAV flight mode, and the accuracy rate can reach 99.5%. In future work, straightforward complexity models should be utilized to reduce the training time without reducing the model performance for SEI.

References

1. Huang, G., Yuan, Y., Wang, X., Huang, Z.-T.: Specific emitter identification for communications transmitter using multi-measurements. Wirel. Pers. Commun. **94**(3), 1523–1542 (2017)
2. Sa, K., Lang, D., Wang, C., Bai, Yu.: Specific emitter identification techniques for the Internet of Things. IEEE Access **8**, 1644–1652 (2020)
3. Al-Emadi, S., Al-Senaid, F.: Drone detection approach based on radio-frequency using convolutional neural network. In: 2020 IEEE International Conference on Informatics, IoT, and Enabling Technologies (ICIoT), pp. 29–34 (2020)
4. Medaiyese, O.O., Syed, A., Lauf, A.P.: Machine learning framework for RF-based drone detection and identification system. In: 2021 2nd International Conference on Smart Cities, Automation & Intelligent Computing Systems (ICON-SONICS), pp. 58–64 (2021)
5. Akter, R., Doan, V.-S., Lee, J.-M., Kim, D.-S.: CNN-SSDI: convolution neural network inspired surveillance system for UAVs detection and identification. Comput. Netw. **201**, 108519 (2021)
6. Basan, E.S., Tregubenko, M.D., Mudruk, N.N., Abramov, E.S.: Analysis of artificial intelligence methods for detecting drones based on radio frequency activity. In: 2021 XV International Scientific-Technical Conference on Actual Problems of Electronic Instrument Engineering (APEIE), pp. 238–242 (2021)
7. Huynh-The, T., Pham, Q.-V., Nguyen, T.-V., Costa, D.B.D., Kim, D.-S.: RF-UAVNET: high-performance convolutional network for RF-based drone surveillance systems. IEEE Access **10**, 49696–49707 (2022)
8. Nemer, I., Sheltami, T., Ahmad, I., Ul-Haque Yasar, A., Abdeen, M.A.R.: RF-based UAV detection and identification using hierarchical learning approach. Sensors **21**(6), 1947 (2021)
9. Mo, Y., Huang, J., Qian, G.: Deep learning approach to UAV detection and classification by using compressively sensed RF signal. Sensors **22**(8), 3072 (2022)
10. Allahham, Mhd.S., Khattab, T., Mohamed, A.: Deep learning for RF-based drone detection and identification: a multi-channel 1-D convolutional neural networks approach. In: 2020 IEEE International Conference on Informatics, IoT, and Enabling Technologies (ICIoT), pp. 112–117 (2020)
11. Al-Sa'd, M.F., Al-Ali, A., Mohamed, A., Khattab, T., Erbad, A.: RF-based drone detection and identification using deep learning approaches: an initiative towards a large open source drone database. Futur. Gener. Comput. Syst. **100**, 86–97 (2019)
12. Swinney, C.J., Woods, J.C.: Unmanned aerial vehicle flight mode classification using convolutional neural network and transfer learning. In: 2020 16th International Computer Engineering Conference (ICENCO), pp. 83–87 (2020)
13. Swinney, C.J., Woods, J.C.: Unmanned aerial vehicle operating mode classification using deep residual learning feature extraction. Aerospace **8**(3), 79 (2021)
14. Wang, Z., Oates, T.: Imaging time-series to improve classification and imputation, pp. 3939–3945 (2015)

15. He, K., Zhang, X., Ren, S., Sun, J.: Deep residual learning for image recognition. In: 2016 IEEE Conference on Computer Vision and Pattern Recognition (CVPR), pp. 770–778 (2016)
16. Szegedy, C., et al.: Going deeper with convolutions. In: 2015 IEEE Conference on Computer Vision and Pattern Recognition (CVPR), pp. 1–9 (2015)
17. Wang, Q., Wu, B., Zhu, P., Li, P., Zuo, W., Hu, Q.: ECA-Net: efficient channel attention for deep convolutional neural networks, pp. 11531–11539 (2020)
18. Szegedy, C., Ioffe, S., Vanhoucke, V., Alemi, A.A.: Inception-V4, inception-ResNet and the impact of residual connections on learning, pp. 4278–4284 (2017)
19. Jie, H., Shen, L., Albanie, S., Sun, G., Enhua, W.: Squeeze-and-excitation networks. IEEE Trans. Pattern Anal. Mach. Intell. **42**(8), 2011–2023 (2020)
20. Allahham, M.H.D.S., Al-Sa'd, M.F., Al-Ali, A., Mohamed, A., Khattab, T., Erbad, A.: DroneRF dataset: a dataset of drones for RF-based detection, classification and identification. Data Brief **26**, 104313 (2019)

Automated Metal Surface Defect Detection

Chi Wee Tan[1]([⊠]) [iD], Joren Mundane Antequisa Pacaldo[1] [iD], Wah Pheng Lee[1],
Gloria Jennis Tan[2] [iD], Siaw Lang Wong[3], and Jun Kit Chaw[4] [iD]

[1] Faculty of Computing and Information Technology, Tunku Abdul Rahman University of
Management and Technology, 53300 Setapak, Kuala Lumpur, Malaysia
chiwee@tarc.edu.my
[2] Faculty of Computer and Mathematical Sciences, Universiti Teknologi MARA, Cawangan
Terengganu, 21080 Kuala Terengganu, Terengganu, Malaysia
[3] HELP International School, 40150 Shah Alam, Selangor, Malaysia
[4] Institute of IR4.0, Universiti Kebangsaan Malaysia (UKM), 43600 Bangi, Selangor, Malaysia

Abstract. Product defect detection is one of the essential steps in quality control
to ensure product safety. Inspection needs to be conducted regardless of during
or at the end of the manufacturing process to ensure all products complies with
specification and requirements. In-process defect detection is conducted to identify any deviations or defects in the product to ensure all pieces are consistent
and safe to use. However, manual quality inspection procedures are often time-
consuming, expensive, and prone to errors especially for manufacturers that conduct large-scale production on a daily basis. Hence, many industries have started
to leverage and incorporate technologies such as IoT devices, Computer Vision,
Artificial Intelligence and Deep Learning in the manufacturing process for a more
robust and efficient defect detection system. This project aims to identify the most
suitable image segmentation method for patch defect and scratch defect respectively and accurately localize the patch defect on metal surfaces and evaluated
using Intersection over Union (IoU). In this project, a total of 3 image segmentation methods are attempted namely threshold-based segmentation, edge-based
segmentation and clustering techniques are implemented and compared for detecting patch and scratch defects. We successfully identified that the threshold-based
segmentation method is more suitable for patch defects whereas the edge-based
segmentation method is more suitable for scratch defects. Among the attempted
threshold-based segmentation, namely simple thresholding, adaptive thresholding and Otsu's Binarization, we discovered that the best technique to detect patch
defects is Otsu's Binarization.

Keywords: product defect · manufacturing · scratches · patches

1 Introduction

Computer vision has come a long way in terms of its capabilities, and it is being applied
in manufacturing industry [1]. As one of the main raw materials of industrial products,
metal will inevitably be damaged on its surface such as patches and scratches due to

© ICST Institute for Computer Sciences, Social Informatics and Telecommunications Engineering 2023
Published by Springer Nature Switzerland AG 2023. All Rights Reserved
X. Jiang (Ed.): MLICOM 2022, LNICST 481, pp. 39–49, 2023.
https://doi.org/10.1007/978-3-031-30237-4_4

inappropriate process and storage. Most of the time, metal defects are visible on the surfaces. Patches are usually formed when unfinished metals are not properly and evenly coated. When this happens, moistures penetrate the coating and get locked under the finish, causing oxidation to occur. The oxidation of metal will possibly lead to rusting and corrosion, an irreversible damage to the metal surface if left untreated [2–4]. Besides, scratches are produced by friction or crushing of metal against other materials during the manufacturing process [5]. It could lower the product strength due to the disruption of the fixed metal molecule structure.

It is crucial to eliminate defective metals because of several reasons. Despite the fact that metal surfaces with patches and scratches are not suitable to be used on the outer appearance of certain products, the quality of the metal is the key concern. Patches and scratches both contribute to the shortening of metal durability. Scratches are also the possible signs of metal fatigue. The damage of the metal surface will seriously affect the quality and appearance of products, leading to serious consequences such as adverse industrial accidents.

However, in traditional manual inspection, there will be problems such as missed detection and low efficiency under the influence of human subjective factors. In this prototype, we propose a machine vision algorithm to facilitate this process. The key direction of this prototype is to develop an accurate and efficient automated metal surface defect detector to replace humans in performing visual inspection. The approach used in this prototype will be image segmentation, one of the popular image processing techniques. The following section will be arranged by Sect. 2 Literature Review, Sect. 3 Methodology and followed by Sect. 4 Result and Discussion. Last but not least, conclusion in Sect. 5.

1.1 Objectives

- To identify the most suitable image segmentation method for patch defect and scratch defect respectively
  Three image segmentation approaches including threshold-based segmentation, edge detection segmentation and clustering techniques. The threshold-based segmentation includes simple thresholding, adaptive thresholding and Otsu's Binarization while the edge detection segmentation methods comprise the Sobel, Laplacian and Canny edge detector. For clustering approach, K-means clustering is attempted. These segmentation approaches will be evaluated, and the best technique will be identified as the most suitable image segmentation method for patches and scratches defect detection respectively.
- To accurately localize the patch defect on metal surfaces
  There are a total of 18 metal surface images with patch defect type will be used to demonstrate the functionality of the system. As we proposed an algorithm that is capable of detecting defects on metal surfaces, we expect to see clear highlights and visualization of the patch defects in the tested images.
- To accurately localize the scratch defect on metal surfaces
  There are 19 metal surface images with scratch defect type will be used to demonstrate the functionality of the system. As we proposed an algorithm that is capable of

detecting defects on metal surfaces, we expect to see clear highlights and visualization of the scratch defects in the tested images.

1.2 Motivation

Automated Visual Inspection in Manufacturing Companies. Automated Visual Inspection is a form of quality control that includes analyzing and examining the production line. For human visual inspection, inspectors have to undergo special training to be equipped with professional knowledge and experience. However, there are many limitations to what humans can achieve. For instance, humans are prone to errors and mistakes which arise from several issues such as fatigue and lack of attention. However, this problem is non-existent and could be overcome with machines and computers. Besides, with the improvements and development of such advanced inspection systems, detection of defects that are hard to be noticed by the human naked eye are made possible. By implementing automotive quality control with the use of cameras connected to a processing unit, product line inspection can be conducted efficiently with minimal human efforts. At the same time, it also greatly prevents issues that arise due to human error. In the long-term, automated visual inspection helps to reduce the overall cost of production as less manpower is needed in the manufacturing quality control process. With machines responsible for inspections, humans can program and monitor the progress remotely. Manufacturing factories can also carry out inspection processes for a longer period of time resulting in better productivity. Lastly, the implementation of automated visual inspection is unchallenging as these systems are capable of adapting quickly to diverse products and surfaces.

Industrial Workplace Safety. Quality control for steels and metals are crucial as they play an important role in the majority of the engineering and constructions industry. It is important to ensure good quality of steel to prevent steel structure fatigue that leads to serious consequences. A defect in metal surfaces could result in weakness that leads to critical accidents. For instance, the presence of defects in steel surfaces can exhilarate great changes on a material's corrosion resistance and its mechanical properties. With surface defects, metals are prone to oxidation which weakens its structural integrity. This makes the metal unsuitable for further usage as it has lost its strengths and durability. Besides for metals used in electronic devices, surface defects tend to bring negative impacts on its electrical conductivity. These imperfections on metal surfaces bring hidden danger to the safety of users as well as affecting the performance of the end products. Hence, metals and steels must be inspected thoroughly to ensure good durability and strength in order to prevent any industrial accidents.

2 Literature Review

2.1 Deep Learning and Computer Vision

Implementation of Artificial Intelligence in manufacturing is getting more popular nowadays. For most AI-based defect detection solutions, deep learning and computer vision are used for visual inspection. A deep learning model is commonly empowered by artificial neural networks for the machine to learn through examples. The deep learning model will analyze input data and extract any common or underlying patterns beneath it for future prediction or classification. In automotive defect detection, a deep neural network is usually trained with many examples of defects it must detect. One of the most common deep learning algorithms is the Convolutional Neural Networks (CNN) where the model learns to perform tasks by computing algorithms and applying weights on the inputs. Each pixel value is analyzed where the neural network layers will convolve features extracted and recognize the landmarks for each type of defect. This information will then be interpreted and helps the deep learning model to learn, understand and recognize similar feature patterns in the future. Hence, the neural networks are capable of recognizing or distinguishing features from different classes in images by analyzing the typed edges and corners detected.

2.2 Image Segmentation

Image segmentation refers to the process of classifying image pixels to a certain class. This computer vision task could be referred to as a classification problem based on image pixels. There are TWO (2) types of segmentation techniques namely semantic segmentation and instance segmentation.

Semantic Segmentation

Semantic segmentation refers to the process of classification of each pixel to its corresponding or belonging label. This type of segmentation does not differentiate distinct instances of the same object label. Instead, it treats multiple objects from the same class as a single entity. For instance, if an image containing two dogs is passed into a semantic segmentation model, the returned output result of the segmentation will assign the same labels to both pixels covering the dog in the image.

Instance Segmentation

Instance segmentation refers to the process of classifying every instance of an object with a unique label. In simple words instance segmentation allows differentiation among similar object instances. For instance, the image with 2 dogs will now be assigned with different colours for pixels of each dog.

3 Methodology

3.1 Description of Dataset

The dataset used in this project is a surface defect database[1] constructed by Northeastern University (NEU) [6]. The image dataset consists of 6 types of defects namely crazing (Cr), inclusions (In), patches (Pa), pitted surface (PS), rolled-in scale (RS), and scratches (Sc). Each type of defect consists of 300 images which gives a total of 1800 gray-scaled images with resolution of 200×200 pixels. The dataset is divided into 1440 training

---

[1] Available at https://www.kaggle.com/datasets/kaustubhdikshit/neu-surface-defect-database.

images and 360 validation images. For each image, the defects are annotated to be used as ground truth for validation. In this study, we focus on patches and scratches which is the two most significant defect category in manufacturing process that is the largest contributing class that lead to the rejections [7] (Fig. 1).

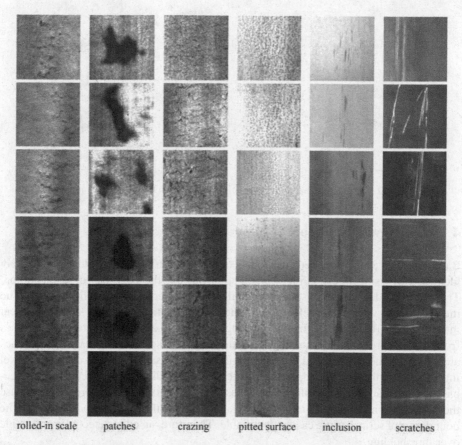

| rolled-in scale | patches | crazing | pitted surface | inclusion | scratches |

Fig. 1. Samples of six kinds of typical surface defects on NEU surface defect database. Each row shows one example image from each of 300 samples of a class

3.2 Technique in View

Figure 2 shows the image segmentation techniques that have been studied and implemented in this project. The techniques attempted are labeled with a green check mark.

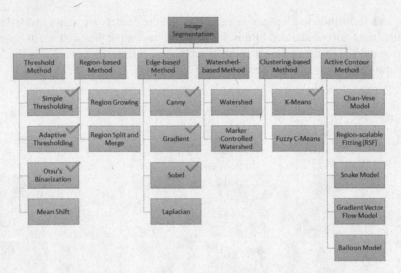

Fig. 2. Attempted Image Segmentation Techniques (Color figure online)

4   Result and Discussion

Based on the results obtained, we found out that patch defects could be accurately identified by using thresholding segmentation but not the edge-based segmentation. This could be due to the noise present in the patch defect images in our dataset. The metal surfaces with patch defects have uneven distribution of patches with different intensities. Therefore, it is difficult for an edge detector to clearly distinguish the patches from the background. Thresholding is a better way in this situation because the patches are darker so the patches and the background could be separated based on their pixel intensities. On the other hand, scratch defects are more distinctly detected using edge-based segmentation instead of threshold-based segmentation. This is probably because the scratches on metal surfaces in our dataset are mostly straight and uniform. The boundaries of scratches are easily identifiable. Therefore, an edge detector is preferable over thresholding.

The best thresholding technique for path defects is the Otsu's Binarization as it uses an optimal threshold that can be specified automatically and yet yields comparable results with a fine-tuned simple thresholded image. The simple thresholding technique is not selected as we want to avoid choosing a threshold manually every time, we take in an input image of different image brightness. Meanwhile, the Canny Edge Detector is shortlisted as the best technique to detect scratch defects. This is because it yields simply a black background with white contour representing the scratches that ease the localization process. The Sobel-filtered image and Laplacian-filtered image could not give a sharp representation of the scratch defects. Hence, when we perform localization, the scratch defects could not be located accurately (Table 1).

Next, we applied Bilateral filter on patch defects images and Gaussian filter on scratch defects image to denoise the images for better results of thresholding and edge detection since the techniques used are very sensitive to noises. The Bilateral filter is shortlisted

Table 1. Comparison of proposed method against ground truth for patch detects detection

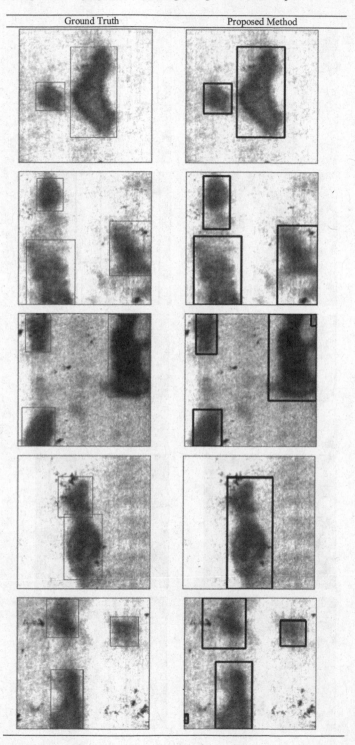

Table 2. Comparison of proposed method against ground truth for scratch detects detection

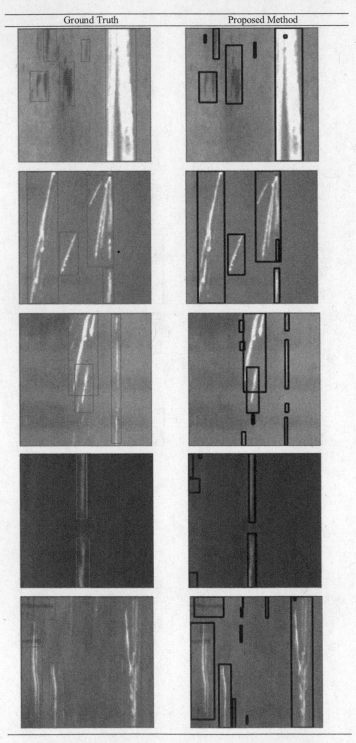

as it gives the best segmentation results with the least noise detection on patch defective metal. Meanwhile, the Gaussian, Average and Median filters return similar results of edge detection. Since Gaussian filters are the most generally used filtering methods in image pre-processing stages, it is selected to be applied on scratch defective metal. As a result, the contour of defects that we have obtained on each image helps us to successfully locate the defects with bounding boxes.

Moreover, the opening operation performed on patch defects images allows us to retain the huge chunks of patches and remove small objects in the foreground. By doing so, we are able to obtain a clearer highlighted defect area for better localization results. In contrast, the closing operation is used on scratch defects because we want to connect the lines or strikes as a result of edge detection on the surface of scratch defects images. This operation helps to improve the localization results on scratch defects images.

Finally, we observed that some IoU values computed for the patch and scratch defects localization have extreme differences. For example, there are 2 detections with 0 IoU values in the patch defects detection, as well as the scratch defects' detection. The reason for this phenomenon is that we extract only the largest bounding box from the ground truth and the detection to compute the IoU. However, the largest bounding box in the ground truth does not necessarily match the one detected by our algorithm.

Nevertheless, we have obtained satisfactory results as most of the defective images tested have an IoU value above 0.6 as illustrated in Fig. 3 and Fig. 4. Besides, all tested images are returned with clear bounding boxes surrounding the defective regions. By visual inspection, the localization of defects is considered accurate as it is impossible to acquire bounding boxes which are identical with the ground truth (Table 2).

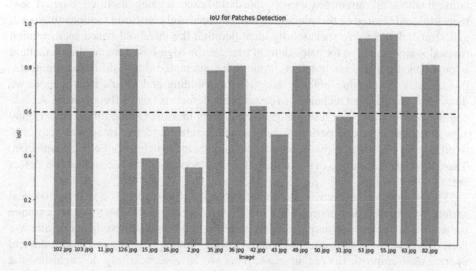

Fig. 3. Evaluation of patch defects detection using IoU

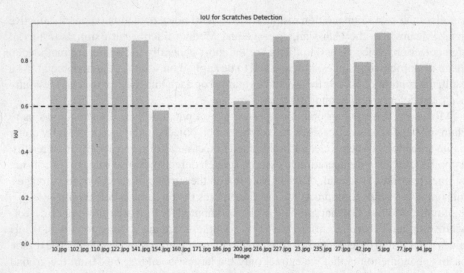

Fig. 4. Evaluation of scratch defects detection using IoU

5 Conclusion

This study has achieved all the objectives mentioned in the previous section.

Foremost, the most suitable image segmentation method for patch and scratch defect respectively are successfully identified. In this project, a total of three image segmentation methods are attempted namely threshold-based segmentation, edge-based segmentation and clustering techniques are implemented and compared for detecting patch and scratch defects. We successfully identified that the threshold-based segmentation method is more suitable for patch defects whereas the edge-based segmentation method is more suitable for scratch defects. Among the attempted threshold-based segmentation, namely simple thresholding, adaptive thresholding and Otsu's Binarization, we discovered that the best technique to detect patch defects is Otsu's Binarization. A clear contour is observed when tested with patch defects images. On the other hand, Canny edge detection algorithm performs the best with scratch defective images as compared to other edge-based segmentation methods implemented such as Sobel and Laplacian. There is a clear distinction in the output edge lines between defect areas and non-defect areas.

Furthermore, the objective to accurately localize patch defects on at least 10 metal surfaces is achieved. In our project, Otsu's Binarization is the final shortlisted technique for patch defect detection and is further optimized in order to achieve better results. We performed several optimization techniques such as image blurring and morphological operations to improve the output mask. After we have successfully distinguished the defective region from the non-defective region, we localize the defect regions by drawing bounding boxes and displaying them on the original image. As a result, we can see clear highlights and accurate visualization of patch defects in more than 10 tested images.

Moreover, the objective to accurately localize scratch defects on at least 10 metal surfaces is achieved. In our project, Canny edge detection is the final shortlisted technique for scratch defect detection and is further optimized in order to achieve better results. We performed several optimization techniques including defining a function to auto-determine the optimum threshold, image blurring and morphological operations to improve the output mask. After we have successfully distinguished the defective region from the non-defective region, we localize the defect regions by drawing bounding boxes and displaying them on the original image. As a result, we can see clear highlights and accurate visualization of scratch defects in more than 10 tested images.

Lastly, the proposed system is capable of achieving an Intersection over Union (IoU) value for at least 0.6 for both defect types. After testing the selected 18 images with the shortlisted and optimized segmentation method, the results are compared and evaluated against the ground truth provided in the original dataset through computing the IoU value. As a result, the system successfully detects defects with more than 0.6 IoU value in more than 10 images tested for each defect type.

References

1. Ong, Z.Y., Chye, K.K., Kang, H.W., Tan, C.W.: A flower recognition system using deep neural network coupled with visual geometry group 19 architecture. In: Conference Proceedings: International Conference on Digital Transformation and Applications (ICDXA 2021). Tunku Abdul Rahman University College, pp. 121–128 (2021). https://doi.org/10.56453/icdxa.2021.1012
2. Whitney, W.R.: The corrosion of iron. J. Am. Chem. Soc. **25**, 394–406 (1903). https://doi.org/10.1021/JA02006A008/ASSET/JA02006A008.FP.PNG_V03
3. Tang, Z.: A review of corrosion inhibitors for rust preventative fluids. Curr. Opin. Solid State Mater. Sci. **23**, 100759 (2019). https://doi.org/10.1016/J.COSSMS.2019.06.003
4. Harsimran, S., Santosh, K., Rakesh, K.: Overview of corrosion and its control: a critical review. Proc. Eng. Sci. **3**, 13–24 (2021). https://doi.org/10.24874/PES03.01.002
5. Yin, Q., Li, C., Dong, L., et al.: Effects of physicochemical properties of different base oils on friction coefficient and surface roughness in MQL milling AISI 1045. Int. J. Precis. Eng. Manuf. Green Technol. **8**, 1629–1647 (2021). https://doi.org/10.1007/S40684-021-00318-7/FIGURES/15
6. Song, K., Hu, S., Yan, Y.: Automatic recognition of surface defects on hot-rolled steel strip using scattering convolution network. J. Comput. Inf. Syst. **10**, 3049–3055 (2014). https://doi.org/10.12733/jcis10026
7. Qamar, S.Z., Arif, A.F.M., Sheikh, A.K.: Analysis of product defects in a typical aluminum extrusion facility. Mater. Manuf. Processes **19**, 391–405 (2004). https://doi.org/10.1081/AMP-120038650

Design and Implementation of Intelligent Truck Based on Azure Kinect

Jingfang Wei[1], Kaiyang Xu[1], Zilin Hu[2], Yuji Iwahori[3], Haibin Wu[1(✉)], and Aili Wang[1]

[1] Heilongjiang Province Key Laboratory of Laser Spectroscopy Technology and Application, Harbin University of Science and Technology, Harbin 150080, China
woo@hrbust.edu.cn
[2] City University of Hong Kong, Hong Kong 610200, China
[3] Computer Science, Chubu University, Kasugai 487-8501, Aichi, Japan

Abstract. In recent years, due to the impact of COVID-19, the market prospect of non-contact handling has improved and the development potential is huge. This paper designs an intelligent truck based on Azure Kinect, which can save manpower and improve efficiency, and greatly reduce the infection risk of medical staff and community workers. The target object is visually recognized by Azure Kinect to obtain the center of mass of the target, and the GPS and Kalman filter are used to achieve accurate positioning. The 4-DOF robot arm is selected to grasp and transport the target object, so as to complete the non-contact handling work. In this paper, different shapes of objects are tested. The experiment shows that the system can accurately complete the positioning function, and the accuracy rate is 95.56%. The target object recognition is combined with the depth information to determine the distance, and the spatial coordinates of the object centroid are obtained in real time. The accuracy rate can reach 94.48%, and the target objects of different shapes can be recognized. When the target object is grasped by the robot arm, it can be grasped accurately according to the depth information, and the grasping rate reaches 92.67%.

Keywords: Automatic Collection · Template Matching · RGB-D · Precise Positioning

1 Introduction

Transportation has always been an indispensable work in various industries. The transportation vehicle can not only solve the manpower problem, but also improve the work efficiency. With the continuous development of intelligent trucker technology, the market is far from saturated and the development potential is huge. Especially in the post epidemic era so far, as far as the reported sources of infection in China are concerned, food contact infection and express contact infection are the main ways of infection at present. Therefore, non-contact handling is the market demand that arises as the times require. With the normalization of nucleic acid testing, how to learn to fight a protracted

© ICST Institute for Computer Sciences, Social Informatics and Telecommunications Engineering 2023
Published by Springer Nature Switzerland AG 2023. All Rights Reserved
X. Jiang (Ed.): MLICOM 2022, LNICST 481, pp. 50–62, 2023.
https://doi.org/10.1007/978-3-031-30237-4_5

war against the epidemic is a very critical issue. Sufficient sampling materials are the premise to ensure the rapid and orderly work of sampling points, and also the work that wastes the most mobile manpower. In order to ensure the safety of medical personnel and community workers, it is often necessary to carry out multiple alcohol disinfection and sealed packaging of materials, which is time-consuming and laborious, as shown in Fig. 1. At this time, non-contact handling can just solve this problem. Therefore, this paper designs an intelligent truck based on Azure Kinect.

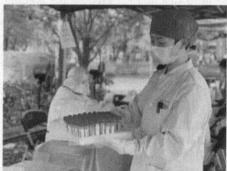

a) Nucleic acid sampling tube transport   b)Non contact distribution of fruits and vege-
tables

Fig. 1. Handling application scenario

In terms of the realization of the transport vehicle, Zou Jun designed a transport robot, which uses UWB and ultrasonic sensors to collect environmental information, and selects fuzzy algorithm to achieve effective obstacle avoidance [1]. Zhang Jun designed a navigation and positioning system by using GPS technology and established a navigation and positioning correction system, so that the transport robot can realize the autonomous following function [2].

In addition, Kalman filter technology has developed rapidly in the application of GPS. Zhu Zhongxiang used dual fuzzy Kalman filter for GPS/IMU/MV sensor information fusion to navigate autonomous tractors [3]. Choi et al. proposed that a vision sensor should be installed above the robot arm to sense the three-dimensional environment information, and obtain the position to be reached by the robot, so as to complete the identification and grasping of the target object [4]. Rosenberger et al. proposed a human-computer interaction method using real-time robot vision to realize the capture and control of target objects through object detector, fast capture selection algorithm and RGB-D camera [5]. In recent years, the target detection algorithm has also been widely opened and applied. Zhang Zhanpeng's team proposed an improved training network to increase the utilization rate of training data and achieve a 94% success rate [6]. Guo Di of Tsinghua University realized the detection of object grasping order in the complex environment of overlapping objects [7].

Azure Kinect provides developers SDKs with four kinds of sensors including depth, vision, sound and direction, through one million pixel TOF depth camera and 12 million pixel RGB high-definition camera. The color camera obtains high-definition RGB images and video information. The infrared emitter projects pulse light to objects within a certain range, receives pulse light through the depth camera, and creates a depth image within a certain range [8]. Therefore, we designed an intelligent truck based on Azure Kinect for the three-dimensional information of the target object can be accurately obtained. Firstly, GPS is combined with Kalman filter algorithm to realize real-time accurate positioning of the target and assist the accurate movement of the car. The Azure Kinect camera acquires depth information, combines template matching algorithm to intelligently identify and determine the distance of the nucleic acid sampling tube, and marks the spatial position of its centroid. The third function is to realize the accurate grasping and placement of the target object through the robot arm module.

2   System Software Design

First, the location of the captured target is obtained through Bluetooth communication, and the positioning is updated in real time by combining Kalman filter algorithm, and the data is transmitted to the GPS module, so that the GPS module can search for the target. Use Azure Kinect to intelligently identify and determine the distance of the target object through template matching algorithm and depth information, draw a rectangular box and mark the centroid, and obtain the centroid space coordinates in real time. Drive the robot arm to grasp the target object accurately. The functional flow chart is shown in Fig. 2.

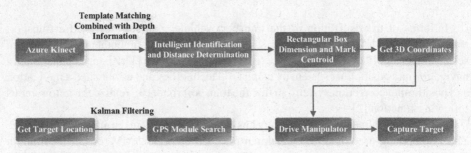

Fig. 2. The functional flow chart of software system

2.1   Accurate Positioning Model Based on Kalman Filter Algorithm

The communication between Arduino and GPS module mainly includes positioning, navigation and path planning of GPS module. In order to improve the positioning accuracy, Kalman filter algorithm is adopted to make the optimal estimation of the state of the system, which carries out an iterative cycle, and the minimum value of the mean square error can be obtained, that is, the optimal estimation value. It is assumed that $\hat{X}_{k-1}$ is the optimal estimation value of the state quantity X_{k-1} is obtained when the filtering algorithm operates at the $k - 1$ time. With the aid of the input data u_{k-1} and the measurement data y_k, the optimal estimation value X_k of the Kalman filter for the system state X_k at the kth time is derived.

The prediction process is as follows:

$$\hat{X}_{k,k-1} = \Phi_{k,k-1}\hat{X}_{k-1} + Bu_{k-1} \tag{1}$$

$$P_{k,k-1} = \Phi_{k,k-1}P_{k-1}\Phi_{k,k-1}^T + Q_{k-1} \tag{2}$$

where $\hat{X}_{k-1}$ is the state vector at time $k - 1$, $\hat{X}_{k,k-1}$ is the state vector at time k, B is the additional transition matrix, and P is the covariance matrix of the state vector.

The update process is as follows:

$$K_k = P_{k,k-1}H_k^T\left(H_kP_{k,k-1}H_k^T + R_k\right)^{-1} \tag{3}$$

$$\hat{X}_k = \hat{X}_{k,k-1} + K_k\left(Z_k - H_k\hat{X}_{k,k-1}\right) \tag{4}$$

$$P_k = (I - K_kH_k)P_{k,k-1} \tag{5}$$

This process represents the correction of the actual value to the predicted value, K is the gain matrix and I is the unit diagonal matrix.

2.2 Intelligent Recognition and Distance Measurement Model Based on Template Matching Algorithm and Depth Information

In real life, object detection can be used for 3D matching, image understanding, image compression, etc. At present, two new research ideas are gradually emerging, namely, significant target detection in RGB and RGB-D image. Compared with traditional RGB image data, depth image can also complete functions in three dimensions that cannot be completed in two dimensions [9]. Due to the accuracy problem of Kinect camera, image noise is unavoidable when obtaining data. Noise has a considerable impact on image recognition, especially on video image processing. Frequent noise will cause unstable recognition results. Therefore, the image is denoised before image recognition [10]. One of the methods that can be considered is median filtering, which is beneficial to retain edge information and remove speckle noise and salt and pepper noise [11]. At the same time, we can analyze a single target image or multiple targets with different perspectives at the same time [12]. The RGB-D image classification process is shown in Fig. 3. The target background segmentation calculation method based on depth is similar to the method based on color.

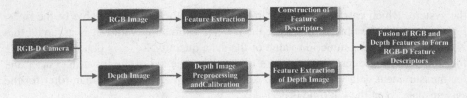

Fig. 3. RGB-D image classification method

$$P(x_i^t \in f_g) = \frac{P\left(x_i^t \in f_g | \text{depth}(x_i^t), h_{fd}^{(t-1)}\right)}{P\left(x_i^t \in f_g | \text{depth}(x_i^t), h_{fd}^{(t-1)}\right) + P\left(x_i^t \in b_g | \text{depth}(x_i^t), h_{bd}^{(t-w1)}\right)} \quad (6)$$

The depth histograms of target and background in the depth image sequence frame $t-1$ are expressed as $h_{fd}^{(t-1)}$ and $h_{bd}^{(t-1)}$ respectively. The Formula 6 calculates the possibility that each pixel in the depth image sequence frame belongs to the target.

In the target detection, this paper uses the image processing technology to process the collected color image, in order to reduce the detection error, and finally converts the collected image into a binary black-and-white image, reducing the impact of environmental factors such as light and background on the detection results during the image acquisition process [13]. This algorithm is template matching, which is a key part of the image processing process. The process of finding and locating the target position in another image according to the known target template map is called template matching. See formula (7) for the calculation method.

$$R(x, y) = \sum_{x', y'} (T(x', y') - I(x + x', y + y'))^2 \quad (7)$$

where $T(x', y')$ is the template image matrix and $I(x, y)$ is the original image matrix.

2.3 Robot Arm Program Design of Grab Control

By adjusting the movement trajectory of the robot arm and the closing angle of the robot claw, the robot claw can grasp the target object. The specific flow chart is shown in Fig. 4.

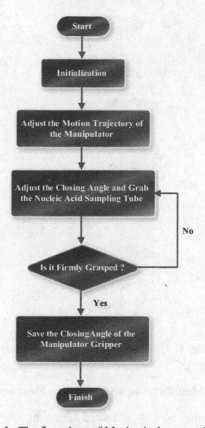

Fig. 4. The flow chart of Mechanical arm module

2.4 Function Programming of Intelligent Search System

The GPS module and the Bluetooth module are used to guide the smart car, so that the smart car can reach the position of the target object. When programming, according to the modular programming idea, each module generates independent sub functions for the main program to call. The program flow chart is shown in Fig. 5.

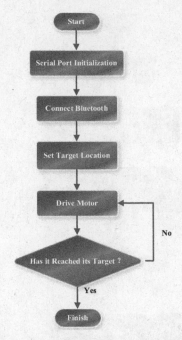

Fig. 5. GPS precise positioning flow chart

2.5 Design Intelligent Identification and Distance Measurement

The Azure Kinect camera needs to be calibrated during the application process to obtain the real position information of the measured object in the three-dimensional space. The flow is shown in Fig. 6.

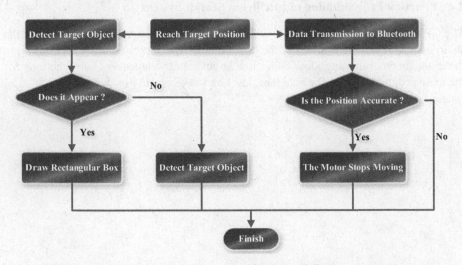

Fig. 6. The flow chart of intelligent identification and distance measurement

3 Hardware Design of the System

The overall scheme design flow chart is shown in Fig. 7.

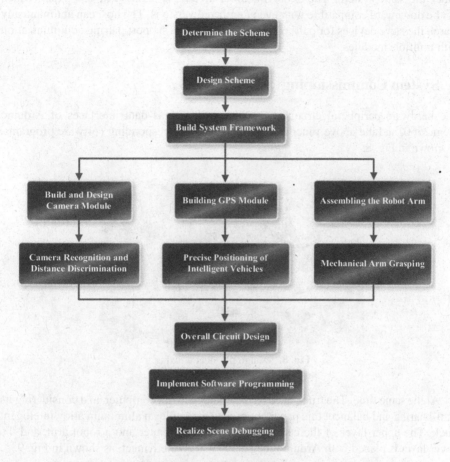

Fig. 7. Overall design scheme of intelligent truck based on Azure Kinect.

The main control module uses Arduino Mega2560 as the control chip, which has 54 channels of digital input and output and is suitable for the design requiring a large number of IO interfaces. It can supply power through three modes, and can automatically select the power supply mode. The GPS module adopts the ATGM332D-5N series, which has 32 tracking channels. Its advantages are high sensitivity, low power consumption and low cost. It is suitable for vehicle navigation, handheld positioning and wearable devices, which can directly replace the U-blox NEO series.

This article uses Azure Kinect DK, which was launched by Microsoft in February 2019, as the camera module to obtain data. Compared with previous products, Azure Kinect DK supports higher resolution for both RGB camera and depth camera. It is more compact and lightweight, and more suitable for vehicle applications. The robot arm module is mainly used to grasp the target object. The opening of the claw can reach 225 mm, the length of the robot arm is 401 mm, and the weight of the robot arm is 460 g. It is applicable to all kinds of bionic robot joints, so it can be used in multiple scenarios under the same system. The hc06 Bluetooth module is adopted in this paper, which can be downward compatible with even numbered versions. The host can automatically search the slave devices for pairing, and the adapter can support pairing communication with multiple modules.

4   System Commissioning

The hardware peripheral circuit is composed of various data interfaces of Arduino Mega2560, and the above functions are realized by corresponding software programs, as shown in Fig. 8.

Fig. 8.   Design physical drawing.

At the same time, The truck needs to be equipped with computer, and considering its load-bearing and balance, this paper chooses to assemble an aluminum alloy intelligent truck. The upper layer of the car is placed with a computer and a robot arm, and the lower layer is placed with Arduino mega2560 and Azure Kinect, as shown in Fig. 9.

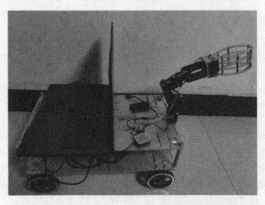

Fig. 9.   Physical image of intelligent truck.

4.1   GPS Precise Positioning Test

When the GPS module is used to locate the car, the received data is analyzed, mainly to extract the longitude and latitude in the GPS module. The specific method is to separate the data according to the comma between the data, extract the longitude and latitude data, and then convert the data to obtain the results. Results as shown in Fig. 10, the positioning function can be accurately completed with an accuracy rate of 95.56%.

Fig. 10.   GPS module of data reception.

4.2   Experiments of Target Recognition and Distance Measurement

In this paper, we use nucleic acid sampling tube, potato and potato bucket to simulate three scenarios. The results show that when the target object appears in the picture, it can be recognized. After many experiments, it is found that the recognition rate can reach 94.48%, which meets the actual needs. The recognition results are shown in Fig. 11, and the obtained centroid space coordinates are shown in Table 1.

4.3   Grasping Accuracy of Manipulator

When the target object is grasped by the robot module, the design of the control method of the robot arm must meet the physical characteristics of the robot arm and the constraint conditions. Otherwise, the robot arm will be seriously damaged and even threaten the personal safety of the user. The grasping control using the robot arm is shown in Fig. 12.

In the experiment, the robot arm is used to grasp the target object, and the rotation angle of the steering gear is recorded, that is, the closing angle of the mechanical claw. After many experiments, when the closing angle of the robot arm is 30°, it can firmly grasp the target object, and the grasping rate reaches 92.67%.

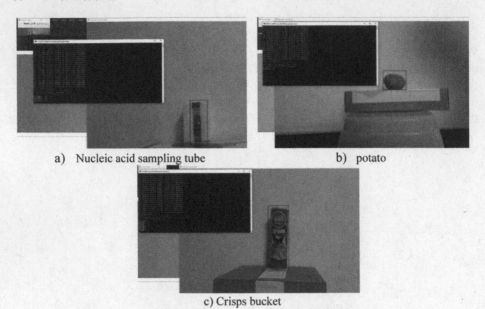

a)   Nucleic acid sampling tube   b)   potato

c) Crisps bucket

Fig. 11. Intelligent recognition and distance measurement experiment.

Table 1. Centroid space coordinates.

Number	Nucleic acid sampling tube	Potato	Crisps bucket
1	(313,243,177)	(275,211,167)	(293,223,170)
2	(314,243,179)	(273,210,166)	(295,225,166)
3	(314,243,178)	(275,213,168)	(292,224,169)
4	(314,243,179)	(274,211,169)	(291,221,171)
5	(317,243,178)	(276,212,165)	(296,220,173)
6	(313,243,181)	(277,210,167)	(295,226,165)
7	(315,243,179)	(275,216,164)	(297,220,172)
8	(314,242,177)	(276,210,167)	(295,219,170)
9	(314,241,178)	(271,211,166)	(296,223,171)
10	(312,241,179)	(273,213,167)	(295,221,170)

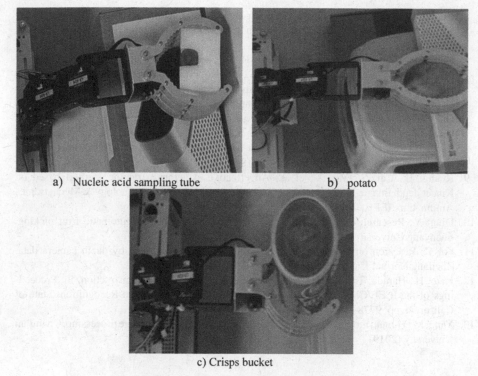

a) Nucleic acid sampling tube   b) potato

c) Crisps bucket

Fig. 12. Grasping control experiment of manipulator.

5   Conclusions

This paper has completed the design of an intelligent truck based on Azure Kinect. Using GPS and Kalman filter algorithm to obtain the position of the target object, and the accuracy rate is 95.56%. Azure Kinect camera obtains depth information, combines template matching algorithm to intelligently identify and determine the distance of the target object, and marks the spatial position of its centroid, with an accuracy rate of 94.48%. When the target object is grasped by the robot arm, it can be grasped accurately according to the different depth information, and the grasping rate reaches 92.67%. It can complete contactless material transfer, improve work efficiency, reduce the burden of staff, reduce the risk of staff infection, and meet the needs of epidemic prevention.

References

1. Zou, J.: Research and development of intelligent robot tracking system. Huazhong University of Science and Technology (2018)
2. Zhang, J.: Research on autonomous tracking control system of tracked agricultural mobile robot. Zhejiang University of Technology (2017)
3. Liu, Y.: Application of Kalman filter in GPS dynamic positioning. Huazhong University of Science and Technology (2009)

4. Choi, C., Taguchi, Y., et al.: Voting-based pose estimation for robotic assembly using a 3D sensor. In: IEEE International Conference on Robotics and Automation, pp. 1724–1731. IEEE (2012)
5. Rosenberger, P., Cosgun, A., Newbury, R., et al.: Object-independent human-to-robot handovers using real time robotic vision. J. IEEE Robot. Autom. Lett. **1**, 17–23 (2016)
6. Glorot, X., Bordes, A., Bengio, Y.: Deep sparse rectifier neural networks. In: International Conference on Artificial Intelligence and Statistics, pp. 315–323 (2011)
7. Guo, D.: Research on target detection and grasping planning for robot operation. Tsinghua University (2016)
8. Yang, P.: Research on gesture recognition based on Kinect and its application in virtual simulation system. Nanjing University (2018)
9. Kuang, H., Cai, S., Ma, X., et al.: An effective skeleton extraction method based on Kinect depth image. In: International Conference on Measuring Technology & Mechatronics Automation. IEEE (2018)
10. Ding, Y.: Research on identification and positioning methods of automatic fruit picking. Shenyang University of Technology (2020)
11. Fu, Y.: Research on humanoid robot motion and algorithm driven by depth camera data. Zhejiang Normal University (2019)
12. Kato, H., Harada, T.: Learning view priors for single-view 3D reconstruction. In: Proceedings of the IEEE/CVF Conference on Computer Vision and Pattern Recognition, State of California, pp. 9778–9787(2019)
13. Yang, M.: Human motion recognition and tracking robot based on image processing. Chang'an University (2019)

A Comparison of Discrete Event Simulator and Real-Time Emulator for Mobile Ad Hoc Network

Jingzhi Wang⑩, Penghui Hu⑩, Yixin Zhang$^{(\boxtimes)}$, and Jian Wang$^{(\boxtimes)}$

School of Electronic Science and Engineering, Nanjing University, Nanjing 210023, China
{zyixin,wangjnju}@nju.edu.cn

Abstract. Network research requires testing tools to evaluate new protocols and algorithms. Since implementing and verifying these protocols and algorithms on real network devices is time-consuming and costly, widely-used tools often run in virtual environments to reproduce the behavior of real networks. These tools can be divided into simulators and emulators. Unlike simulator, which is mature and widely used in network research, emulators are relatively new and still developing, especially those based on the latest virtualization technologies. The most common application scenario of an emulator is Software Defined Network (SDN). Still, it has a great development prospect in Mobile Ad hoc Network (MANET) research. In an ad hoc network, nodes are equivalent; each node acts as a router. Large-scale MANET simulations with a simulator often take a long time, while real-time emulators do not. However, although the strong expansion capability of the newly proposed emulator is suitable for MANET, it lacks the mobility and scenario model necessary. In this paper, the discrete event simulator and real-time emulator are thoroughly compared, the parameters and performance of the classical simulator and emulator are compared, the development trend of the emulator is summarized, and open issues are proposed.

Keywords: Network Simulator · Emulator · MANET · SDN · Docker

1 Introduction

As network technology evolves, researchers pursue simulation tools to evaluate and analyze newly proposed architectures, algorithms, and protocols. The simulation tools can verify the throughput, end-to-end delay and other performance parameters of a protocol or algorithm without implementing a complex and large-scale network prototype system. Network simulation tools typically support network modeling with different topologies by defining the behavior of communication channels and network nodes [1].

There are many simulation tools on the market, and they can be classified differently. They can be divided into discrete event simulators and real-time emulators from the implementation principle. Also, they can be divided into general tools and special tools from the applicable field, and they can be divided into open source tools and commercial

X. Jiang (Ed.): MLICOM 2022, LNICST 481, pp. 63–74, 2023.
https://doi.org/10.1007/978-3-031-30237-4_6

tools. This paper mainly discusses the differences between discrete event simulator and real-time emulators and their capacities for MANET research.

Mobile Ad hoc Network (MANET) is a wireless Network in which nodes can communicate with each other through radio. The nodes are equivalent to each other and have mobility. MANET does not rely on pre-existing infrastructure communications and can be applied to tactical communications, emergency medical rescue, rescue, and disaster relief [2]. Each node of a MANET is equivalent to a router in a traditional network, and each node in the network needs to perform forwarding and run routing protocols. Existing research on MANET covers the whole protocol stack from top to bottom, including the physical layer, MAC layer, network layer and node mobility model. It is usual to study the signal model in the mobile scenario and the fading resistant physical layer protocol for the physical layer. And for the MAC layer, the access problem under unstable communication links and mobile scenarios needs to be studied. The routing decision problem in dynamic changing topology in the network layer is a research hotspot. Classical MANET routing protocols include active, reactive and hybrid routing protocols. Active routing protocols include Optimized Link State Routing Protocol (OLSR), the Destination Sequenced Distance Vector (DSDV), etc. Reactive routing protocols include the Temporally Ordered Routing Algorithm (TORA), Ad Hoc on-demand distance vector routing (AODV), etc. Hybrid routing protocols include border gateway protocol 1 (BGP) and zone routing protocol (ZRP) [3]. When studying the above MANET protocols at each layer, the network simulators and the emulators are adopted to verify their behavior and analyze their performance.

The remaining part of this paper is organized as follows: In Sect. 2, we compare the simulator and emulator, analyzing their implementation principles and characteristics. Section 3 surveys some classical network simulators, and Sect. 4 introduce two well-known emulators. Section 5 comprehensively compares the above tools from the aspects of running speed, scalability, protocol support, etc. Section 6 discusses the recent development direction of network emulators and proposes several problems to be solved in MANET emulation. In the last section, we summarize the whole paper and propose some suggestions for MANET emulator development.

2 Fundamentals of Discrete Event Simulation and Real-Time Emulation

The discrete-event simulation tool uses software programs to simulate the operation of real devices and their interactions, such as NS-3 [4], OPNET [5], OMNET++ [6], etc. Compared to running real operating systems and applications on real devices, running simulators on PC is low-cost, flexible, controllable, and scalable. They run in virtual tick time instead of real-time. However, if the model used in the simulator is not correct enough, the results will be biased from the actual experimental results. Real-time online emulators, such as Mininet [7] and EstiNet [8], are generally based on virtualized nodes and run actual applications. Most classical network simulation tools are based on the discrete event simulation paradigm.

A discrete event simulator simulates the random events of nodes in the network, as shown in Fig. 1. For example, when a packet starts to send, the simulator puts it into the event queue according to the time. And then, the event in the queue will be processed sequentially, according to the actual network behavior. When an event in the queue is finished, the global variable is changed to trigger the next event.

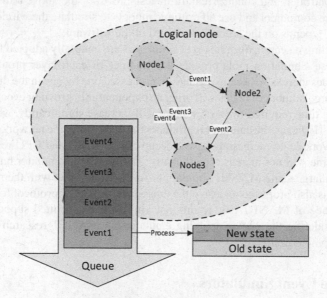

Fig. 1. Discrete event simulation

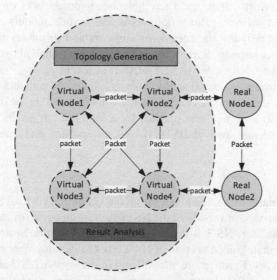

Fig. 2. Realtime emulation based on virtualization

Real-time emulation tools are usually based on virtualization technology and resource isolation technology. Real applications can flow in virtual nodes to send and receive data packets to each other in real time, mimicking the behavior of a real network, as shown in Fig. 2. Emulators are most commonly used in SDN simulation. It can easily build network topology, control the behavior of each virtual node through a centralized controller, and conduct real traffic tests. Most of the above tools can be run on one or more computers and use algorithmic models to simulate the wireless channel. The accuracy depends on the algorithm defined in the software.

In the existing research, discrete event simulators are generally adopted for MANET research. These simulation tools provide the modules of each layer protocol. As the number of nodes increases, because events are processed one by one in the discrete event simulator, a large number of nodes will bring an exponentially growing event queue, and the processing time required by the simulator will increase significantly, which may be unacceptable. However, the emulator reproduces the behavior in the network in real time. With the network scale increasing, it will occupy more RAM and CPU resources, but the running time will not increase significantly. Therefore, the emulator has more time advantages in large-scale MANET simulation. At the same time, with the rise of SDN, SD-MANET is also proposed to design the cross-layer MANET protocol for improving the performance of MANET [9]. Traditional Simulator has limited support for these aspects. Considering the above, applying emulators in MANET research may be the future development trend.

3   Discrete Event Simulators

The large number of network simulation tools brings difficulties to the selection of researchers and network engineers. There have been some works on the comparative study of simulation software. But no protocols and mobile models are mentioned in [10]. Paper [11] investigates the common simulators and discusses the protocols and mobility models they support. Some simulation tools mentioned above have developed new features and provided more MANET support in recent years.

This section introduces several well-known simulators. Simulators for other specific scenarios, such as SensorSim, and GrooveNet, are not included in the description. Some older simulators that have not been updated for a long time or are inconvenient to use are also out of the picture, such as JiST/SWANS, GlomoSim, and QualNet.

3.1   Ns-2&NS-3

The Network Simulator project originates from the US military's Real Simulator Project [12]. NS-2 [13], the second version of the NS project, is an open-source object-oriented discrete event Simulator. NS-3 is the third version of Network Simulation, started in 2006. NS-3 is not an upgraded version of NS-2 but a re-development of core functional modules based on C++. Furthermore, the API and framework of NS-3 are not completely consistent with NS-2. NS-3 also provides an optional Python extension interface, which greatly reduces the programming complexity for users [14].

The simulation layers of NS-3 are similar to the OSI model. It encapsulates data in the device, network, transport, and application layers sequence. The process of the packet transmission is simulated according to the protocol of the classes in C++. NS-3 is an event-driven simulator. Events are triggered by network nodes, the core module extracts and processes events in the queue, and the interaction of pointers completes the packet forwarding process, so it has a fast running speed and less memory consumption. The tracing system of NS-3 is also convenient for users to analyze the output using software such as Wireshark [4].

Currently, NS-2 has stopped updating. NS-3 is still developing rapidly. Although the model and protocol library are not as perfect as NS-2, it provides a better user interface and higher performance. The disadvantages of NS-3 include: (1) limited GUI support, which requires the development of additional plug-ins; (2) inadequate model libraries and protocol libraries, which require user customization.

3.2 OMNET++

OMNET++ is also an object-oriented discrete event network simulator, and the latest version was released in 2022. It is not only designed to simulate a network but can theoretically be used to simulate any system that transmits information to each other.

OMNET++ has been applied in several problem areas, such as communication network modeling, protocol simulation, network queueing, modeling of multiprocessors and other distributed hardware systems, hardware architecture verification, and performance evaluation of complex software systems [6].

OMNET++ has good GUI support, which makes it easy to modify models and observe results under the graphical interface. OMNET++ uses C++ programming, of which the architecture can realize the parallel simulation and is scalable. OMNET++ has the following disadvantages: (1) it does not organize simulation levels according to OSI standards; (2) it has limited support for communication protocols; (3) it has poor support for mobility modeling; and (4) it is not easy to analyze performance metrics.

3.3 NetSim

NetSim [11] is used for network design, planning, research, and development, supporting the simulation of many networks, such as TCP, IP, WIMAX, WLAN, wireless sensor networks, and MANET. And it also supports the simulation of 802.11, LTE, 5G and other protocols. NetSim is also a discrete event simulator. TECOS developed it with Indian Institute of Science and enabled end-to-end, full-stack, packet-level event simulation. An advanced feature of NetSim is the ability to debug custom code at various levels, including each packet interval, which avoids a time-consuming programming process. NetSim has an excellent GUI, friendly interface, programmability, and built-in data analysis framework. As commercial software, it has detailed documentation and user tutorials. The downside of NetSim is that com-mercial software costs money, and the code is not open-source.

4 Real-Time Emulators

Real-time emulators are often called SDN emulators. In fact, both of emulators and simulators can be used to conduct MANET research. This section presents two widely used emulators.

4.1 Mininet

Mininet [15] is a virtual network simulation platform developed by Stanford University. It started in 2010 and has been widely used in SDN emulation. Mininet can be developed to validate various communication protocols. Because the code on the Miniet node is a Linux executable, its protocols can be better ported to hardware.

Mininet creates virtual hosts using the process-based virtualization method and network namespace mechanism to separate network interfaces, routing tables and ARP tables of different virtual hosts. Namespace and group have been supported since Linux version 2.2.26, and these features also support container development. The virtual switch in Mininet is a software OpenFlow switch named "Open vSwitch". The link between the virtual host and the virtual switch is achieved by using the virtual Ethernet pair provided by the Linux kernel. The Linux kernel protocol stack parses data sent from one virtual host to another [16]. Mininet uses the Python API to set up network topologies.

Mininet has good scalability. Its lightweight structure makes it easy to simulate a network with thousands of nodes on a single host and verify and test a complete network system, including hosts, links, switches, etc. Mininet can also be used to verify the routing algorithm of the MANET network. However, Mininet has the following disadvantages: (1) limited protocol support and dependence on Linux kernel protocol stack, (2) the node lacks mobility modeling support, (3) CPU can not accurately schedule the sequence of the virtual host, virtual switch and controller, and its simulation results are not accurate and difficult to reproduce.

4.2 EstiNet

EstiNet is a novel commercial simulator. EstiNet originated from NCTUns and became commercial software in 2011, which can run network emulation at high speed without losing fidelity. EstiNet's network simulation layer includes the physical, MAC, network, transport, and application layers, which correspond to the actual network structure [17].

Unlike the virtual nodes in Mininet that completely depend on the Linux protocol stack, EstiNet uses a method called "CR" kernel re-entry. EstiNet captures the IP packets sent by the Linux kernel to the lower layer through the tunnel network interface and sends them to EstiNet's simulation engine. Each virtual node has its simulation protocol stack in the simulation engine, including the MAC and physical layers, which can simulate parameters such as link delay and bandwidth. As a commercial software, EstiNet is much better than Mininet in terms of accuracy and repeatability [18]. At the same time, EstiNet also has good scalability and superior performance in large-scale network simulation.

EstiNet is mainly used in SDN to emulate the interaction between the Openflow switch and the Openflow controller. However, this architecture is also very suitable for MANET emulation. EstiNet also provides examples of MANET protocol emulation. The disadvantages of EstiNet include: (1) commercial software with no open source and (2) limited support for MANET and node mobility.

5   Comparison and Analysis

This paper investigates the five well-known simulation and emulation tools, each with its characteristics, applicable fields, and shortcomings. Table 1 summarizes the basic characteristics of these tools.

Table 1. Comparison List of Basic Characteristics

Name	NS-3	OMNET++	NetSim	Mininet	EstiNet
Type	simulator	simulator	simulator	emulator	emulator
License	Open Source	Open Source	Commercial	Open Source	Commercial
OS	windows, linux, macOS	windows, macOS	windows	linux	linux
Program Language	C++, python	C++	C, JAVA	python	–
Released	2008	1997	2002	2010	2011
Latest	2022	2022	2021	2021	2021

Table 2. Comparison List of Performance and Supported Network

Name	NS-3	OMNET++	NetSim	Mininet	EstiNet
Memory Usage	excellent	poor	good	good	excellent
Velocity	Good	average	average	good	good
scalability	excellent	good	good	excellent	good
User Guide	Good	good	excellent	good	average
Supported Network Scenario	Ethernet, 4G, 5G, Ad hoc, mesh, WIFI, VANET, MANET	5G, Ad hoc, WiFi, Ethernet, VANET, MANET, LTE	5G, WiFi, Ad hoc, mesh, MANET, VANET, IOT/WSN, SDN	SDN, Ad hoc, MANET	SDN, WiFi, Ad hoc, MANET, VANET

Literature [19] evaluated the performance of mainstream simulation tools at that time, and literature [20] evaluated the performance of discrete event simulation tools. The simulation tools mentioned in this paper are compared based on the existing work and the author's practice. Table 2 summarizes the performance differences of the application scenarios for these simulation tools.

In MANET research, simulation tools are needed to support the wireless channel model, standard communication protocol (such as 802.11), MANET routing protocol

Table 3. Comparison List of Protocol and Mobility Models

Name	NS-3	OMNET++	NetSim	Mininet	EstiNet
Radio Propagation Models	Friis Loss Model, 3GPP Loss Model, Random Loss, etc.	Rician Fading, Rayleigh Fading, Free space path loss, etc.	Friis Loss Model, Free Space, Log Distance, COST231, HATA, indoor, Rayleigh, Nakagami	Friis Loss Model, Log-Distance Loss Model, Two-Ray Ground Loss Model, etc.	Friis Loss Model, Two-Ray Ground Loss Model, Rician Fading, Rayleigh Fading, etc.
Device (MAC&PHY)	3GPP, LTE, IEEE 802.11, Ethernet	Ethernet, IEEE 802.11, 5G, 3GPP, LTE	5G, LTE, IEEE 802.11 a/b/g/n/ac/e/p, Ethernet	IEEE 802.11	5G, Ethernet, IEEE 802.11 a/g, LTE, 3GPP
MANET Routing	AODV, TORA, DSR, DSDV	AODV, DSDV, DYMO, GPSR	DSR, AODV, ZRP, OKSR	BATMAN OLSR, BABEL	OLSRD2
Internet Protocol Stack	TCP, UDP, IPv4, IPv6	TCP, UDP, IPv4, IPv6, OSPF, BGP	TCP, IP, UDP	TCP, UDP, IP	TCP, UDP, IPv4, IPv6, OSPF, RIP, BGP,
APP	HTTP, FTP, TELNET	HTTP, FTP, TELNET, DNS	HTTP, FTP, P2P, Video Traffic, Email, Custom Model	User Defined	HTTP, FTP, DHCP, NAT, VPN, DNS, SSH, etc.
Mobility models	Random, Constant Acceleration, Constant Acceleration	Tractor, Random, GaussMarkov, Chiang Mobility, Deterministic Model	Random way point model, Group mobility, File Based Mobility, etc.	Random Walk, Gauss Markov, Truncated Levy Walk, etc.	Random

and mobility model. Table 3 investigates the protocols supported by various simulation tools, including application layer protocols. The content in Table 3 includes the functions of this software and the plug-in functions provided by their communities. The perfect ecology is also an important part of the simulation tool.

Through comparative studies, we find that the simulators are mature but limited performance of time for large-scale MANET, while the emulator has limited model support but has great potential.

With the continuous development of technology, network simulation technology is also developing. Regarding requirements, the development goals of network simulation are faster simulation speed, more simulation nodes, more accurate simulation results, easier use and easier to expand the software architecture.

1. With the development of parallel computing and distributed theory, more and more simulation software began to develop distributed processing and parallel simulation mechanisms to improve the computing speed of large-scale simulation.

2. The design of modularity is emphasized constantly. Network simulation tools should abstract hierarchical modules that conform to the OSI network model, improve logicality and readability, make simulation event mechanisms more similar to the real network, and improve the accuracy and credibility of simulation results.

3. Better user support and friend GUIs. The tools tend to abandon specialized programming languages in favor of widely used general-purpose programming languages such as C++, Python, and JAVA.

4. Various extension packages and tools are developed on open-source frameworks to meet different needs. For example, node mobility models and scene modeling are required in MANET, while many traditional simulation tools lack these functions. The open source community can work closely with users and update tools. For example, Mininet-WiFi [21], provided by the Mininet community and INET framework [22], provided by the OMNET++ community, offer MANET support.

Despite these developments, the architecture of the discrete event simulator itself is limited. For large-scale MANET simulations, the interactions between the nodes cause the simulator to perform long-time computations before the result is obtained. However, after the above summary comparison, we can find that the current emulator is still not very mature. Compared to the rich simulation tools, the only widely used open-source emulator is Mininet. Emulators are still evolving rapidly, and we'll look at their prospects and current problems in the next section.

6   Future Enhancement of Emulators for Large-Scale MANET

For large-scale MANET, discrete event simulators cost too much time, while the existing real-time emulators cannot provide rich models and the simulation results are not accurate enough. Therefore, there is still room for further development of MANET emulation tools, such as optimizing memory usage, providing more mobility models and scene modeling for real-time simulation tools, and developing emulation architectures with higher fidelity.

6.1 High Performance Open Source Emulators Based on Container

With the development of virtualization technology, container technology and cloud computing have been widely used, the container is suitable to act as the node of a network emulator, so the real-time simulation tool based on the container is also proposed. Such tools have better scalability and lower resource consumption.

Docker [23] is currently the most popular container technology, and real-time online simulators based on Docker have appeared. NestedNet [24] is an emulation environment for hierarchical SDN systems, and it also provides an example MANET with 12 nodes. The inter-node throughput in NestedNet can reach 32 Gbps. DockSDN [25] is a SDN emulator based on a docker container, and its performance is better than Mininet. Kathara [26] is an open-source real-time simulation system, and it is designed to be used in the teaching of standard computer networks.

However, the scale of emulator nodes generally does not exceed hundreds, and no MANET emulators can scale up to thousands of nodes horizontally. The performance of a single computer is limited, and the software running on it cannot strike a balance between simulation speed and memory footprint. One possible idea is to build distributed real-time emulators. In the Internet industry, thousands of containers can be managed using server clusters and Kubernetes [27] tools to deploy microservices in containers. The emulator can learn from the successful experience of the data center. A high-performance container overlay network is first required to build a distributed emulator. Container networks can provide a virtual layer on top of the real network with vnet and OvSwitch [28]. We need a tool to easily define the topologies of a virtual overlay network for real-time emulation. Then we can define the link parameters during the transmission of the virtual network to emulate the scenario in the real MANET.

6.2 High Fidelity Emulators with Physical Layer Emulation Capability

So far, all the emulators we have discussed are software running on single or several computers, and they can only provide link-level simulations. For wireless channel level emulation, we inevitably need to integrate simulation with emulation, as Mininet-WiFi and EstiNet do. This requires software to compute the result when packets transmit between nodes, which will destroy real-time performance.

DARPA has developed the Colosseum, an emulation platform that runs on a cluster of servers. Colosseum has real RF systems for traffic and high-precision wireless channel simulation based on FPGA and USRP (Universal Software Radio Peripheral). The Colosseum system provides both packet-level emulation in software and IQ radio-level emulation. It's a semi-physical emulator, and it builds a 256×256 RF channel simulator that can compute and simulate more than 65000 channel interactions between more than 256 wireless devices in real time. The Colosseum is well suited for MANET emulations. However, the Colosseum relies on high-performance servers and expensive radio frequency devices, which are more complex. The Colosseum only supports a fixed and limited number of nodes. It is necessary to design an emulation environment that provides both link-level and IQ-level emulation, and the number of nodes can be easily extended.

6.3   High Scalability Emulator with Real Devices and Virtual Nodes

Another issue that needs to be addressed is an emulating interface with real devices. Existing simulators can only provide limited interactive support for real devices, such as NS-3 and OMNET++. However, emulators based on containers can provide a more integrated heterogeneous emulation method. The virtual nodes simulated by containers should be equivalent to the physical nodes in the virtual topology. They should be able to send and receive protocol packets in real time with each other.

7   Conclusion

The discrete event simulator has a mature simulation paradigm and a lot of early research, while the real-time emulator has better scalability but lacks the MANET model. Open source simulators have a better community ecosystem and a richer model base, and commercial simulators have better user support, prettier GUIs, and better performance. NS-3 would be a better choice in open source simulators, and its performance is the best in discrete event simulators. This paper investigates and summarizes various simulators and emulators, which will help researchers in the field of MANET to select appropriate tools for protocol and algorithm research. We also found that none of the existing emulators can fully meet the research needs in the field of MANET, and a new emulator may be designed to meet all the requirements of network researchers in the future. The new emulator must support all types of networks, protocols, and mobility models. It must be extensible, scalable and provide good emulation support with real devices.

Acknowledgements. This work is supported by Science and Technology Project of State Grid Shanghai Municipal Electrical Power Company. (SGSHXT00YJJS2100140).

References

1. Fujimoto, R.M., Riley, G.F., Perumalla, K.S.: Network Simulators, pp. 5–17. Springer, Cham (2007)
2. Bang, A.O., Ramteke, P.L.: MANET: history, challenges and applications. Int. J. Appl. Innov. Eng. Manage. (IJAIEM) **2**, 249–251 (2013)
3. Ramphull, D., Mungur, A., Armoogum, S., Pudaruth, S.: A review of mobile ad hoc network (MANET) protocols and their applications. In: 2021 5th International Conference on Intelligent Computing and Control Systems (ICICCS), pp. 204–211 (2021)
4. Gustavo, C.: NS-3: network simulator 3. In: UTM Lab Meeting, April 2010
5. OPNET NETWORK SIMULATOR. https://opnetprojects.com/opnet-network-simulator/. Accessed 29 Aug 2022
6. What is OMNET. https://omnetpp.org/intro/. Accessed 29 Aug 2022
7. Mininet overview. http://mininet.org/overview/. Accessed 29 Aug 2022
8. Wang, S., Chou, C, L., Yang, C, M.: EstiNet openflow network simulator and emulator. IEEE Commun. Mag. **51**(9), 110–117 (2013)
9. Kafetzis, D., Vassilaras, S., Vardoulias, G., Koutsopoulos, I.: Software-defined networking meets software-defined radio in mobile ad hoc networks: state of art and future directions. IEEE Access **10**, 9989–10014 (2022)

10. Manpreet, Malhotra, J.: A survey on MANET simulation tools. In: 2014 Innovative Applications of Computational Intelligence on Power, Energy and Controls with their impact on Humanity (CIPECH), pp. 495–498 (2014)
11. Dorathy, I., Chandrasekaran, M.: Simulation tools for mobile ad hoc networks: a survey. J. Appl. Res. Technol. 437–445 (2018)
12. Keshav, S.: REAL: a network simulator. Technical report. UCB/CSD-88-472, EECS Department, University of California, Berkeley (1988)
13. The Network Simulator - NS2. http://www.isi.edu/nsnam/ns/. Accessed 29 Aug 2022
14. Sharma, P., Gupta, R., Sharm, S.: A comparative study of NS-2 and NS-3. Int. J. Sci. Res. Dev. 2(3), 428–431 (2014)
15. Lantz, B., Heller, B., McKeown, N.: A network in a laptop: rapid prototyping for software-defined networks. In: ACM Hotnets 2010, Monterey (2010)
16. Pfaff, B., Pettit, J., Koponen, T., Amidon, K., Casado, M., Shenkerz, S.: Extending networking into the virtualization layer, January 2009
17. Wang, S., Chou, C., Lin, C.: The design and implementation of the NCTUns network simulation engine. Simul. Model. Pract. Theory 15(1), 57–81 (2007)
18. Wang, S.: Comparison of SDN OpenFlow network simulator and emulators: EstiNet vs. Mininet. In: 2014 IEEE Symposium on Computers and Communications (ISCC). pp. 1–6 (2014)
19. Yang, L.-Y., Li, Y.-K., Han, S.-S., Wang, X.: Network simulation and computational experiment platforms: the overview and prospect. J. Command Control 4(4), 281–290 (2018)
20. Admassu, T.: Performance analysis of emulated software defined wireless network. Indonesian J. Electr. Eng. Comput. Sci. 16, 311 (2019)
21. Fontes, R.R., Afzal, S., Brito, S.H., Santos, M.A., Rothenberg, C.E.: Mininet-WiFi: emulating software-defined wireless networks. In: 2015 11th International Conference on Network and Service Management (CNSM), pp. 384–389. IEEE (2015)
22. INET Framework. https://inet.omnetpp.org/. Accessed 29 Aug 2022
23. Docker Homepage. https://www.docker.com/. Accessed 29 Aug 2022
24. Zhang, X., Prabhu, N., Tessier, R.: NestedNet: a container-based prototyping tool for hierarchical software defined networks. In: 2020 International Workshop on Rapid System Prototyping (RSP), pp. 1–7 (2020)
25. Petersen, E., To, M.A.: DockSDN: a hybrid container-based SDN emulation tool. In: 2020 IEEE Latin-American Conference on Communications (LATIN-COM), pp. 1–6 (2020)
26. Scazzariello, M., Ariemma, L., Caiazzi, T.: Kathará: a lightweight network emulation system. In: NOMS 2020 IEEE/IFIP Network Operations and Management Symposium, pp. 1–2 (2020)
27. Bernstein, D.: Containers and cloud: from LXC to Docker to Kubernetes. IEEE Cloud Comput. 1(3), 81–84 (2014)
28. Dua, R., Kohli, V., Konduri, S.K.: Learning Docker Networking. Packt Publishing, Birmingham (2016)

A Data-Driven Algorithm for Large-Scale Multi-camera Calibration

Zijun Wang(iD), Yuhui Wan(iD), Kunlin Zhong(iD), Yixin Zhang(✉),
and Jian Wang(✉)

School of Electronic Science and Engineering, Nanjing University,
Nanjing 210023, China
{zyixin,wangjnju}@nju.edu.cn

Abstract. Multi-camera calibration, which is the establishment of a mapping relationship between the 2D coordinates of individual cameras and the 3D world coordinates, has been a major challenge in computer vision technology. The model-driven multi-camera calibration, which starts from the imaging model of the camera, is computationally complex and difficult to consider the imaging distortion comprehensively, while the data-driven multi-camera calibration is often difficult to meet the needs of large-scale scenes in terms of the calibration range. To solve the above two common problems, this paper designs a multi-camera image acquisition system, which collects millions of point cloud coordinate samples in a large-scale space and uses neural networks to infinitely approximate the transformation model of 2D images and 3D world. After the calibration experiments, the scheme is simple and effective, and it can accomplish the requirement of high precision calibration for large-scale space in both spatial positioning and reprojection.

Keywords: Multi-camera calibration · Large-scale · Data-driven · Neural networks

1 Introduction

With the continuous development of computer vision technology, multi-camera has gained widespread attention in the fields of 3D reconstruction, part measurement, defect detection, and autopilot due to their advantages such as extensive measurement range, multiple perspectives, and rich 3D information [1]. The accuracy of the calibration results and the stability of the algorithm directly affect the subsequent 3D reconstruction work. The size of the calibration space also directly limits the use of multi-camera, so how to perform high-precision calibration in large-scale space is the focus of this work.

The current multi-camera calibration work can be broadly divided into two categories. One is defined as model-driven from the imaging model of the camera. And another is defined as data-driven camera calibration from the coordinate data of pairs of massive 2D pixel points and corresponding 3D world

X. Jiang (Ed.): MLICOM 2022, LNICST 481, pp. 75–85, 2023.
https://doi.org/10.1007/978-3-031-30237-4_7

points. Based on the model-driven calibration method, the geometric camera imaging model must be established to consider various possible aberrations in the imaging process. However, the more cameras there are, the more comprehensive the aberrations are considered, and the more accurate the imaging model is. Still, the more computationally tricky it is to perform the calibration work. Unlike model-driven calibration methods, data-driven multi-camera calibration does not require complex model computation and analysis. The mapping relationship between two-dimensional images and the three-dimensional world can be accurately solved using the powerful fitting ability of neural networks. Based on the above reasons, this paper establishes a mapping model with the help of neural networks using a data-driven calibration method. It verifies the feasibility of performing high-precision multi-camera calibration work even in a large-scale range.

2   Related Works

A new algorithm is proposed in [2] for calibrating cameras using occlusion contours of spheres, requiring the camera to observe the sphere at three or more locations. By specifying the problem in dyadic space, [2] recovers the camera parameters optimally using semidefinite planning. The solution is simple, flexible, enabling simultaneous calibration of multiple cameras. However, this approach can be susceptible to degradation or camera aberrations. Lu and Li [3] have designed a theodolite coordinate measurement system (TCMS), a global calibration scheme. The system determines the 3D coordinates of the feature points. Then, the global calibration is performed by direct and indirect transformation methods according to the calibration target position of the camera. But the calibration accuracy of the system depends on the theodolite coordinate measurement system, and its establishment process is slow. Other calibrations of multi-camera use auxiliary tools such as mirrors [4] [5]. Shen and Hornsey [6] present a novel non-planar target for fast calibration of inward-looking visual sensor networks (VSNs). Two spheres built on a supporting rod are used as calibration targets. However, the non-planar targets are applied separately rather than to all cameras. All of the above work is model-driven, but model-driven starts from a complex imaging model, which is difficult to derive, challenging to estimate distortions, and computationally complex and time-consuming.

As artificial neural network technology [7] continues to develop and advance, more and more problems in computer vision can be solved using neural network methods [8]. The same is true for camera calibration. Ahmed et al. [9] propose a method for camera calibration using neural networks, whose network solves the perspective projection matrix between the world's 3D points and the associated 2D image pixels, solving four calibration problems: (i) Estimating all camera parameters simultaneously. (ii) Estimating other parameters given the image center. (iii) Estimating extrinsic parameters given intrinsic parameters. (iv) Estimating intrinsic parameters given extrinsic parameters. However, this algorithm is only suitable for single-camera calibration work. Chen [10] proposes an improved genetic simulated annealing algorithm to optimize Back Propagation neural networks for binocular camera calibration, which has high calibration accuracy and significantly improves the calibration speed but has a limited calibration space size.

3   Method

To solve the problems of complex calculation and limited calibration range, this paper designs the following system for data acquisition and uses a neural network algorithm for high-precision multi-camera calibration.

3.1   Image Acquisition System

In this paper, we design an auto-system using the multi-camera to acquire images of calibrators at different heights. Based on the system, a large and highly dense calibration point cloud [11] is generated, which provides data support for data-driven multi-camera calibration based on 8 cameras, arranged in the order shown in Fig. 1, with the image acquisition logic shown in Fig. 2.

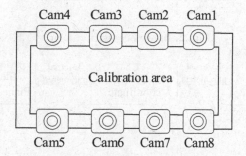

Fig. 1. Camera Array.

3.2   Multi-camera Calibration Process

The camera calibration aims to solve the mapping relationship between the world and pixel coordinate systems, involving the coordinate transformation relationships shown in Fig. 3.

The model-driven calibration of a multi-camera relies on an accurate mathematical imaging model. However, it is challenging to consider the full range of imaging aberrations and accurately describe the non-linear aberrations between the ideal image plane and the actual image plane. All non-linear factors are included in the neural network. Only the coordinates of many point clouds in the camera imaging space are needed to infinitely approximate the mapping between 3D world coordinates and pixel coordinates. In summary, the data-driven calibration method solves the pain points of the model-driven method with the amount of data and skips the intermediate transformation process. The mapping relationship between the two is shown in Fig. 3.

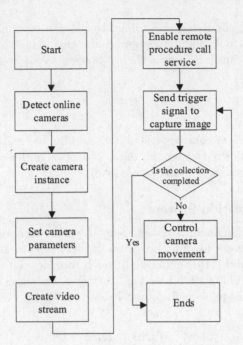

Fig. 2. Image acquisition logic.

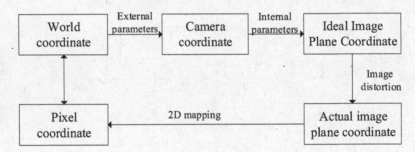

Fig. 3. Coordinate conversion relationships.

Neural Network Structure and Principles. With the development of artificial intelligence, it has been shown that neural networks are capable of approximating arbitrary continuous functions with infinitely minor errors, incorporating all non-linearities. Based on this property, using neural networks makes it possible to perform multi-camera calibrations.

A neural network consists of three parts, an input layer, hidden layers and an output layer. The neural network structure used in this paper is shown in Fig. 4.

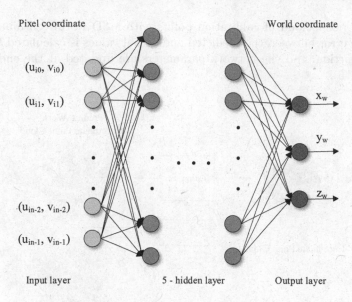

Fig. 4. Neural network structure.

Input Layer. Receives the pixel coordinates from the multi-camera and passes the pixel coordinate information to the hidden layers.

Hidden Layers. The hidden layers used in this paper are all fully connected, the number of neurons in each layer is 32, 64, 128, 64, and 32, respectively, and the principle of action is as in Eq. 1.

$$output = input \times kernel + b \tag{1}$$

Input is a fully connected network input, the output of the fully connected layer, kernel is the internal weight matrix, and b is the bias. The function of the fully connected layer is to perform an affine transformation on the feature data. And the multiple superimposed affine transformations are still essentially affine transformations. The appropriate activation function can introduce non-linear parameters that perfectly fit the mapping relationship between the pixel and 3D world space.

Output layer. The network predicts three neurons for the 3D world coordinates.

Evaluation Indicators. The calibration network uses a multi-layer fully-connected neural network for multi-camera calibration. The core operation of a fully connected neural network is matrix multiplication, which is essentially a feature space transformation. The neural networks-based multi-camera calibration method is driven by data, which first requires extracting the pixel coordinates of calibration points in the chessboard image and establishing a pixel coordinate point cloud of calibration points with a 3D world coordinate point cloud. The error between the predicted and actual values is calculated based on the loss function, and the network parameters are updated at the end of each epoch (Fig. 5).

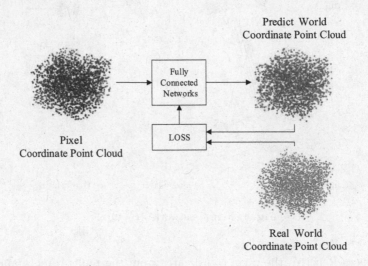

Fig. 5. Schematic of a fully connected calibration network

The neural network loss function is set to MAE(Mean Absolute Error), as shown in the following:

$$MAE = \frac{\sum_{i=1}^{n} \left[|x_w - x_w'| + |y_w - y_w'| + |z_w - z_w'| \right]}{n} \tag{2}$$

where x_w', y_w', z_w' are the corresponding predicted values, respectively. Through continuous iterative training, different weights and biases in the three-dimensional error space will cause the mean absolute error between the true and predicted values to change, so the magnitude of the MAE value is also an indicator of intuitively understanding the performance of the calibration network.

4   Experiments and Results

4.1   Calibration Data Set Processing

Experiments will be conducted to verify whether the fully connected network can calibrate the multi-camera with high accuracy in large-scale space. As the chessboard [12] calibration board has the characteristics of perspective invariance and high accuracy in large-scale calibration space, it can present apparent edge features at any position and accurately identify saddle points, which helps to improve spatial positioning accuracy. Therefore, this paper adopts the chessboard calibration board as a calibration tool to accurately and conveniently prepare 3D world coordinates and pixel coordinates datasets to provide tremendous data support for the neural network.

Figure 6 shows the use of a chessboard specification with a grid size of 3.81 mm×3.81 mm, and the calibration points are arranged as 200 × 299. The chessboard has 59800 calibration points, covering 1143×765.81 mm^2 of space.

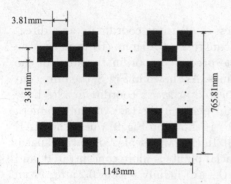
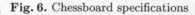

Fig. 6. Chessboard specifications

Fig. 7. Neural network train point cloud

The multi-camera calibration system designed in this paper has 8-cameras with an image resolution of 4608 × 3456. There are 76 images on the z-axis of the calibration board, which is uniformly at 4 mm intervals.

Using the OpenCV tool library to identify chessboard corner points with subpixel accuracy, a total of 4.5 million samples were obtained, forming a calibrated coordinate point cloud in 3D space, as shown in Fig. 7.

4.2 Calibration Results and Accuracy Analysis

The neural network was trained on a GPU (Graphics Processing Unit), with the number of iterations set to 1000, the learning rate set to 0.0001, and the MAE defined by equation (1) as the loss function.

Spatial Positioning Results. Divide the collected samples according to the ratio of the train set, validation set, and test set 8:1:1. The calibration results from pixel space to 3D world space are shown in Table 1.

Table 1. Spatial positioning accuracy (mm)

MAE for each coordinate axis	Value
x-axis	0.14
y-axis	0.12
z-axis	0.15
Average	0.14

The average spatial positioning accuracy of all three coordinate axis directions in the large-scale calibration space can reach 0.15 mm. To evaluate the prediction effect more intuitively, we fit the predicted coordinate values of the 3D world by the network with the actual values. As shown in Fig. 8, the fully connected network-based multi-camera is calibrated at x, y, z coordinate axes have a high degree of agreement, all of which can perform the task of multi-camera calibration at large scales well. The accuracy is shown in Fig. 9, where the MAE of the test sample is fitted on the 3D surface. In the large-scale calibration space, the local positioning accuracy of the 3D spatial points is more concentrated, and calibration errors in fully connected networks are mainly within 0.2 mm. From the error surface, the calibration accuracy is poorer at the edges, and extreme points with significant errors can occur, probably due to less information around the edge calibration points.

Reprojection Results. Reprojection is an inverse operation with spatial localization to map the 3D world coordinates to the pixel coordinates of the eight cameras. The projected pixel errors for the eight cameras are averaged, and the reprojection accuracy is shown in Table 2.

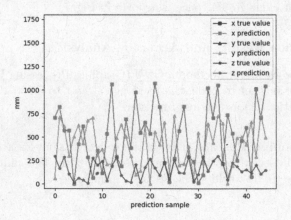

Fig. 8. Results of fitting each axis of the fully connected network.

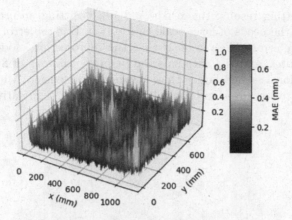

Fig. 9. Fully connected network error surfaces.

Table 2. Reprojection accuracy (in pixels)

MAE for each coordinate axis	Value
x-axis	0.29
y-axis	0.31
Average	0.30

Reprojecting from the 3D world space to the pixel plane, the difference between the results in the x and y axes is small, with an average value of 0.30 pixels. The reprojection error of 0.3 pixels satisfies the need for high precision calibration in large-scale calibration. The reprojection results for each camera are similar, so we selected the results of one of them. The results are as shown in Fig. 10. Figure 11 shows its reprojection error surface.

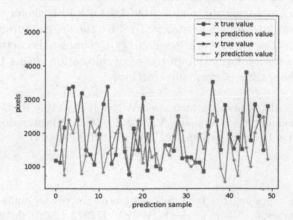

Fig. 10. Results of reprojection fitting for fully connected networks

From the fitting results, the x-axis and y-axis fitting accuracies are high, fully satisfying the needs of large-scale calibration. But the error surface shows an obvious edge error. The reason is that the reprojection model input is 3D spatial coordinates, and the output is the pixel coordinates of 8 cameras. The output dimension is much larger than the input dimension, which makes the model difficult to converge, and the calibration accuracy is relatively poor.

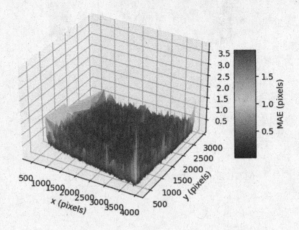

Fig. 11. Fully connected network error surfaces.

5   Conclusion

This paper designs and implements an 8-camera calibration image acquisition system, and the system size is $1143 \times 765.81\,\text{mm}^2$. A fully connected network calibration was carried out using 4.5 million data in a large-scale scene. Based on the experimental results, the network achieves an accuracy of 0.14 mm from pixel coordinates to 3D world coordinates and a reprojection accuracy of up to 0.3 pixels. The result demonstrates the effectiveness of the network in calibrating multi-camera in large-scale space and provides a sound basis for subsequent 3D reconstruction work with high accuracy. To solve the edge accuracy degradation problem, in the subsequent work, we can try to change the network structure or enrich the position information of the edge calibration points to improve the multi-camera calibration performance further.

Acknowledgements. This work was supported by Jiangsu Key R&D Plan (Industry Foresight and Common Key Technology) (BE2018114) and Postgraduate Research & Practice Innovation Program of Jiangsu Province (SJCX22_0014).

References

1. Olagoke, A.S., Ibrahim, H., Teoh, S.S.: Literature survey on multi-camera system and its application. IEEE Access **8**, 172892–172922 (2020). https://doi.org/10. 1109/ACCESS.2020.3024568

2. Agrawal, M., Davis, L.S.: camera calibration using spheres: a semi-definite programming approach. In: Proceedings of the Ninth IEEE International Conference on Computer Vision, ICCV 2003, vol. 2, p. 782. IEEE Computer Society, USA (2003)
3. Lu, R., Li, Y.: A global calibration method for large-scale multi-sensor visual measurement systems. Sens. Actu. A Phys. **116**(3), 384–393 (2004). https://doi. org/10.1016/j.sna.2004.05.019, https://www.sciencedirect.com/science/article/ pii/S0924424704003279
4. Lébraly, P., Deymier, C., Ait-Aider, O., Royer, E., Dhome, M.: Flexible extrinsic calibration of non-overlapping cameras using a planar mirror: application to vision-based robotics. In: 2010 IEEE/RSJ International Conference on Intelligent Robots and Systems, pp. 5640–5647 (2010). https://doi.org/10.1109/IROS.2010.5651552
5. Xu, Z., Wang, Y., Yang, C.: Multi-camera global calibration for large-scale measurement based on plane mirror. Optik **126**(23), 4149–4154 (2015). https://doi. org/10.1016/j.ijleo.2015.08.015, https://www.sciencedirect.com/science/article/ pii/S0030402615007743
6. Shen, E., Hornsey, R.: Multi-camera network calibration with a non-planar target. IEEE Sens. J. **11**(10), 2356–2364 (2011). https://doi.org/10.1109/JSEN.2011. 2123884
7. Abiodun, O.I., Jantan, A., Omolara, A.E., Dada, K.V., Mohamed, N.A., Arshad, H.: State-of-the-art in artificial neural network applications: a survey. Heliyon **4**(11), e00938 (2018). https://doi.org/10.1016/j.heliyon.2018.e00938, https://www.sciencedirect.com/science/article/pii/S2405844018332067
8. Zhou, Y.T., Chellappa, R.: Computational Neural Networks, pp. 6–14. Springer, New York (1992). https://doi.org/10.1007/978-1-4612-2834-9_2
9. Ahmed, M., Hemayed, E., Farag, A.: Neurocalibration: a neural network that can tell camera calibration parameters. In: Proceedings of the Seventh IEEE International Conference on Computer Vision, vol. 1, pp. 463–468 (1999). https://doi.org/ 10.1109/ICCV.1999.791257
10. Chen, L., Zhang, F., Sun, L.: Research on the calibration of binocular camera based on bp neural network optimized by improved genetic simulated annealing algorithm. IEEE Access **8**, 103815–103832 (2020). https://doi.org/10.1109/ACCESS. 2020.2992652
11. Guo, Y., Wang, H., Hu, Q., Liu, H., Liu, L., Bennamoun, M.: Deep learning for 3D point clouds: a survey. IEEE Trans. Pattern Anal. Mach. Intell. **43**(12), 4338–4364 (2021). https://doi.org/10.1109/TPAMI.2020.3005434
12. De la Escalera, A., Armingol, J.M.: Automatic chessboard detection for intrinsic and extrinsic camera parameter calibration. Sensors **10**(3), 2027–2044 (2010). https://doi.org/10.3390/s100302027, https://www.mdpi.com/1424-8220/ 10/3/2027

Efficient Transmission Protocols for the Satellite-Terrestrial Integrated Networks

Yunjie Xiao[1], Hao Zhang[2], Qianyu Ji[3], Yixin Zhang[3(✉)], and Jian Wang[3(✉)]

[1] State Grid Shanghai Municipal Electrical Power Company, Shanghai 200002, China
[2] Global Energy Internet Research Institute Co.Ltd., Nanjing 210003, China
[3] School of Electronic Science and Engineering, Nanjing University,
Nanjing 210023, China
{zyixin,wangjnju}@nju.edu.cn

Abstract. The satellite-terrestrial integrated network (STIN) can provide ubiquitous coverage.However, the eature longer transmission delays, higher bit error rates and frequency switches, which challenge the design of the transmission communication protocols to perform well. In particular, users usually have a very short view time of the satellites. The improvement of transmission efficiency cannot be ignored to complete the transmission of a certain amount of information. The multi-path methods are promised to facilitate the efficiency of packet transmission, which can provide service even the links between the satellite and the ground in poor channel conditions. This paper proposes a multi-path transmission control protocol for STIN, named MPTCP. The proposed MPTCP decomposes the data in the network into multi-flows and then transmits the flows on multi-unrelated paths. We implement the MPTCP in a simulation SDN environment of STIN. The results show that the proposed MPTCP performs better than traditional TCP and ECMP (Equal Cost Multipath Routing) schemes in end-to-end and pack loss.

Keywords: Satellite-Terrestrial Integrated Networks · SDN · TCP · MPTCP

1 Introduction

With the development of communication systems, the satellite-terrestrial integrated communication network (STIN) has gradually become a hot research field for communication systems. In STIN, the Low Earth Orbit (LEO) satellites play an important role because of their low transmission power, low transmission delay, high real-time and strong anti-destructive capability [1]. However, satellite-terrestrial links feature long delay, high error codes and intermittency compared with terrestrial links. In this case, the widely used TCP/IP based protocols are unsuitable for the STIN [2].

Currently, the multi-path transmission technology is rapidly rising, hoping to improve the end-to-end communication performance in the parallel transmission

X. Jiang (Ed.): MLICOM 2022, LNICST 481, pp. 86–96, 2023.
https://doi.org/10.1007/978-3-031-30237-4_8

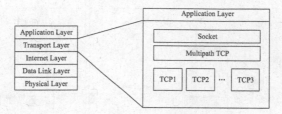

Fig. 1. The Proposed Multi-path TCP Protocol Structure.

of multi-path data. Multi-path TCP (MPTCP) is a multi-path transmission scheme at the transport layer that guarantees the quality of the network operation. MPTCP can split the data stream into multi-flows and transmit the flows on multi-paths individually so that when one of the paths in the network is congested or fails, the data in the network can still be transmitted normally. There are already technical solutions to implement multi-path transmission at the application layer [3,4], transport layer [5] and network layer [6] as well as at the data link layer [7].

This paper aims to improve the information transmission efficiency in the satellite-terrestrial integrated networks (STIN). We propose a multi-path transmission scheme based on the SDN architecture to decompose the data in the network into multi-flows and then transmits the flows on multi-unrelated paths. The remainder of this paper is as follows. Section 2 introduces the MPTCP protocol about the structure and the communication mechanism. Section 3 implements the proposed access MPTCP algorithm based on SDN in detail. The proposed method is eventually validated through simulation in Sect. 4. Finally, the conclusions of this paper are drawn in Sect. 5.

2 The Proposed Multi-path TCP Protocol (MPTCP) for STIN

2.1 The Structure of MPTCP

The proposed MPTCP protocol is located between the transport and application layers, using multi-paths simultaneously for data transmission and in the form of a single TCP protocol at higher levels [8]. The structure of the MPTCP protocol is shown in Fig. 1. At the transport layer, MPTCP is divided into two layers. The upper layer performs functions such as path management of the network, while the lower layer is responsible for splitting the packets into multiple sub-flows for propagation over different wireless paths. Individual sub-flows are propagated using the same transport capabilities as TCP [9].

When the application data stream generated by upper arrives, MPTCP splits it into sub-flows. Then the different sub-flows are transferred by multiple links in the network. If there are redundant links in the network, MPTCP will make good use of them. So MPTCP can improve the efficiency of the network and the utilization of the network links. If the client and server want to use MPTCP, both

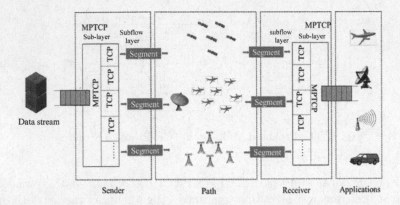

Fig. 2. The System model and the Proposed MPTCP transmission diagram for STIN.

need to support the MPTCP protocol. The MPTCP protocol is still transmitted in a single path at the transport layer. The MPTCP protocol at the transport layer receives the data, splits the data stream, adds sequence and acknowledgment numbers to the sub-paths and then sends it to the network. The server receives the data and recombines it using the sequence and acknowledgment numbers on the packets before passing it on to the upper layer applications (Fig. 2).

The communication mechanism of MPTCP consists mainly of initializing the connection, establishing sub-paths, transferring data and disconnecting. The connection is initialized similarly to TCP, established by employing three hand-shakes during the connection establishment phase. Upgraded from the TCP protocol, the MPTCP adds the MP_CAPABLE technology in the handshake to determine if the communicating parties have chosen to use the MPTCP protocol. The process is shown in Fig. 3.

2.2   The Communication Mechanism of the MPTCP

The communication mechanism of MPTCP mainly includes initializing the connection, establishing a sub-path, transmitting data, and disconnecting the connection, and the details are as follows:

1 In the control message, the key values of the sender and receiver are used to detect the origin of the packet. After the detection, the subsequent packets are continued to be processed. This key value is still used to detect if it is a MPTCP connection when adding a sub-path [10].
2 The sub-path establishment starts when the initial connection completed. The difference from initialization is that the MP_JOINT field needs to be added to the handshake message. After MPTCP initialed, the two communicate entities can acquire the source and destination IP addresses. The IP addresses

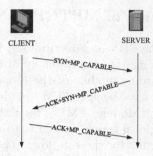

Fig. 3. The initialization of MPTCP by the three-way handshake.

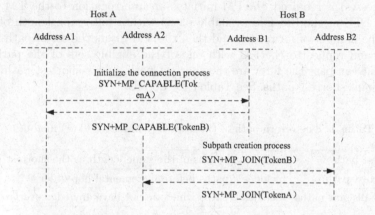

Fig. 4. MPTCP sub-path creation flowchart [11].

obtained by both communicating parties form a binary for both parties to distinguish between different sub-flows, as shown in Fig. 4.

3 When transmitting data, MPTCP split the data into multiple sub-flows and sequences the different sub-flows for propagation in different paths. After the propagation is completed at the transport layer, MPTCP transmits the data to the application layer. The sub-flow Sequence Mapping field is used to count the sequence of sub-flows during data transfer.

4 The closure of MPTCP sub-flows requires the same four-way handshake as TCP to complete the link disconnection. To ensure independence between sub-paths, each wave of the sub-path affects only its own connection relationship. It is not until the application layer has finished transferring data that the application layer calls the close function, and MPTCP acknowledges each sub-flow with a message with MP_DFIN. After receiving the control message, the server initiates an acknowledgment message to the sender, which receives and completes the match and disconnects.

3   The Implementation of MPTCP in SDN

The solution is based on the SDN architecture and is based on programming the Floodlight controller to manage the topology of the MPTCP network and to forward data. The forwarding module of the Floodlight controller adds the TOPO_MANAGER (Topology Manager, TM) module and the FORWARD-ING_MODULE (Forwarding Module, FM). The TM is responsible for monitoring and calculating the global topology, and the FM provides path selection and OpenFlow forwarding rules for the sub-flows. The TM module can sense a global view of the topology with information between the SDN controller and the switch. Whenever a path between a pair of source-destination address pairs (IP addresses) is required, the FM initiates an interrogation to the TM, which uses the DFS method to find available paths with a full graph length of up to k (k is the number of forwards), and then the TM filters the set of paths found by DFS and replies to the FM with one of the eligible sets of the path. The paths that can pass the filter are the shortest path, and k-shortest path, and k edge-disjoint shortest paths. See Table 1 for details.

Table 1. The return path of the Topology Manager (TM) module.

Shortest path	Includes all paths of the same length as the shortest path
k-shortest path	Includes k paths before incremental hop order
k-edge-disjoint paths	Includes k paths which do not have any edge overlap

3.1   The Design of the Topology Manager Module

The TM module selects the right set of paths to significantly improve the transmission efficiency of the network. If the TM adequately brings redundant links in the network into play, the utilization of the network links is increased, thus improving the efficiency of the network transmission. The FM module uses two ways of assigning sub-paths. One is random allocation, and the other is deterministic allocation. If the random allocation scheme is used, the TM returns the shortest set of paths, and this method is equivalent to ECMP. If the deterministic allocation method is used, then FM assigns sub-flows to different paths, thus implementing the MPTCP method. The deterministic allocation scheme avoids the problems that arise when the ECMP on-the-fly allocation scheme allocates different sub-flows to the same paths.

3.2   The Design of the Forwarding Module

The path-cache and flows tables are maintained in FM. The set of paths returned by TM is stored in the path-cache, and when MPTCP splits the packet into multiple sub-flows, FM searches the path-cache. If there is a matching path in the path-cache, then the flows table reads in that path and initiates an MPTCP connection between the pair of addresses MPTCP connection between the pair of addresses. Otherwise, FM issues a query to TM and then stores the result returned by TM into the two hash tables mentioned above. The path-cache refresh time can be adjusted to meet the dynamic requirements of the STIN network.

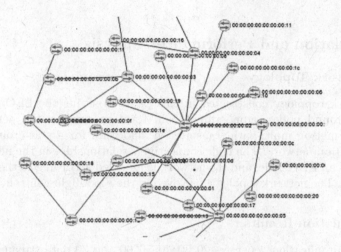

Fig. 5. Network topology observed within the controller

3.3   The Design of Flow Table Entry

The flows table includes each pair of MPTCP connection relationships, and each pair of MPTCP connection relationships also contains the sub-connection relationships within that connection relationship and is assigned to the IpEntry. The IpEntry caches the path set obtained after this source-destination IP interrogation TM and assigns it to the sub-flow.

Each time the first sub-flow in a connection arrives at the first switch in the network, the FM needs to extract the IP address and port number of the source-destination node in the sub-flow and identify the MP_CAPABLE or MP_JOIN command during this process since the switch has not yet acquired the relevant forwarding rules. If the command identified by FM is the MP_CAPABLE command, then this is an initialized sub-flow of MPTCP as described in Sect. 2.2, and address pairs needs to be stored in the Primary_IP set, then queried to the path-cache table for the set of paths that satisfy the communication requirements of this address pair, and the path set assigned to the sub-flow to prevent different sub-flows from being assigned to the same path. If the command recognized by FM is MP_JOIN, then MPTCP has completed initialization, at which point FM extracts the token from the stream and obtains the existing MPTCP connection. If the token does not exist in the stream, then this is the first additional sub-flow generated in the path, and FM uses this token to create a new connection in the network. If the token already exists in the network, then FM looks up the token corresponding to Ip_Entry and assigns the next sub-path in the path-cache that has not yet been assigned to a sub-flow and updates IpEntry. Boosts the consumption of controller computation by constantly maintaining two hash tables.

4   Simulation and Performance Analysis

4.1   Network Topology

The network topology constructed in this paper contains the LEO constellation and ground nodes, numbering 110 in total, to analyze the performance of the information multi-path transmission algorithm for a star-ground fusion communication network. The node connectivity relationships in the network are exported as an EDGE file, and the network is modeled according to the exported parameters. The network topology displayed in the Floodlight controller is Fig. 5.

4.2   Simulation Results

Firstly, the application generates $20, 30, 40, 50, 60$ and 70 data streams between node h12 and h13 in the network, causing network congestion. The performance of TCP, ECMP and the multi-path algorithm MPTCP constructed in this paper are analyzed by counting the data streams received at the server side. We use the Reno congestion control algorithm [12], and the path set in the global-aware multi-path transmission scheme was chosen as the k-disjoint path set with k being 8. The simulation time was 50 s.

The results are shown in Fig. 6. As can be seen in the figure, with 20 data streams in the network, the network is not yet congested, and no data streams are lost in any of the three scenarios. As the number of streams in the network rises, the traditional TCP protocol loses streams in the presence of network congestion, and performance degrades more quickly. The other two algorithms both used a multi-path transmission scheme in the network and were able to maintain good communication performance without experiencing significant data loss problems.

Then we initiate hundred data streams, and the traffic received on the web server side is counted for 200 s of simulation time with a 5-s interval. As the multi-path transmission algorithm needs to operate on the paths in the network and construct the path set during the initial communication, the data for the first 5 s of the simulation was discarded and analyzed. The fluctuations of the

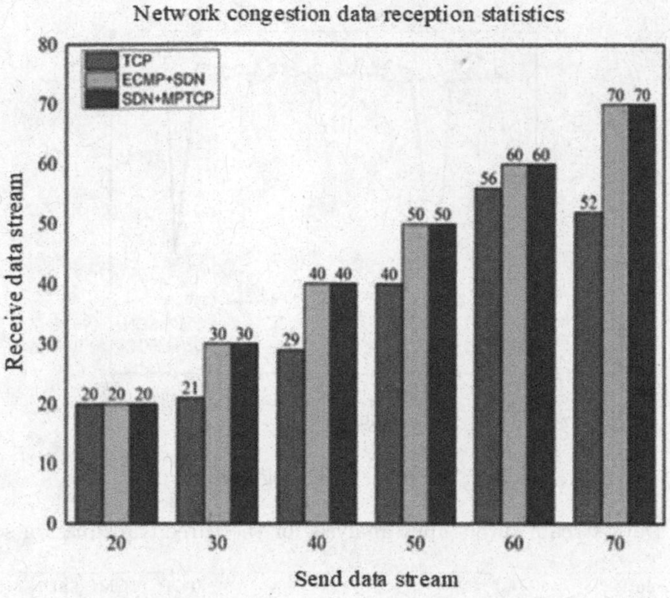

Fig. 6. Network congestion data reception statistics.

conclusion information are shown in Fig. 7. In the event of congestion in the network, the traffic received by the server in the traditional TCP scheme fluctuates considerably, with large peaks and valleys occurring during congestion, resulting in severe fluctuations and poor network stability. The ECMP and globally aware multi-path algorithms are relatively smooth. As can be seen in the figure, the ECMP scheme has slightly higher traffic fluctuations than the globally aware multi-path algorithm.

Then, we select four data streams in each scenario to see how the streams are transmitted. For comparison, one data stream is selected from each of the three transmission schemes. The simulation results are shown in Fig. 8, 9 and 10. The simulation results show that the traditional TCP protocol has large differences between data streams in the network when transmitting data and that the throughput varies dramatically when the data streams are delivered. The ECMP and MPTCP+SDN transmission schemes have relatively low network fluctuations. Looking at the data for the four data streams, the results of which are shown in Table 2. It shows that the ratio of the lowest value to the highest value of throughput for the same data stream in the network is as low as 12.9% in the traditional TCP transport scheme, 19.9% in the ECMP+SDN scheme, and 25.9% in the MPTCP+SDN scheme, which has the best performance.

The statistics of the transmission traffic of each stream in the network are shown in Fig. 11. The transmission volume of each data stream in the network

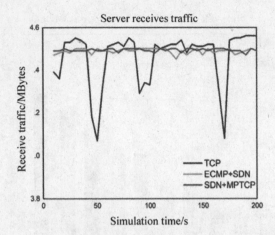

Fig. 7. Server receiving traffic.

Table 2. Data stream throughput analysis for the three transmission schemes.

Transmission solutions	TCP	ECMP+SDN	MPTCP+SDN
Single link throughput minimum/Kbytes	9.9	9.76	13.9
Maximum single link throughput/Kbytes	229	97.6	106
Ratio of minimum to maximum throughput of a single data stream	12.9%	19.9%	25.9%

fluctuates greatly in the traditional TCP transmission scheme, while the ECMP and global-aware multi-path algorithms fluctuate less. The ECMP+SDN scheme and MPTCP scheme are relatively smooth, with the lowest value of the ECMP scheme compared to the highest value of 51.1% over 100 data streams. The lowest to highest MPTCP transmission ratio was 51.9%, an improvement of 0.8 percentage points. Also, the MPTCP+SDN solution has a relatively higher minimum and maximum value than the ECMP solution, with the highest amount of network data transmitted (Table 3).

Table 3. Data stream throughput analysis for the three transmission schemes.

	TCP	ECMP+SDN	MPTCP+SDN
Minimum data stream transfer volume/KB	920.15	1259	1363.7
Maximum value of data stream transfer/KB	3497.4	2460.4	2626.1
Ratio	26.3%	51.1%	51.9%

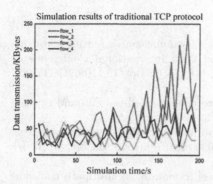

Fig. 8. Traditional TCP protocol simulation results.

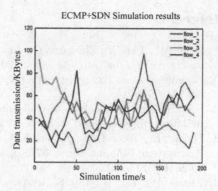

Fig. 9. ECMP+SDN simulation results.

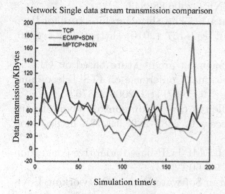

Fig. 10. ECMP+SDN simulation results.

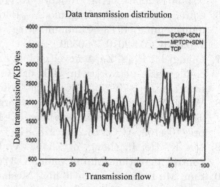

Fig. 11. Data flow distribution in the network.

5 Conclusion

This paper proposes a multi-path transmission scheme MPTCP based on the SDN architecture to improve the throughput and efficiency of the Satellite-Terrestrial Integrated Network (STIN). The proposed multi-path transmission scheme MPTCP is implemented in SDN simulation, which decomposes the data streams transmitted in the STIN network into multiple sub-flows and transmits the sub-flows in multiple unrelated paths. It merges them after the transmission is completed, thus ensuring the efficiency of network information transmission even when the link communication in the STIN is ineffective. Simulation tests demonstrate that this solution has good performance in STIN and can improve the efficiency of network transmission and the stability of link data transmission, thus improving the transmission throughput in the network.

Acknowledgement. This work is supported by Science and Technology Project of State Grid Shanghai Municipal Electrical Power Company. (SGSHXT00YJJS2100140).

References

1. Peng, W., Jian, Y., Zhi-gang, C., Jing-lin, W.: Dynamic source routing algorithm in low-earth orbit satellite constellation. In: 2006 International Conference on Communication Technology, pp. 1–4 (2006). https://doi.org/10.1109/ICCT.2006.341754
2. Bao, S., Luo, L.: Analysis of transmission protocol in satellite-to-ground communication. Dig. Commun. World **3**(3), 28–29, 32 (2018)
3. Habak, K., Youssef, M., Harras, K.A.: An optimal deployable bandwidth aggregation system. Comput. Netw. **57**(15), 3067–3080 (2013). https://doi.org/10.1016/j.comnet.2013.07.012
4. Zhang, W., Lei, W., Liu, S., Li, G.: A general framework of multipath transport system based on application-level relay. Comput. Commun. **51**, 70–80 (2014)
5. Iyengar, J., Amer, P., Stewart, R.: Concurrent multipath transfer using SCTP multihoming over independent end-to-end paths. IEEE/ACM Trans, Netw. **14**(5), 951–964 (2006). https://doi.org/10.1109/TNET.2006.882843
6. García-Martínez, A., Bagnulo, M., Beijnum, I.V.: The Shim6 architecture for IPv6 multihoming. IEEE Commun. Mag. **48**(9), 152–157 (2010). https://doi.org/10.1109/MCOM.2010.5560599
7. Qiang, L., Ping, Z.: A novel mobility management architecture based on GLL in configurable networks. In: 2006 6th International Conference on ITS Telecommunications, pp. 70–73 (2006). https://doi.org/10.1109/ITST.2006.288763
8. Wang, W., Wang, X., Wang, D.: energy efficient congestion control for multipath TCP in heterogeneous networks. IEEE Access **6**, 2889–2898 (2018). https://doi.org/10.1109/ACCESS.2017.2785849
9. Ma, K., He, J., Zhang, Z., Zhang, X., Fan, L.: MPTCP-based adaptive congestion control algorithm. Mob. Commun. **37**(20), 55–60 (2013)
10. Sun, M.: Research on Switching Mechanism in Software-Defined Networking Environment. Master's thesis, Nanjing University of Aeronautics and Astronautics (2016)
11. Wei, W.: Research on coupled congestion control and data scheduling mechanism in MPTCP-based multipath transmission. Ph.D. thesis, University of Science and Technology of China (2020)
12. Padhye, J., Firoiu, V., Towsley, D., Kurose, J.: Modeling TCP reno performance: a simple model and its empirical validation. IEEE/ACM Trans. Netw. **8**(2), 133–145 (2000). https://doi.org/10.1109/90.842137

A Reinforcement Learning Based Resource Access Strategy for Satellite-Terrestrial Integrated Networks

Jiyun Qiu[1], Hao Zhang[2], Li Zhou[3], Penghui Hu[3], and Jian Wang[3(✉)]

[1] State Grid Shanghai Municipal Electrical Power Company, Shanghai 200002, China
[2] Global Energy Internet Research Institute Co. Ltd., Nanjing 210003, China
[3] School of Electronic Science and Engineering, Nanjing University, Nanjing 210023, China
wangjnju@nju.edu.cn

Abstract. The satellite-terrestrial integrated network (STIN) has recently attracted considerable attention. The problem studied in this paper is how the access controller located at the ground station selects the best-joining satellite for multi-users, who are covered by multi-satellites with limited onboard resources and high-speed moving in STIN. This paper proposes a multi-objective satellite selection strategy for multi-user based on reinforcement learning. We adopt Q-learning to continuously confirm the optimal access choice in the continuous interactive learning with the environment. We consider the multi-parameters of the integrated satellite network, including satellites' elevation angle and coverage time for users and the available channel related to the overall capacity and the traffic load. Finally, a multi-LEO satellite system for multi-user is established in STK, based on which the access algorithm is implemented. Based on the simulation, we analyze the convergence of the algorithm, and the results show that the proposed access algorithm can improve selection efficiency and user satisfaction.

Keywords: LEO Satellite · Satellite-Terrestrial Integrated Networks · Access Algorithm · Multi-targets · SDN · Reinforcement Learning

1 Introduction

The Satellite-Terrestrial Integrated Network (STIN) is promised to provide land, sea, air, and space users with any time, global coverage, on-demand services, and safe and reliable information services [1]. The Low Earth Orbit (LEO) satellites based on STIN, such as OneWeb, SpaceX, and Telesat systems, have been providing broadband Internet access services for areas with underdeveloped telecommunication infrastructure [2].

However, STIN features a heterogeneous structure with wide-area distributed and highly dynamic nodes, limited onboard wireless resources, non-negligible delay, and severe fading. Moreover, moving at a rapid speed at a low altitude,

© ICST Institute for Computer Sciences, Social Informatics and Telecommunications Engineering 2023
Published by Springer Nature Switzerland AG 2023. All Rights Reserved
X. Jiang (Ed.): MLICOM 2022, LNICST 481, pp. 97–107, 2023.
https://doi.org/10.1007/978-3-031-30237-4_9

LEO satellites have a relatively short period of view, causing frequent handovers between the ground terminal and the satellites. To continue communication with the counterpart, the user has to switch among the covered satellites. Up to now, SpaceX has launched nearly 3108 satellites for Starlink [3]. In this scenario, it is increasingly common to see multi-satellites covering the same area simultaneously. Such a complex and dynamic environment greatly challenges wireless resource management.

In the current STIN access selection scheme, the single target access algorithm and multi-target weighting algorithm [4] are unsuitable for access decisions for dynamic networks and fail to ensure the QoS requirements of different users flexibly. Recently, AI (artificial intelligence) algorithms have been applied to communication. Especially, Q-learning was proposed to continuously confirm the optimal access choice in the continuous interactive learning with the environment.

This paper proposes an intelligent access resource strategy based on reinforcement learning for STIN, aiming to select the best-joining satellite for multiple users covered by multi-LEO satellites with limited onboard resources at high speed. The remainder of this paper is as follows. Section 2 illustrates the reference scenario and introduces the system model. Section 3 presents the proposed access algorithm based on reinforcement learning in detail. The proposed method is eventually validated through simulation in Sect. 4. Finally, the conclusions of this paper are drawn in Sect. 5.

2   System Model

2.1   Scenario

We introduce a general formalism for the general multi-star coverage scenario. The area covered by the satellite in the ground plane is as shown in Fig. 1(a). $user_1$ is simultaneously located under the signal coverage of the satellites LEO_1 and LEO_2. After the satellite returns the result, the ground control center sends it to the user to complete the satellite access. Supposing the network composed of n users and m satellites, we get :

$$U = \{u_1, u_2, u_3, \ldots, u_n\} \tag{1}$$

$$S = \{s_1, s_2, s_3, \ldots, s_m\} \tag{2}$$

where U is the user set and S is satellite set. We assume multi-satellites covering the same area simultaneously. For example, if two satellites cover $user_i$, the set of satellites S_i that can serve the user is:

$$S_i = \{s_1, s_2\} \tag{3}$$

where $i \in \{1, 2, \ldots, n\}$.

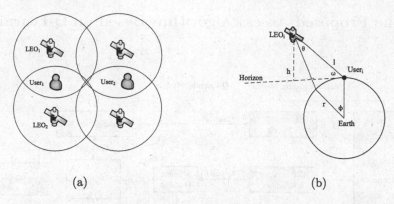

(a)   (b)

Fig. 1. Figure 1(a) shows the multi-star coverage model, and Fig. 1(b) shows the satellite coverage map of the earth . In Fig. 1(b), r represents the radius of the earth. ω represents the elevation angle of the satellite, which is the angle between the user and the satellite connection to the horizontal line, h is the height of the satellite relative to the ground, l represents the distance from the user to the satellite, and ϕ represents the satellite service area on the ground. θ represents the included angle of the satellite relative to the user.

2.2   Parameter Evaluation

We consider the multi-parameters of the integrated satellite network from the physical parameters of a single low-orbit satellite and the overall capacity of the traffic load, including the satellite elevation angle, coverage time, and the available channels.

Figure 2 shows the satellite-to-ground diagram, in which the ϕ is:

$$\varphi = \cos^{-1}\left[\frac{r}{r+h}\cdot\cos\omega\right] - \omega \tag{4}$$

Then we get the average radius of coverage area:

$$r' = r\cdot\sin\varphi \tag{5}$$

So size of the area is:

$$s = 2\pi r^2\cdot(1-\cos\varphi) \tag{6}$$

Assuming satellites move around the earth in a uniform circular motion. The period T can be obtained as:

$$T = 2\pi\sqrt{\frac{(r+h)^3}{\mu}} \tag{7}$$

where $\mu = 398601.58$ km^3/s^2 is the Kepler constant. Therefore, the coverage time of the satellite to the ground is:

$$T_s = \frac{2\varphi}{360}\cdot T \tag{8}$$

3   The Proposed Access Algorithm Based on Q-Learning

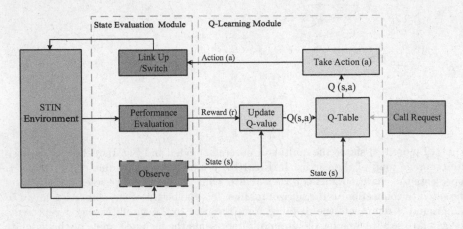

Fig. 2. Structure diagram of multi-satellite access scheme based on Q-learning.

3.1   Q-Learning Algorithm

Markov Decision Process (MDP) [5] is defined by a tuple (S, A, p, r) with explicit state transition properties. In the tuple, S represents states' finite set, A represents actions' finite set, p is a transition probability, and r represents the immediate reward obtained from state s to state s' after the execution of the action a. π is denoted as a "policy" that represents a mapping from a state to action. The goal of a time-infinite MDP is to maximize the expected discounted total reward or maximize the average reward:

$$\max_{\pi} \mathbb{E} \left[\sum_{t=0}^{T} \gamma r_t(s_t, \pi(s_t)) \right] \tag{9}$$

where $\gamma \in [0, 1]$ represents the discount factor, which determines the great significance of future rewards compared with the current reward. We aim to find an optimal policy $\pi\prime : \mathcal{S} \to \mathcal{A}$ and define value function $\mathcal{V}^{\pi} : \mathcal{S} \to \mathbb{R}$ that represents the expected value obtained by following policy π from each state $s \in \mathcal{S}$. The value function is:

$$\begin{aligned} \mathcal{V}^{\pi}(s) &= \mathbb{E}_{\pi} \left[\sum_{t=0}^{\infty} \gamma r_t(s_t, a_t) \, | s_0 = s \right] \\ &= \mathbb{E}_{\pi} \left[r_t(s_t, a_t) + \gamma \mathcal{V}^{\pi}(s_{t+1}) \, | s_0 = s \right] \end{aligned} \tag{10}$$

As we need to find the optimal policy π^* , an optimal action at each state can be found through: $\mathcal{V}^*(s) = \max_{a_t}\{\mathbb{E}_\pi[r_t(s_t,a_t) + \gamma\mathcal{V}^\pi(s_{t+1})]\}$.

We define $\mathcal{Q}^*(s,a) \triangleq r_t(s_t,a_t) + \gamma\mathbb{E}_\pi[\mathcal{V}^\pi(s_{t+1})]$ as the optimal Q-function for all state-action pairs, then the optimal value function can be expressed as $\mathcal{V}^*(s) = \max_a\{\mathcal{Q}^*(s,a)\}$. For all state-action pairs, this can be done through iterative processes [6]:

$$
\begin{aligned}
\mathcal{Q}_{t+1}(s,a) =&\mathcal{Q}_t(s,a) \\
&+\alpha_t\left[r_t(s,a)+\gamma\max_{a'}\mathcal{Q}_t(s,a')-\mathcal{Q}_t(s,a)\right]
\end{aligned}
\tag{11}
$$

The core idea behind this update is to find the Temporal Difference (TD) between the predicted Q-value.

3.2   Algorithm Structure

The overview of the proposed method is as shown in Fig. 2. State Evaluation Module is to collect the observed information of the STIN. And the Reinforcement Learning Module is the decision-making center to explore optimal access links by interacting with environmental information. The algorithm is shown in Algothrim 1. We denote $\mathcal{Q}_t^*(s,a)$ as the optimal Q-function at t. s^* and a^* is the corresponding state and action.

Algorithm 1. Q-learning-based resource access strategy for STIN

Input: For each (s,a), initialize the table entry $\mathcal{Q}(s,a)$ arbitrarily. Observe the current state s, initialize the learning rate α and the discount factor γ as Table 5.
When calls arrive **do**
1 Observe ω, t, and c in the STIN environment to get s as (12).
2 Generate random variable ρ, as (13):
if $0 \le \rho \le \varepsilon$ **then** Select random action a.
else Select the action $a = \arg\max Q(s,a)$.
3 Execute action a to get access
4 Obtain the immediate performance reward r as (15).
5 Update the Q-table entry:
    $\mathcal{Q}_{t+1}(s,a) \leftarrow \mathcal{Q}_t(s,a)+\alpha_t\left[r_t(s,a)+\gamma\max_{a'}\mathcal{Q}_t(s,a')-\mathcal{Q}_t(s,a)\right]$
Until $|\mathcal{Q}_t^*(s,a) - \mathcal{Q}_{t+1}^*(s,a)| \le 0.1$
Output: Access strategy $\pi^*(s) = \arg\max_a\{\mathcal{Q}_t^*(s,a)\}$

3.3   Q-Learning Based Access Resource Strategy Based Design

The proposed scheme designs the satellite network state as the state set, the alternative satellites as the action set, and the comprehensive network performance as the reward function of the selection strategy. The details are as follows:

Table 1. Parameter for Multi-satellite Environment in STK.

Parameter	Value
LEO number	$m = 48$
Orbit number	6
LEO number in per orbit	8
LEO height	550(km)
Orbit inclination	$53°$
Call arrival model	Poisson Distribution, $r \sim P(10)$
Number of calls arriving	Uniform Distribution, $n \sim U(5, 25), n \in \mathbb{N}$
Call duration	Exponential Distribution, $T \sim E(180)(s)$
The sampling period in STK	$T_s = 1(\min)$
Channel capacity	240
Minimum services angle	$\omega_{\min} = 15°$ or $\pi/12$
Elevation angle	$\omega \in [\pi/12, \pi/2]$
Cover time	$t \in [0, 11.94]$ (min) as (7) and (8)
Number of available channels	Uniform Distribution, $c \sim U(1, 240), c \in \mathbb{N}$

State Space. Three parameters, i.e., the satellite elevation angle ω, the coverage time t, and the number of available channels c, are considered as the state space of Q-learning. These parameters are selected based on signal strength, service continuity, and load balancing considerations. So the state space of Q-learning is: This paper considers the double-satellite coverage scenario. So the state space complete formula is as follows:

$$S(\omega, t, c) = \{(\omega_1, t_1, c_1), (\omega_2, t_2, c_2)\} \tag{12}$$

Action Space. The action for the satellite access scenario is the set of satellites to be selected for access. In Fig. 1(a), the set of satellites covered by the user in the action space is as follows:

$$A_i = \{a_1, a_2\} \tag{13}$$

This paper adopts ϵ-greedy strategy, in which ϵ is the exploration probability. The system generates a random $\rho \in [0, 1]$ to determine whether to take the action with the maximum value or a random action according to ρ. The ϵ-greedy strategy is as follows:

$$a_\tau = \begin{cases} \arg\max Q(s, a), \varepsilon \leq \rho \leq 1 \\ random(A), 0 \leq \rho \leq \varepsilon \end{cases} \tag{14}$$

Reward Function. The observed QoS of the entire communication network is designed as the reward, including packet loss, jitter, and delay. Considering the comprehensive impact of the selection strategy on network performance, we define a utility function:

$$r(s, a) = \alpha_\omega U_\omega(\omega^*) + \alpha_t U_t(t^*) + \alpha_c U_c(c) \tag{15}$$

Table 2. Influence of state parameters on performance indicators.

	Pack Loss	Delay Jitter	Delay
Satellite elevation	✓		✓
Coverage time		✓	
Load Balancing	✓	✓	

Table 3. Weight of the parameters affecting business in (15).

Parameters	α_w	α_t	α_c
Value	0.6	0.2	0.2

where $U_\omega(\omega^*), U_t(t^*)$, and $U_c(c)$ represent the satellite elevation angle, coverage time, and the benefit function of the available channel, respectively. α_ω, α_t, and α_c can be thought of as weights to the corresponding parameters. As shown in Table 3.

For the satellite elevation angle, the benefit function is:

$$U_\omega(\omega^*) = \sigma \left(\frac{\omega^* - \omega_{\min}}{\omega_{\min}} \right)^2 \qquad (16)$$

where ω^* represents the current elevation angle, and $\omega_{\min}$ is the minimum angle that the system can provide services. $\sigma \in (0,1)$ is a normalization parameter selected according to factors such as the geographical environment. This formula reflects that the larger the satellite elevation angle, the better the signal quality.

For the utility function of satellite coverage time, the definition is given as follows:

$$U_t(t^*) = \begin{cases} \mu \left(\frac{t_{\max}}{t_{\max} t^*} \right)^2, t_{\max} \neq t^* \\ 1, t_{\max} = t^* \end{cases} \qquad (17)$$

where t^* represents the current coverage time, $t_{\max}$ is the longest satellite coverage time, and μ is a normalization parameter. This formula shows that the longer the coverage time, the better the communication quality of the user. For the load situation of the channel, we use change in the available channels before and after the action is taken to measure whether the action is beneficial for load balancing. And the function is defined as:

$$U_c(c^*) = \begin{cases} 0, \Delta c^* - \Delta c < 0 \\ 1, \Delta c^* - \Delta c > 0 \end{cases} \qquad (18)$$

where c^* represents the current number of available channels. The difference in the number of available channels after the action selection measures whether the action benefits load balancing. If the difference is negative, the reward is 0. Otherwise, the reward is 1.

Finally, it is necessary to design the weights of α_ω, α_t, and α_c. We comprehensively consider delay, jitter, and packet loss rate as the QoS measure.

The effects of three state parameters ω, t, and c on these performances are in Table 2, which shows that pack loss is affected by both satellite elevation and the available channel. In contrast, the delay is only affected by the elevation. The value of the weights factor is as shown in Table 3.

4   Simulation and Result Analysis

4.1   Environment and the Parameters

We try to evaluate the availability of the algorithm in practical scenarios. The proposed access algorithm is simulated and verified. First, STK is used to build a low earth orbit (LEO) satellite to obtain satellite parameters, as shown in Table 1. After the parameters are obtained from the environment, they must be loaded into the reinforcement learning module for training through quantization processing. The specific quantization range is shown in Table 4.

Table 4. The actual parameter range corresponding to the quantized value in $U_\omega(\omega^*)$, $U_t(t^*)$, and $U_c(c^*)$ about the elevation angle, coverage time, and the number of available channels.

	Level 1	Level 2	Level 3	Level 4	Level 5	Level 6
Elevation Angle(ω^*)	$[15°, 33°)$	$[33°, 60°)$	$[60°, 90°)$			
Cover Time(t^*)	$[0\,\text{s}, 3.98\,\text{s})$	$[3.98\,\text{s}, 7.96\,\text{s})$	$[7.96\,\text{s}, 11.94\,\text{s})$			
Channel Number(c^*)	$[0, 40)$	$[40, 80)$	$[80, 120)$	$[120, 160)$	$[160, 200)$	$[200, 240)$

The parameters of Q-Learning Module are as shown in Table 5.

Table 5. Parameter for Q-Learning Model.

Parameter	Description	Value
α	Learning rate	0.5
γ	Discount factor	0.8
ϵ	Probability choose to explore in the ϵ-greedy strategy	0.8
ρ	Decay coefficients for the probability of exploration	0.08
τ	Decay cycles for the probability of exploration	$10(s)$

4.2   Result Analysis

For this algorithm, we set the number of training rounds to 500. Then we analyze the impact of the access selection algorithm on communication performance. And the convergence process of the Q-learning algorithm model based on a real-time communication system is first analyzed. We use a single utility function adopting the weighted sum of the satellite elevation angle, coverage time, and available channel for comparison. CLWA represents comprehensive weighting and static access algorithms in the following figures, and Q-Learning illustrates the proposed method.

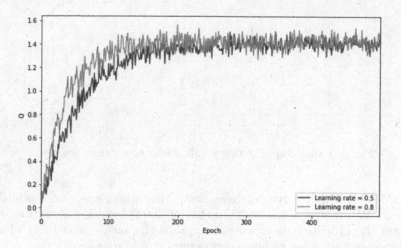

Fig. 3. Convergence Process of Q-learning.

Convergence Analysis. As the training progresses, Fig. 3 shows that the Q-learning algorithm is converging. It shows that the agent can obtain the optimal access strategy from the satellite elevation angle, coverage time and the number of available channels to explore the STIN environment. It also shows the difference in algorithm convergence when the learning rates α are 0.8 and 0.5, respectively. As demonstrated by the curve, when the learning rate is 0.8, the Q value changes faster and stabilizes earlier. α determines the learning ability. The larger the α, the faster the learning speed under the premise of convergence.

Successful Access Rate Analysis. We measure this performance with access probability, which refers to the number of calls successfully connected to the satellite to the total number of calls. The access probability is related to the access algorithm and the busyness of the network. As shown in Fig. 4, when the number of call arrivals per unit time increases from 5 to 25, the access probability of the curves corresponding to the two algorithms first remains close to 100%, then gradually decreases, and finally remains around 50%. It is because when the call arrival is relatively low, the network load is relatively small, the call requests of all users can be satisfied, and the access probability is 1. As the call arrival rate increases, the network load gradually increases. As demonstrated in Fig. 4, compared with the Q-Learning algorithm, the access probability of

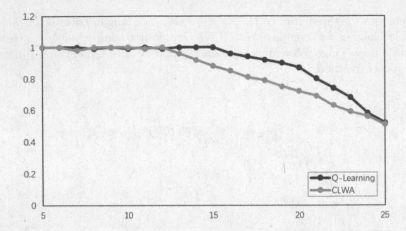

Fig. 4. Probability of complete call versus new call arrival rate.

the CLWA algorithm curve decreases first. Meanwhile, the access probability of the CLWA algorithm is lower than that of the Q-Learning algorithm, which indicates the proposed algorithm can improve the access probability of users, thereby providing higher communication quality and user satisfaction.

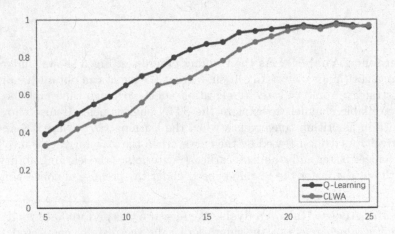

Fig. 5. Satellite channel utilization versus call arrival rate.

Network Resource Utilization Analysis. We consider the impact of this algorithm on the utilization of the entire network resources. Channel utilization refers to the difference between the successfully utilized channels and the channel capacity in STIN. As shown in Fig. 5, as the number of calls increases, the channel utilization rises and then tends to stabilize, and its value is close to 1.

When the call arrival rate is low, the network load is small, fewer channels are needed at this time, and the channel utilization rate is low. At the same time, it shows that the channel utilization rate of the CLWA algorithm is lower than that of the Q-Learning algorithm, and the time to reach the highest channel utilization rate is relatively late. It shows that the proposed Q-Learning-based access algorithm can better allocate the channel resources of the STIN and improve channel utilization.

5   Summary

This paper proposes a multi-objective integrated satellite access algorithm based on Q-learning for the satellite-terrestrial integrated network (STIN), aiming to select the optimal access satellite for multiple users covered by multi-LEO satellites with limited channel resources. We consider the multi-parameters, including the elevation angle of satellites, the coverage time, and the available channel related to the traffic load. According to the QoS requests, we design the access problem as a multi-objective optimal problem and adopt reinforcement learning to select the satellite. Finally, an LEO-based STIN is simulated in STK, and the proposed algorithm is implemented. Based on the results, we analyze the convergence of the algorithm and verify that the algorithm provides more efficient access selection by analyzing user satisfaction and network resource utilization.

Acknowledgement. This work is supported by the Science and Technology Project of State Grid Shanghai Municipal Electrical Power Company. (SGSHXT0 0YJJS2100140).

References

1. Liu, J., Shi, Y., Fadlullah, Z.M., Kato, N.: Space-air-ground integrated network: a survey. IEEE Commun. Surv. Tutor. **20**(4), 2714–2741 (2018). https://doi.org/10. 1109/COMST.2018.2841996
2. del Portillo Barrios, I., Cameron, B., Crawley, E.: A technical comparison of three low earth orbit satellite constellation systems to provide global broadband. Acta Astronautica **159** (2019). https://doi.org/10.1016/j.actaastro.2019.03.040
3. Wikipedia: Starlink – Wikipedia, The Free Encyclopedia (2022). https://en. wikipedia.org/wiki/Starlink. Accessed 26 Aug 2022
4. Li, C., Zhang, Y., Hao, X., Huang, T.: Jointly optimized request dispatching and service placement for MEC in LEO network. China Commun. **17**(8), 199–208 (2020). https://doi.org/10.23919/JCC.2020.08.016
5. Lowe, R., Wu, Y., Tamar, A., Harb, J., Abbeel, P., Mordatch, I.: Multi-agent actor-critic for mixed cooperative-competitive environments. In: Proceedings of the 31st International Conference on Neural Information Processing Systems, NIPS 2017, pp. 6382–6393. Curran Associates Inc., Red Hook (2017)
6. Luong, N.C., et al.: Applications of deep reinforcement learning in communications and networking: a survey. IEEE Commun. Surv. Tutor. **21**(4), 3133–3174 (2019). https://doi.org/10.1109/COMST.2019.2916583

A RF Fingerprint Clustering Method Based on Automatic Feature Extractor

Pinhong Xiao, Di Lin[✉], and Mengjuan Wang

University of Electronic Science and Technology of China, Chengdu, Sichuan, China
202022090634@std.uestc.edu.cn, lindi@uestc.edu.cn

Abstract. RF fingerprint technology has received extensive attention and research in recent years due to its immutable nature. RF fingerprinting technology can be used as a wireless network security mechanism alone or combined with existing security mechanisms to enhance wireless network security. The early RF fingerprint research widely used the method of artificial feature extraction, but this method relies too much on expert experience. This paper proposes a semi-supervised learning approach for RF fingerprint recognition. This work directly uses the original I/Q sequence data, designs a fingerprint extractor based on the convolutional neural network (CNN), and uses K-means and DBSCAN algorithms to cluster the fingerprints. The experimental results demonstrate that after training with a small amount of labeled data, the fingerprint extractor can effectively extract features of unknown signals, and these features can well allow unknown similar devices to be clustered together by the clustering algorithm.

Keywords: RF fingerprint identification · Semi-supervised Learning · Feature extraction

1 Introduction

RF fingerprints are widely present in wireless communication equipment. Just like everyone has different fingerprints, each wireless device also has different RF fingerprints. RF fingerprints arise from hardware differences within the device, including manufacturing tolerances generated during the production of electronic components and drift tolerances generated during use [1], and are both unique and short-time invariant. By analyzing the received RF signal, various features of the device can be extracted, and the multi-dimensional features together constitute the RF fingerprint library of the device. This method of extracting device hardware features based on communication signals is called RF fingerprint extraction, and the method of using RF fingerprints to identify different wireless devices is called RF fingerprint identification. The traditional wireless network protection scheme is usually a security protocol based on a password mechanism, but the security protocol may have flaws, and attackers can crack the authentication mechanism by cracking passwords, statistical analysis, and other methods. RF fingerprint extraction and identification both work at the physical layer and cannot be tampered with. It can

Published by Springer Nature Switzerland AG 2023. All Rights Reserved
X. Jiang (Ed.): MLICOM 2022, LNICST 481, pp. 108–116, 2023.
https://doi.org/10.1007/978-3-031-30237-4_10

be used as an authentication mechanism alone or combined with traditional security mechanisms to bring higher wireless network security performance.

Traditional RF fingerprinting methods rely heavily on expert experience, which requires expert experience and expertise to analyze and feature the signal, and then input the features into the classifier for classification. With the rise of deep learning, deep learning-based RF fingerprinting methods have been widely studied. Literature [2] generates device fingerprint data through MATLAB simulation and proposes a RF fingerprint recognition method based on CNN model. It uses the original IQ signal to input the CNN model without analyzing or extracting signal features, and has achieved good results, greatly reducing the dependence on expert experience.

In the field of RF fingerprinting, in addition to supervised machine learning and deep learning research, a small amount of unsupervised learning research has also appeared. In contrast to supervised learning, unsupervised RF fingerprinting techniques do not require training data registered in advance. This approach must find the implied structure in the signal and cluster similar signals together then map them to a device. In [3], an infinite Gaussian mixture model are used to detect the number of devices and classify them based on two features: frequency bias and phase shift deviation. At present, the unsupervised RF fingerprint identification method still needs further research.

In this paper, we propose a semi-supervised RF fingerprint recognition method based on CNN and DBSCAN algorithm. This method requires only a small amount of labeled data to train the CNN for signal feature extraction, and then unsupervised clustering can be performed on completely unknown data. Experiments show that the method can effectively extract signal features and achieve good clustering results in unknown signals.

2 Related Work

2.1 Supervised Learning

Methods Based on Manual Feature Selection: The manually selected features mainly include many parameters with actual physical meaning and statistical features after Fourier transform, Hilbert transform, and other transformations on the target signal segment. According to the different target signal types, the selected features are also different. Generally, the RF fingerprint features are divided into two types: RF fingerprint features based on transient signals and RF fingerprint features based on steady-state signals. The features extracted based on transient signals mainly include transient signal duration, spectral features, wavelet domain features, fractal dimension, envelope features, etc. Early studies almost all revolve around transient signal RF fingerprinting techniques. With the development of technology, almost all digital communication systems include a leading sequence before the data segment to simplify the design of the receiver [4]. Stable leads provide a stable identifiable steady-state signal, so the focus of research in this area is beginning to shift to steady-state signals. After feature selection and feature extraction, the signal features are input into the machine learning classification model or deep learning classification model for supervised training, and then the trained classification model is obtained. Reference [5] extracts the parametric features such as information dimension, constellation features, and phase noise spectrum in RF signals and classified them by machine learning models such as BaggedTree and Fine-GaussianSVM. Reference [6] uses spectral correlation function to extract signal features and proposed a deep confidence network to classify signals. In the method of manual feature selection, both the selection of features and the construction of classifiers have a great impact on the final experimental results. However, feature selection often relies on expert experience and has defects such as poor feature generalization ability. It often performs poorly in the face of a large number of devices or in low signal-to-noise ratio environments.

Methods Based on Raw I/Q Data: This method uses the target I/Q signal directly as model input. In earlier studies, the original signal was used directly as a device fingerprint for identification and authentication, using different methods of similarity measures, including Euclidean distance, Marxian distance, cosine similarity, Pearson correlation coefficient, etc. [7]. However, such fingerprints contain too much redundant information and dimension, which leads to insufficient recognition efficiency and dimension disaster. Moreover, such methods are easily affected by the environment, and their performance fluctuates greatly with noise. In recent years, with the development of deep learning technology, compared with traditional machine learning technology, the characteristics of deep learning automatic feature extraction have natural advantages in the face of complex original signals. Kevin Merchant [8] et al. built a CNN model for automatic feature extraction, using the time-domain complex baseband error signal to train the CNN. Tong Jian [9] et al. also used the CNN model to perform RF fingerprinting on the processed I/Q signals, and also considered some feature engineering to reduce the influence of the channel in the case of low signal-to-noise ratio and low computing power.

2.2 Semi-supervised Learning and Unsupervised Learning

Supervised RF fingerprint technology has proven its effectiveness in a large number of literature. However, in the actual environment, it is often infeasible to register the fingerprint database in advance. At present, there is still relatively little research on semi-supervised and unsupervised RF fingerprint recognition technology. Reference [3] proposes a non-parametric Bayesian clustering method to detect the number of devices, selected frequency difference and phase shift difference as features, and performed unsupervised passive classification of multiple devices. When the environment contains 4 devices, this method achieves high accuracy. Reference [10] applies unsupervised and semi-supervised methods to the field of radio modulation classification. They first constructed a convolutional self-encoder for the unsupervised extraction of modulation features of radio signals, while a CNN was used for the supervised feature extraction. Finally, the extracted features are clustered using a clustering algorithm.

3 Approach

3.1 Dataset

In this work, multiple transmitters and one receiver are simulated using MATLAB, and the RF fingerprint dataset is generated by simulation. The AWGN channel is simulated between the transmitter and the receiver. The signal is modulated by QPSK, the signal-to-noise ratio is 20 db, the sampling rate is 20 Mbps, the sampling time interval is 0.05 us, and the number of sub-carriers is 52, including 4 pilot signals and 48 data signals. We generate the RF fingerprint of the device by simulating conditions such as DC offset, phase offset, I/Q imbalance, etc. In recent years, there are also studies on the application of CNN in the field of I/Q signal processing. In [2], the I/Q signal is directly input into the CNN for device classification. Reference [10] uses CNN to extract the features of raw I/Q data, then carry out the modulation classification of the signal.

3.2 CNN Model

Compared with ordinary feedforward neural networks, CNNs are locally connected and have shared parameters. CNNs perform mathematical convolution operations locally on the input data through convolution kernels, enabling them to discover meaningful features of the input data and making the amount of computation in the network reduced. CNNs have been widely used in the field of image processing and image recognition with great success. CNNs have also been applied to sequence data such as natural language processing and audio processing, and achieved remarkable results [11]. In recent years, there are also studies on the application of CNN in the field of I/Q signal processing. In [2], raw I/Q data is directly input into the CNN model for device classification. Reference [10] uses CNN to extract the features of the I/Q signal, then carry out the modulation classification of the signal. The architecture c the CNN feature extractor designed in this paper is shown in Fig. 1. Our network has a total of five layers, including two convolutional layers, two fully connected layers, and an output layer. Our simulation produces the raw I/Q sequence, containing both real and imaginary parts, and we treat it as $2 \times N$ dimensional vector. As shown in Fig. 2, inspired by [2], we divide the I/Q sequence in the form of a sliding window in order to enable the model to detect the damage at any position on the I/Q sequence. The size of the window is 128, the step size of each slide is 1, and each input sample of the model is a 2×128 dimensional vector. The input sample is first processed in two convolutional layers. In order to fully extract the sample features, we use a 2×5 convolutional kernel and a 1×5 convolutional kernel for convolution in the first and second convolutional layers. Between the second convolutional layer and the fully connected layer, we dropout at a ratio of 0.5 to control overfitting. The first fully connected layer has 128 neurons and the second fully connected layer has 28 neurons. The output of the second fully connected layer will be used to input the Softmax layer to train the CNN model. When the CNN training is completed, we will use the output of the second fully connected layer as the feature of the I/Q sample, which is the RF fingerprint. This feature has dimension 28 and it will be fed into the clustering model for unsupervised clustering.

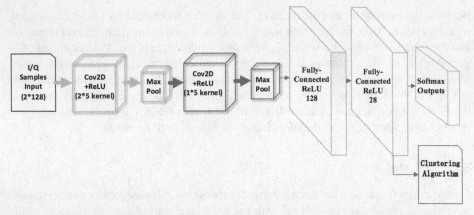

Fig. 1. The CNN model designed to extract features of raw I/Q in this work.

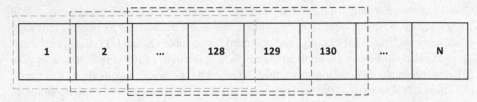

Fig. 2. An example of sliding operation using a window of length 128 over I/Q sequences.

3.3 Clustering Algorithm

After extracting the RF fingerprints of the signals, we use unsupervised clustering algorithms to cluster similar fingerprints to the same transmitting device. The dimensionality of the features extracted by CNN is 28. To improve the clustering effect, we firstly use PCA to reduce the dimensionality of the features. After experiments, we find that when the dimension is reduced to 7, more than 90% of the variance of the original fingerprint can be retained.

Once the CNN model is trained and deployed, we no longer need any prior information and can perform RF fingerprinting in a completely new unknown environment. We consider both an environment with a known number of devices and a totally blind environment with an unknown number of devices. In an environment where the number of devices is known, we use the K-means algorithm for clustering. In a completely unknown environment, we use the DBSCAN algorithm for clustering, because the DBSCAN algorithm does not require information about the number of clusters, and it can achieve better results in irregular shape data. When the number of devices is small, the DBSCAN algorithm shows good performance. However, as the number of devices increases, the clustering performance of the DBSCAN algorithm shows a more significant decrease.

4 Experimental and Results Analysis

In this work, we use MATLAB to simulate and generate RF fingerprints of 30 devices, with about 300,000 pieces of data. We use 2, 5, 8, and 10 devices to train the CNN feature extraction model, taking 15% of the data as the validation set and 15% of the data as the test set. The test accuracy is shown in Table 1. When the number of devices is less than 10, the test accuracy of our model has reached more than 98%, which shows that the feature extraction model can effectively extract the fingerprint features of the device.

Table 1. The Testing Accuracies of CNN feature extractors

Number of devices	Testing Accuracy
2 devices	1.00
5 devices	0.990
8 devices	0.989
10 devices	0.988

In addition to the above 10 devices, we used different sampling rates and random RF fingerprint parameters to generate 20 brand new devices. It is worth noting that these devices are completely unknown to our feature extraction model, which can reflect the feature extraction ability of the model for unknown signals. We use K-means and DBSCAN algorithms to cluster the signals respectively, and use normalized mutual information(NMI) to measure the similarity of the clustering results. The experimental results are shown in Fig. 3 and Table 2. We can see that the K-means algorithm has relatively stable performance when the number of devices is known. Within 10 devices, the NMI index of K-means can reach more than 0.95. In the environment of 10 to 20 devices, with the increase of the number of devices, the performance of K-means does not decrease significantly, and the NMI index remains at 0.9. This proves that the CNN feature extraction model can effectively extract signal features. When the number of devices is small, the DBSCAN algorithm shows good performance. However, as the number of devices increases, the clustering performance of the DBSCAN algorithm decreases significantly. Considering the performance of K-means, this performance drop may be caused by some limitations of the DBSCAN algorithm. The DBSCAN algorithm is highly sensitive to the domain threshold (Eps) and the point threshold (MinPts), which may need to be dynamically adjusted as the number of devices changes [12].

As described in Sect. 3, the feature dimension extracted by CNN is 28, and we use PCA to reduce the feature dimension to 3. For visualization in two-dimensional space, we use the t-SNE algorithm to map the features to the two-dimensional space. When the number of devices is 10, the clustering results using K-means algorithm and DBSCAN algorithm are shown in Fig. 4 and Fig. 5. We can see that the DBSCAN algorithm does not discover all device classes.

Table 2. The normalized mutual information score using K-means and DBSCAN algorithm

Number of devices	NMI using K-means	NMI using DBSCAN
2 devices	1.00	1.00
3 devices	1.00	1.00
5 devices	0.956	0.906
10 devices	0.968	0.909
15 devices	0.891	0.651
20 devices	0.899	0.526

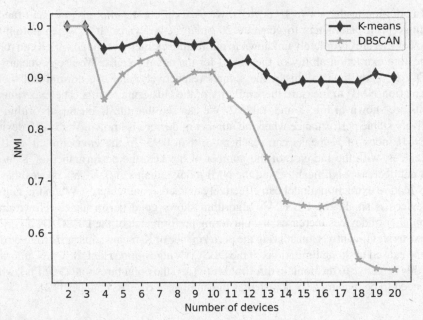

Fig. 3. The normalized mutual information score using K-means and DBSCAN algorithm.

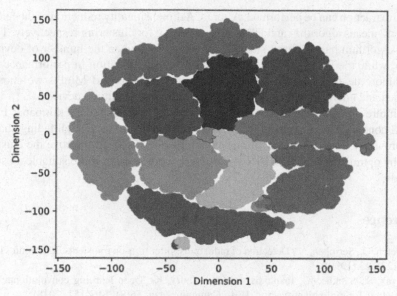

Fig. 4. Visualization of K-means clustering results using t-SNE

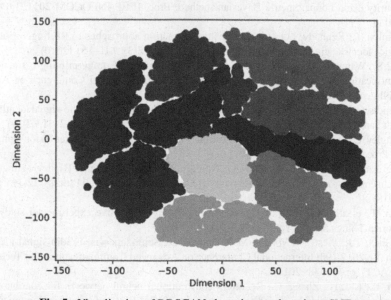

Fig. 5. Visualization of DBSCAN clustering results using t-SNE

5   Conclusion

This paper applies a semi-supervised method to RF fingerprinting, constructs a CNN feature extraction model, and uses only a small amount of data to train the model, avoiding the dependence on expert experience. After the deployment of CNN model, automatic feature extraction can be performed. After PCA dimensionality reduction of the features, we use K-means algorithm and DBSCAN algorithm for clustering respectively. The K-means algorithm has achieved stable and good results when the number of devices is known, while the DBSCAN algorithm shows some degradation in performance when facing more devices. The possible reason is that the Eps and MinPts we chose are solidified and not dynamically adjusted to accommodate multiple devices.

In future work, we will make some improvements to the method of this paper. Firstly, we will conduct experiments on low SNR environments and Rayleigh fading channels to improve the noise immunity of our model. Besides, we will improve the clustering effect by optimizing the DBSCAN algorithm, or choose other more suitable clustering methods.

References

1. Ureten, O., Serinken, N.: Detection of radio transmitter turn-on transients. Electronics Letters 35(23), 23 (1999)
2. Riyaz, S., Sankhe, K., Ioannidis, S., Chowdhury, K.: Deep learning convolutional neural networks for radio identification. IEEE Commun. Mag. **56**(9), 146–152 (2018)
3. Nguyen, N.T., Zheng, G., Han, Z., Zheng, R.: Device fingerprinting to enhance wireless security using nonparametric Bayesian method. Proc. IEEE INFOCOM **2011**, 1404–1412 (2011)
4. Scanlon, P., Kennedy, I.O., Liu, Y.: Feature extraction approaches to RF fingerprinting for device identification in femtocells. Bell Labs Tech. J. **15**(3), 141–151 (2010)
5. Hu, S., Wang, P., Peng, Y., et al.: Machine learning for RF fingerprinting extraction and identification of soft-defined radio devices. In: The International Conference on Artificial Intelligence in China (2019)
6. Mendis, G.J., Wei-Kocsis, J., Madanayake, A.: Deep learning based radio-signal identification with hardware design. IEEE Trans. Aeros. Electron. Syst. **55**(5), 2516–2531 (2019)
7. Langley, L.E.: Specific emitter identification (SEI) and classical parameter fusion technology. In: Proceedings of WESCON 1993, pp. 377–381 (1993)
8. Merchant, K., Revay, S., Stantchev, G., Nousain, B.: Deep learning for RF device fingerprinting in cognitive communication networks. IEEE J. Sel. Topics Signal Process. **12**(1), 160–167 (2018)
9. Jian, T., et al.: Deep learning for RF fingerprinting: a massive experimental study. IEEE Internet Things Mag. **3**(1), 50–57 (2020)
10. O'Shea, T.J., West, N., Vondal, M., Clancy, T.C.: Semi-supervised radio signal identification. In: 2017 19th International Conference on Advanced Communications and Technology (ICACT), pp. 33–38 (2017)
11. Cui, R., Liu, H., Zhang, C.: Recurrent convolutional neural networks for continuous sign language recognition by staged optimization. In: 2017 IEEE Conference on Computer Vision and Pattern Recognition (CVPR), pp. 1610–1618 (2017)
12. Ester, M., Kriegel, H.P., Sander, J., Xu, X.: A density-based algorithm for discovering clusters in large spatial databases with noise. In: AAAI Press, pp. 226–231 (1996)

Across Online Social Network User Identification Based on Usernames

Zijian Li, Di Lin[⊠], and Peidong Li

University of Electronic Science and Technology of China, Chengdu, Sichuan, China
202021090329@std.uestc.edu.cn, lindi@uestc.edu.cn

Abstract. Cross social network user identification aims to identify the same entity on various online social networks to enhance the completeness and accuracy of the persona. There are three broad categories of cross-social network user identification methods: user identification on account of basic user information, user identification on the basis of network topology graphs, and user identification based on the user's origin. This paper analyzes users' display names from different social networks to determine whether they are the same person. The process consists of three steps: first, we obtain information about users and bring their display names from social networking sites. Secondly, we analyze the user's name, get a series of values from the user's name through similarity calculation methods, and match the similarity. We perform similarity matching on the real dataset by using some classification models. Our model performs well, with F1 values reaching 97.07%, 94.65%, and 92.05% for the three datasets, respectively. This paper can provide a high-quality dataset for downstream NLP tasks of high research significance and value.

Keywords: Across Social Network · Similarity · Feature Extraction

1 Introduction

With the spread of computers and the rapid Internet development, social media sites have become increasingly popular and diverse. More people are participating in various social networks to enjoy the convenient and exciting services they offer. In the real world, user information among social networks is isolated from each other due to user privacy leakage. It is difficult for online social network operators to access other users' information on other social networks, which readily forms data silos and makes it difficult to make a complete character portrait of users. Therefore, it is necessary to recognize users' accounts on different social networks, maximize the integration and perfection of user information, mine the user's social data, and build a relatively complete portrait image base for each user, Provide knowledge assurance for downstream tasks such as recommendation systems, entity alignment, etc.

Account association encounters many challenges: there are few public datasets, and there is still no unified public and comprehensive association dataset that allows all algorithms to make uniform comparisons; privacy breaches are involved, and crawling

X. Jiang (Ed.): MLICOM 2022, LNICST 481, pp. 117–127, 2023.
https://doi.org/10.1007/978-3-031-30237-4_11

data from websites will encounter rate and permission limitations, making it difficult to crawl complete information about users' friendships and user attributes; the number of user association pairs required for the training set may be small, and the distribution may be very uneven, all of which affect the accuracy of the association.

In this paper, we use our user information collected from different social networks as a dataset to classify virtual users from various websites using similarity calculation methods and similarity matching methods to find the same person who points to the natural person in different social networks. Meanwhile, our job only analyzes the display name of users, making obtaining data less challenging, and the experiment shows that the model performs well on the actual dataset.

The remainder of this article is as follows: Section 2 describes some related work, Sect. 3 introduces the acquisition of the dataset and some methods for similarity calculation, and Sect. 4 presents the model for user identification. Finally, the conclusion is given in Sect. 5.

2   Related Work

2.1   Social Network

The term social networking was first used by J. A. Barnes in 1954 [1]. Social networking originated from online social networking [2], which started with E-mail. The Internet is intrinsically a network among computers; the early E-mail figures out the problem of remote mail transmission, and it is still the most famous application. It is also the starting point for online social networking. Behavior-Based Safety (BBS) is a step further. The "group" and "forwarding" normalized, theoretically achieving the function of posting information and discussing topics with all people. Behavior-Based Safety (BBS) to the network social step forward from the simple p2p communication cost lowered to the price of p2p communication. Instant messaging and blogs are likely improved versions of the two aforementioned social tools. The former improves the immediate effect (speed of transmission) and the ability to communicate simultaneously (data processing). The latter began to reflect psychological and sociological theories. That is, the distribution of information nodes start to reflect a stronger individual sense, as this can aggregate distributed information in the temporal dimension to become the "image" and "personality" of the distribution of information node. Commonly used social networks include Weibo, Foursquare, Twitter, Facebook, etc.

2.2   User Identification Based on Online Social Networks [3]

Current techniques for user identification across online social networks have two steps.

Similarity Calculation of User Account.   User account similarity calculation methods include similarity calculation based on user attribute information [4], similarity calculation based on network topology map information, and similarity calculation based on user behavior. For the analysis of user attributes, user attributes contain efficient identification information such as user hobbies, occupation, age, etc. The identification methods based on user relationships and user-generated content are difficult to quantify and model, compared with user attributes, which are relatively easier to "get started," so this method is the most widely studied and popular among scholars. Since user data can be stored as strings [5], we can obtain the similarity values of the corresponding user data items by computing the similarity between the string sequences. The related similarity calculation methods include Levenshtein Distance, Dice Coefficient, Jaro Distance, Named Match Distance [6], etc. For network topology similarity calculation mainly depends on the degree of similarity between different network topologies between two nodes to decide whether these accounts point to the same entity. In other words, the more similar the nodes of the network topology are, the higher possibility that the person of two accounts refer to the same in real life. Followership and followings can be easily gained by open application programming interfaces (APIs) in social networks. Similarity matching between nodes contains methods such as Common Neighbor, Adamic-Adar indicator, resource allocation algorithm, etc. User behavior information, also known as user-generated content (UGC), is shared, exchanged, and posted by users using social networks. The UGC will play an essential role in user identification if it can be fully utilized. The similarity of behavioral information between different social accounts is then used to determine whether the user's identity matches. Related methods include Latent Semantic Analysis and Latent Dirichlet Allocation.

Matching User Account [7]. After the similarity values of two accounts from different social networks are obtained using the above methods, matching among accounts can be implemented using relevant matching algorithms. Mainly including the Kuhn-Munkres algorithm [8], stable marriage matching [9], and ranking-based cross-matching (RCM) [10]. RCM aims to find more matching pairs accurately [11]. Thus the identification of seed set users is decomposed into a distributed iterative process. The seed is a collection of one or more pairs of accounts that are known in advance to be pointing to the same entity in reality. Each iterative process has three stages: the selection of accounts, account matching, and cross matching. Matching funds are checked in each iteration, and the iteration ends when there is no user-matched pair is identified. However, if the precision or accuracy of the seed is too low, it can lead to a reduction in the effectiveness of the model. After the accounts are matched, the feasibility and robustness of the algorithm are determined by measuring the evaluation metrics such as accuracy rate [12] and recall rate [13].

3   Data Collection and Feature Extraction

3.1   Dataset

There is no complete public dataset so far, so we have to use crawlers to get the relevant dataset. Usually, most OSN sites do not allow a specific IP to generate too many requests simultaneously, so we used a distributed crawler system to obtain the data. The whole crawling structure is rough as follows (Fig. 1):

The user information of Foursquare may contain one or more links on Facebook, Twitter, and Instagram of the user. We get these links through Foursquare and then go to the corresponding websites to get the user information through these links. Since

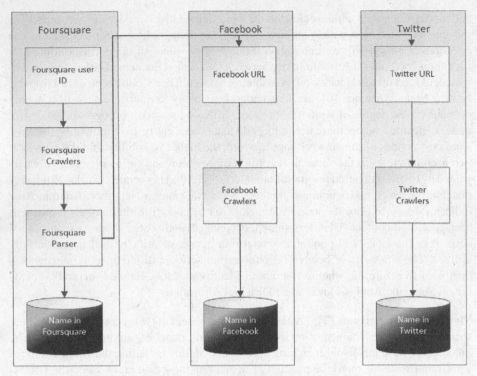

Fig. 1. Procedure of data collection

there were too few users with Instagram links in Foursquare, we only obtained users' Facebook and Twitter links. We got 408,723 user information, among which 225,173 users included Foursquare and Facebook account information, 130,584 users included both Foursquare and Twitter account information, and 9,996 users had both Twitter and Facebook account information. The relevant information is shown in Table 1, and each dataset contains two columns, which are the names of the users of the two platforms.

Table 1. Number of instances in datasets

Name of dataset	Size
FS-TW	225,173
FS-FB	130,584
FB-TW	9,996

The data in Table 1 we call positive samples. At the same time, we construct the negative sample dataset relative to it according to the size of the dataset, and the negative sample dataset is formed by putting different people from different platforms together. It should be noted that we assume that the user's name is unique in the platform and do not include the case of renaming. At the same time, the language of user names may vary widely, considering the possible inaccuracy when the characters are translated. We only obtain information about users whose user names are in English.

3.2 Feature Extraction

As we all know, user names contain rich meanings. We can calculate the similarity of names by some similarity calculation methods to provide rich information for the subsequent similarity matching. The similarity calculations we use include the following methods (Table 2):

Table 2. Similarity calculation methods

No.	Name of method
1	Average of Best Match
2	Max of Best Match
3	Longest Common Substring Similarity
4	Longest Common Substring Comparing Minimum Length
5	Longest Common Substring Comparing Maximum Length
6	Longest Common Subsequence Comparing Minimum Length
7	Longest Common Subsequence Comparing Maximum Length
8	Edit Distance
9	Normalized Edit Distance
10	Longest Common Substring
11	Longest Common Subsequence
12	Edit Distance Comparing Minimum Length
13	Edit Distance Comparing Maximum Length
14	Normalized Edit Distance Comparing Minimum Length
15	Normalized Edit Distance Comparing Maximum Length
16	Jensen-Shannon Divergence of Alphabet Distribution

The relevant methods are calculated as follows:

Max (Average) of Best Match.   Usually, the user's name includes < [first name], [middle name], [last name] >. If the user's name is only taken as a whole, then much information will be lost, so we calculate the similarity of the users' display names by the Average (Max) of Best Match. The specific method is as follows: In the first step, the user's display name is split into words, and for each word, their similarity is calculated first, and the formula for calculating the similarity is as (1).

$$Sim(s_1, s_2) = \frac{len(lcs(s_1, s_1))}{(len(s_1) + len(s_2))} \tag{1}$$

where $len(s)$ refers to the length of s and $lcs(s_1, s_2)$ refers to the length of the longest common substring of s_1 and s_2. Each user name can be split into one or more words so that two arrays Arr_1 and Arr_2 can be obtained.

For $w_i \in Arr_1$ and $w_j \in Arr_2$, the second step uses (1) to calculate their similarity to obtain matrix $A = \{a_{ij}\}$, where $a_{ij} = Sim(s_1, s_2)$.

The maximum value is calculated and recorded for matrix A in the third step. Then, delete the row and the column where the maximum value is located, and the third step is repeated until the size of matrix A becomes zero. And then, we get a list containing the maximum value of matrix A after each change, and the maximum value is the result of the Max of Best Match, and the value of the Average of Best Match is the result of the change of the matrix A. The value of the Average of Best Match is obtained by averaging it.

Longest Common Substring Similarity. Longest Common Substring Similarity aims to compute the longest substring of two strings [14]. The calculation is as follows: In the first step, a counter called cn is defined to indicate the number of comparisons and initialized to zero. In the second step, for $name_1$ and $name_2$, unless the length of the longest common substring of the two strings is zero, the following calculation is performed to calculate the length of the longest common substring of both and record it in a list, and the counter is added by one. And then, for $name_1$ and $name_2$, we delete the substring and repeat the second step until the length of the longest common substring of both is zero. Step two is repeated until the length of the longest common substring is zero. In the third step, we determine whether cn is zero. If it is zero, set it to 1, which means there is no common substring between two strings, and then sum the list to get the total and calculate the Longest Common Substring Similarity of $name_1$ and $name_2$, the calculation formula is as follows (2).

$$Sim_{LCS}(name_1, name_2) = \frac{sum - cn + 1}{len(name_1) + len(name_2) + sum} \tag{2}$$

Longest Common Substring Comparing Minimum (Maximum) Length. We also take the length of the names into account. Generally speaking, the longer the common substring length of two names, the more similar the two names are. We calculate the Longest Common Substring Comparing Min (Max) Length for users by considering the following relevant formula

$$Sim_{LCSmin}(name_1, name_2) = \frac{len(lcs(name_1, name_2))}{\min(len(name_1), len(name_2))} \tag{3}$$

$$Sim_{LCSmax}(name_1, name_2) = \frac{len(lcs(name_1, name_2))}{\max(len(name_1), len(name_2))} \tag{4}$$

Normalized Edit Distance. Similar to the Edit Distance, Normalized Edit Distance performs steps add one when adding and deleting, but steps add two when replacing. The specific formula is as follows.

$$Sim_{ned}(name_1, name_2) = \frac{len(name_1) + len(name_2) - Sim_{edd}(name_1, name_2)}{len(name_1) + len(name_2)} \tag{5}$$

Jensen-Shannon Divergence of Alphabet Distribution. As mentioJensen-Shannon Divergence of Alphabet Distribution.ned in [15] and [16], the display names "gateman" and "nametag" are very similar because one is the reverse spelling of the other. [17]. The formula for calculating the JS Divergence is as follows.

$$Sim_{JSD} = \tfrac{1}{2}(KL(p_{name1}|p_{name}) + KL(p_{name2}|p_{name})) \tag{6}$$

$$p_{name} = \tfrac{1}{2}(p_{name1} + p_{name2}) \tag{7}$$

$$KL(p_{name1}|p_{name}) = \sum_{i=1}^{|p_{name1}|} p_{name1_i} \cdot log \frac{p_{name1_i}}{p_{name_i}} \tag{8}$$

where p_{name} is the alphabet distribution of name, taking David Lee and Dave Wan as an example, the alphabet distribution of both of them is shown below.

Table 3. Alphabet distribution of David Lee and Dave Wan

d		a	v	i	l	e	w	n
$p_{DavidLee}$	2/8	1/8	1/8	1/8	1/8	2/8	p_0	p_0
$p_{DaveWan}$	1/7	2/7	p_0	p_0	p_0	1/7	1/7	1/7

Where p_0 means that the letter does not appear in the string, and we set the position to our preset minimum value of 0.25e−16.

4 Model

This paper is based on users' names to determine whether it is the same person who are using various online social networks, we use a series of supervised machine learning classification models to accomplish this task. The structure of the whole model is as follows (Fig. 2):

4.1 Classifier

For the same dataset, different classification models will have different effects. In this paper, There are ten classification models, including Support Vector Machine (SVM), Logistic Regression (LR), K-Nearest Neighbor (KNN), Gaussian Bayes (GB), Decision Tree (DT), Bagging, Random Forest (RF), Extreme Random Tree (ERT), AdaBoost, and Gradient Boosting Decision Tree (GBDT), are used to classify the data, which are provided by scikit-learn. The result shows that SVM performs best in the three datasets with the accuracy of 92%, 94.5%, 97.1% and AUC values of 95.6%, 95%, 94.4% respectively (Fig. 3, Fig. 4 and Fig. 5).

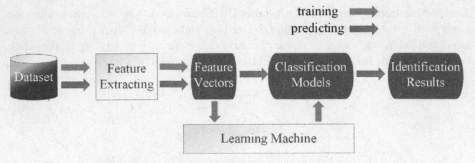

Fig. 2. Identification model procedure

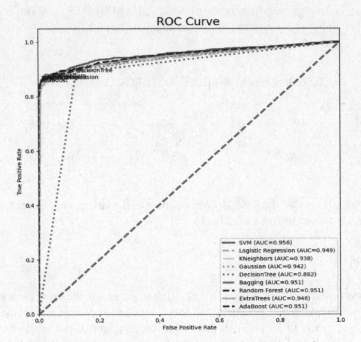

Fig. 3. Identication results of different classfiers in dataset fs-tw

4.2 Evalution Metrics

We introduced the confusion matrix to calculate the goodness of the model. Where a denotes the number of correct predictions in the positive sample, b means the number of wrong predictions in the positive sample, c denotes the number of wrong predictions in the negative sample, and d means the number of correct predictions in the negative sample. Depended on the confusion matrix, our evaluation metrics include ACC, PRE, REC, FNR, and F1 (Table 4).

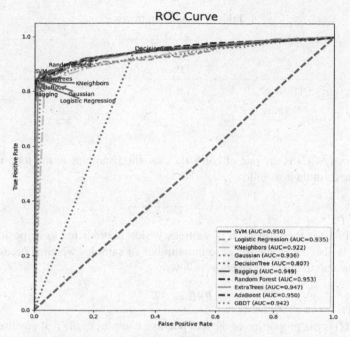

Fig. 4. Identication results of different classfiers in dataset fs-fb

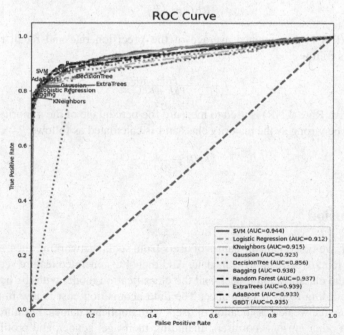

Fig. 5. Identication results of different classfiers in dataset fb-tw

Table 4. Confusion matrix

		Predicted	
		Positive	Negative
True	Positive	a	b
	Negative	c	d

Accuracy (ACC) is the rate of correctly classified samples to the total number of samples, the formula is as follows:

$$ACC = \frac{a+b}{a+b+c+d} \tag{9}$$

Precision (PRE) is the proportion of samples which is predicted to be positive by the model that is also actually positive to the number of samples which is predicted to be positive. The calculation formula is as follows:

$$PRE = \frac{a}{a+c} \tag{10}$$

Recall (REC) is the proportion of the real positive samples to the real positive samples. The formula is as follows:

$$REC = \frac{a}{a+b} \tag{11}$$

F-measure (F1) is the summed average of the precision rate and recall rate and is calculated as follows:

$$F1 = \frac{2 \times PRE \times REC}{PRE + REC} \tag{12}$$

False Negative Rate (FNR) is used to measure the percentage of the minority class that is judged to be wrong as the majority class and is calculated as follows:

$$FNR = \frac{b}{a+b} \tag{13}$$

5 Conclusion

In this paper, we first obtain the names of users from social networking sites, after which we perform feature extraction on the data. And then, the generated feature vector is used as input to the classification model, and the classification model with the best effect is selected according to its performance. The data acquisition cost is low in this paper, which results in a weak classification of users with duplicate names. In future work, we will analyze other attributes of users, including their age, gender, and profile. We will also analyze the user's followership, followings, and the comments made by the user to improve the model's ability to identify users in different data dimension environments.

References

1. Shu, K., Wang, S., Tang, J., et al.: User identity linkage across online social networks: A review. ACM SIGKDD Explorations Newsl **18**(2), 5–17 (2017)
2. Li, H.X., Zhu, H.J., Du, S.G., Liang, X.H., Shen, X.M.: Privacy leakage of location sharing in mobile social networks: Attacks and defense. IEEE Trans. Dependable Secure Comput. **15**(4), 646–660 (2018)
3. Xing, L., Deng, K., Wu, H., et al.: A survey of across social networks user identification. IEEE Access **7**, 137472–137488 (2019)
4. Li, Y., Peng, Y., Zhang, Z., Xu, Q., Yin, H.: Understanding the user display names across social networks. In: Proceedings of International World Wide Web Conference Committee (IW3C2), pp. 1319–1326 (2017)
5. Ma, J., et al.: Balancing user profile and social network structure for anchor link inferring across multiple online social networks. IEEE Access **5**, 12031–12040 (2017)
6. Li, Y., Peng, Y., Zhang, Z., Yin, H., Xu, Q.: Matching user accounts across social networks based on username and display name. World Wide Web **22**(3), 1075–1097 (2018)
7. Ma, J.: Social account linking via weighted bipartite graph matching. Int. J. Commun. Syst. **31**(7) e3471 (2018)
8. Deng, K., Xing, L., Zheng, L., Wu, H., Xie, P., Gao, F.: A user identification algorithm based on user behavior analysis in social networks. IEEE Access **9**, 47114–47123 (2019)
9. K. Deng, L. Xing, M. Zhang, H. Wu, and P. Xie, "A multiuser identification algorithm based on Internet of Things," Wireless Commun. Mobile Comput., vol. 2019, May 2019, Art. no. 6974809
10. Zhao, D., Zheng, N., Xu, M., Yang, X., Xu, J.: An improved user identification method across social networks via tagging behaviors. In: Proceedings of IEEE 30th International Conference on Tools with Artificial Intelligence, pp. 616–622 (Nov 2018)
11. Li, Y., Zhang, Z., Peng, Y., Yin, H., Xu, Q.: Matching user accounts based on user generated content across social networks. Future Gener. Comput. Syst. **83**, 104–115 (2018)
12. Chen, L., Tan, F.: Identity recognition scheme based on user access behavior. In: Proceedings of IEEE 8th Joint International Information Technology and Artificial Intelligence Conference, pp. 125–129 (May 2019)
13. Qi, M., Wang, Z., He, Z., Shao, Z.: User identification across asynchronous mobility trajectories. Sensors **19**(9) (2019), Art. no. 2102
14. Liu, D., Wu, Q., Han, W., Zhou, B.: User identification across multiple websites based on username features. Chin. J. Comput. **38**(10), 2028–2040 (2015)
15. Zafarani, R., Liu, H.: Connecting users across social media sites: A behavioral-modeling approach. In: Proceedings of KDD, pp. 41–49 (2013)
16. Zafarani, R., Tang, L., Liu, H.: User identification across social media. ACM Trans. Knowl. Dis. Data (TKDD) **10**, 1–30 (2015)
17. Li, Y., Peng, Y., Ji, W., Zhang, Z., Quanqing, X.: User identification based on display names across online social networks. IEEE Access **5**, 17342–17353 (2017)

A Weakly Supervised Text Classification Method Based on Vocabulary Construction

Peidong Li, Di Lin[✉], and Zijian Li

University of Electronic Science and Technology of China, Chengdu, Sichuan, China
202022090635@std.uestc.edu.cn, lindi@uestc.edu.cn

Abstract. Text classification is an important research direction in natural language processing. The computer can automatically classify and label texts according to certain classification standards through text classification technology. Traditional text classification tasks require a large amount of labeled data. However, human-labeled data is not only expensive, but also susceptible to the subjective consciousness of the labelers. Therefore, unsupervised text classification using computers becomes relevant. In most cases, the label name of each category is instructive for the classification task. In this paper, we design a weakly supervised text classification method. This method only needs to provide the label names that guide the classification to complete the automated text classification. Our method was tested on several publicly available datasets and performed well.

Keywords: Text Classification · Weak Supervision · Word Vocabulary

1 Introduction

We are in an era of information explosion, with billions of people active on the Internet every day, and more and more people expressing their views and opinions by publishing text messages. The automatic classification of a large amount of text is a very important part of natural language processing tasks. Efficient classification can provide a good dataset for other applications and is a great help in filtering out useful information on the Web. Examples include summary generation, spam detection, and sentiment analysis. To build an automatic text classification, it is generally necessary to use human-labeled documents as the basis for model's learning and training. Some deep learning-based classifiers such as CNN [1] and RNN [2] possess powerful representation learning capability and can effectively capture the semantic information of text sequences. By inputting a large amount of human-labeled texts to train the classifier, a more accurate classification can be achieved.

In June 2017, Google team proposed the classic work of NLP, Transformer, in their paper "Attention Is All You Need" [3], using a new model to completely replace RNN. The Transformer model proposed in this paper outperforms RNNs and CNNs in machine translation tasks, using only encoder-decoder and attention mechanisms. Decoder and attention mechanisms to achieve good results, and its biggest advantage is that it can

X. Jiang (Ed.): MLICOM 2022, LNICST 481, pp. 128–136, 2023.
https://doi.org/10.1007/978-3-031-30237-4_12

be efficiently parallelized. In 2018, the BERT [4] model was born. It performed well in SQuAD1.1 and recorded the best results in 11 different NLP tests. The release of the Transformer architecture creates a new baseline for deep learning text classification methods. Many new models and methods based on the Transformer architecture are created [5]. Lan et al. [6] proposed the ALBERT model to achieve cross-layer parameter sharing while retaining the original Transformer encoder architecture, and the improved model surpasses BERT in all aspects. In order to solve the problem of context fragmentation that BERT is not able to encode the whole article input at one time, Transformer-XL [7] adopts two levels of sentence and paragraph looping mechanism and relative position encoding scheme. This means that the input sequence does not need to be split into arbitrary fixed lengths, but can follow natural linguistic boundaries, such as sentences and paragraphs. This not only helps to understand the deep context of multiple sentences, paragraphs and possibly longer texts, but also enables training on larger datasets. RoBERTa [8] makes several adjustments based on BERT: 1) longer training time, larger batch size, and more training data; 2) remove the next predict loss; 3) longer training sequences; 4) use dynamic adjustment Masking mechanism on training strategy.

Weakly supervised approaches in text classification have attracted a lot of attention from researchers in recent years, as it relieves experts from the burden of annotating a large number of documents, especially for specific domains. In general, in a weakly supervised model, each category contains some tag document or seed word and other open data [9]. Although these forms are much weaker than a fully labeled data, they still require additional knowledge from language experts.

In this paper, we design a weakly supervised text classification method that only need to use the textual information of category names. we expand the description information for classes by constructing a vocabulary. Then, the text with high confidence is added to the training set, and pseudo labeled according to the weighted algorithm we designed. Finally, the pseudo labeled data set is input into the classification model for training.

We conducted experiments on some publicly available datasets for comparison between different methods, and the experimental results shows that our method is more effective than previous methods mentioned in this paper.

2 Related Work

2.1 BERT

BERT is an autoencoder language model, and it uses two tasks to pre-train the model.

The first task is the using of "Mask". In order to make the model learn the ability of bidirectional coding effectively, BERT used masking language model (MLM) in the training process, that is, masking some positions in the input sequence at random, and then predicting them through the model. Because the MLM prediction task can make the result of model coding contain the context information of the context at the same time, it is beneficial to train a deeper BERT network model.

The second task adds a sentence level continuity prediction task on the basis of the bidirectional language model, that is, two sentences were input into the model at the same time, and then the second sentence was predicted to be the next sentence of the first sentence.

Compared with RNN, which relies on the previous calculation to calculate the features of the current word, self-attention in BERT's Transformer-encoder uses context information to calculate the features of the current word. Moreover, it extracts relational features from different levels, which can solve the problem of ambiguity of a word and reflect sentence semantics more comprehensively. Due to the advantages mentioned above, the BERT model has been widely used [10] in natural language processing tasks. In our work, we use BERT for two purposes: (1) representing documents by vector and (2) training a text classifier.

2.2 Weakly Supervised Text Classification

Weakly supervised text classification aims to classify text documents based only on word-level descriptions of each category such as their class names, avoiding the dependence on any labeled documents. Weakly supervised methods can make use of external knowledge [11], such as Gabrilovich et al. who represent text with pre-defined natural concepts that are weighted and easy to understand. An important advantage is that it makes use of a large amount of human-edited knowledge in the encyclopedia. A machine learning approach is used to build a "semantic interpreter" that can shadow natural language text fragments to a weighted vector of wiki concepts. We also can make use of keyword information. For example, ConWea [12] automatically group the same word into an adaptive number of different interpretations based on the contextual representation and the seed information provided by the user, and use the contextual corpus to disambiguate the keywords. WeSTClass [13] contains two modules. One is a text generation module, which is used to generate training set with labels based on the seed information. Another one is a self-training module, which refines the model on the labeled dataset using bootstrap method. WeSHClass [14] extends WeSTClass to hierarchical labels. XClass [15] classifies the data by the idea of clustering. Specifically, a comprehensive category representation is first estimated by incrementally adding the most similar words in each category until inconsistencies arise. Following a tailored hybrid class-holding mechanism, the authors obtain document representations by a weighted average of content-oriented labeled representations. Then, the documents are clustered and the prior of each document is assigned to its closest class. Finally, the most plausible documents from each clustering class are selected to train a text classifier. The method proposed in this page is improved on the basis of LOTClass [16]. Considering the words in vocabulary have different weights for the classification guidance, we use a weighed calculation mechanism. Finally, we use Baidu's translation API to expand the dataset.

3   Method

The classification method in this paper mainly includes two parts. The first part is to predict the replaceable words through the Bert model to construct the vocabulary. In the second part, we use the vocabulary to filter out documents as training set and train the classifier.

3.1 Vector Representation of Text

Firstly, the model takes a single character in the text as the minimum unit token and performs token ID conversion word by word. Then each ID corresponds to a specific vector expression. BERT model adds CLS vector at the initial position of each text. The CLS position vector is randomly assigned at the beginning of training, there is no obvious semantic information, and the CLS vectors of each language segment are independent of each other. The purpose is to take the CLS vector as an object that integrates the global semantic information of the text. The dashed box in the figure represents the preprocessed single text data matrix x0, the first column represents CLS vector, X1 to Xn represent each character vector, and the length of each vector has 768 dimensions (Fig. 1).

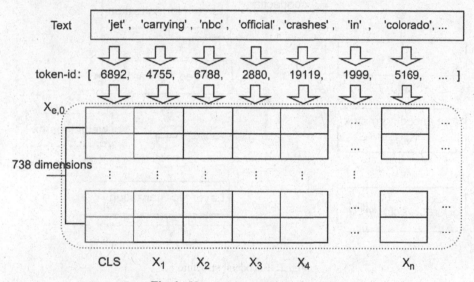

Fig. 1. Vector representation of text.

Each coding module includes multi head attention mechanism and feedforward neural network. Residual connection and layer normalization are used to solve the problem of saturation of feature extraction ability. The loaded pre training BERT model parameters include the weight matrix of each layer to replace the randomly generated values in the original BERT model. Each encoder of BERT has an output, and each output can be used to represent the text vector (Fig. 2).

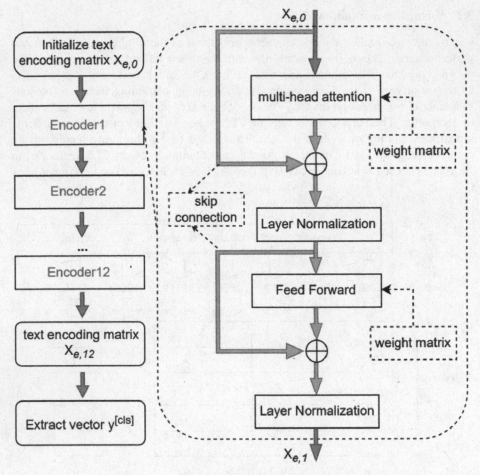

Fig. 2. Encoders' structure.

3.2 Expanding the Description of a Category by Label Name

In the original sentences, there must exist sentences containing label names. In these sentences, we do replaceable word prediction for the location of these label names and get the top-50 replaceable words for each sentence, and the replaceable words are those with similar meaning to the category labels. Each sentence is expanded with category description information using such method. Finally, each category has a certain number of words, and we filter these words to get the top-110 words in terms of frequency of occurrence. We show the predict top-50 task's result in Table 1. The result of the vocabulary for each category are shown in Table 2.

Table 1. Sentence and the predict top words.

Sentence	Predict words
On standby, set to fly. TORONTO -- Last week of August, the playoff race is heating up, and a Red Sox player's thoughts turn to... Football? In some ways, these guys are no different from the typical **sports** fan on the cusp of an NFL season. Sure, they're focused on the business at hand, winning a spot in their own postseason tournament...	'athletics', 'baseball', 'team', 'players', 'teams', 'athletes', 'club' ...
Chain Store Sales Up 0.1 Percent - Report. NEW YORK (Reuters) - U.S. chain store sales rose in the latest week, but business continued to fluctuate from the effects of Hurricane Charley and high gasoline prices, a report said on Tuesday	'trade', 'shop', 'money', 'market', 'commerce', 'store', 'venture' ...

Table 2. Category vocabulary.

Label Name	Vocabulary
politics	'politics', 'politicians', 'government', 'elections', 'democratic', 'party', 'state', 'leadership', 'election', 'politically', 'affairs', 'issues', 'governments', 'voters', 'debate', 'cabinet', 'congress', 'democrat', 'administration', 'president', 'religion', 'republican', 'history', 'war', 'crisis', 'legislature', 'candidates', 'governance', 'opposition', 'problems', 'relations', 'finance', 'justice', 'struggle', 'rhetoric' ...
sports	'sports', 'athletics', 'game', 'national', 'news', 'athletic', 'espn', 'basketball', 'arts', 'baseball', 'tv', 'hockey', 'pro', 'press', 'team', 'red', 'home', 'bay', 'kings', 'legends', 'city', 'winning', 'miracle', 'olympic', 'go', 'giants', 'champions', 'ball', 'players', 'boxing', 'teams', 'athletes', 'tennis', 'club', 'coaches', 'gold', 'west', 'toronto', 'classic', 'pittsburgh', 'super', 'nfl', 'magic', 'key' ...
business	'business', 'trade', 'commercial', 'enterprise', 'shop', 'money', 'market', 'commerce', 'corporate', 'global', 'future', 'sales', 'general', 'group', 'retail', 'companies', 'management', 'operations', 'operation', 'corporation', 'store', 'division', 'firm', 'venture', 'brand', 'contract', 'revenue', 'economic', 'branch', 'subsidiary', 'personal', 'cash', 'short', 'line', 'bank', 'customer', 'concern', 'family', 'work', 'products', 'big', 'scientific', 'virtual' ...
technology	'technology', 'tech', 'software', 'technological', 'device', 'equipment', 'hardware', 'devices', 'system', 'technique', 'digital', 'technical', 'concept', 'systems', 'functionality', 'material', 'process', 'facility', 'feature', 'capability', 'content', 'security', 'ability', 'network', 'internet', 'computing', 'modern', 'communication', 'language', 'mechanism', 'computer', 'design', 'cyber', 'standard', 'tool', 'development', 'format', 'protocol', 'wireless' ...

3.3 Pseudo-Tagging of Text Data by a Word List of Categories

We use the Mask method to make replaceable predictions for each word of each sentence, extracting the top 50 replaceable words at that position. For the word list of each category in the previous step, which has a size of 110, the higher ranked words appear more frequently, we weight the word list. Every ten words are divided into a group, and the weight of each group decreases from 1.5 to 0.5. By weighting calculation, we can get the weight of each sentence corresponding to different categories. If the weight is greater than 25, then we think the sentence can be pseudo-labeled as belonging to a certain category, and if there are more than one categories with weights greater than the threshold of 25, we take the category with the highest weight.

3.4 Classify Task

We use back-translation method to enhance the data set to make the classification more stable. For the problem that the number of documents in each category may vary too much, we use the resample approach to alleviate. The classifier is then trained by the BERT classification model.

4 Experiment

4.1 Dataset

We used AgNews and IMDB datasets for our experiments. The AgNews is a news article dataset, which contains four categories, politics, sports, business and technology, with 120,000 documents in the training set and 7,600 documents in the test set. IMDB is the review text data of movies, containing both categories of positive and negative, with 560,000 documents for training documents and 70,000 documents for testing.

4.2 Expirement Designing

The BERT model inserts a [CLS] symbol in front of the text and uses the output vector corresponding to this symbol as the semantic representation of the whole text. It can be understood that this symbol with no obvious semantic information will "fairly" integrate the semantic information of each word in the text compared with other words in the text. Therefore, we use the first position as the vector representation of the text, instead of the Mean approach where all positions are considered.

We use the BERT-base-cased as the basis of the experiment and leave all hyper-parameters unchanged.

4.3 Result

The Fig. 3 shows the accuracy and the variation of loss when training the classification model on the AgNews dataset.

After experiment, the results show that our method has some improvement in accuracy compared to other methods on AgNews as well as IMDB datasets. The following

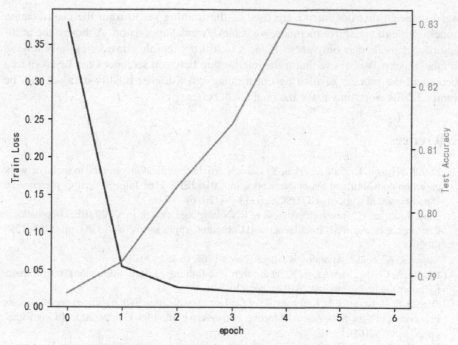

Fig. 3. Experiment's train loss and test accuracy.

data is the result of the experiment when the vocabulary size is 110. In fact, when we take a smaller vocabulary size of 80, the accuracy of pseudolabeling improves from 79.7% to 81.4% and the performance in the testing set also improves a little, although we obtain 13% less pseudo-labeled documents. Controlling the size of the vocabulary for different datasets may make the results better. Table 3 shows our experiment' results.

Table 3. Accuracy comparison.

Method	AgNews	IMDB
BERT simple match	0.752	0.677
WeSTClass	0.823	0.774
Our method	0.829	0.812

5 Conclusion

We design and implement a weakly supervised text classification method and achieved good experimental results. In our work, the Mask method is used for constructing a vocabulary of category description information and pseudo-label documents. These pseudo-labeled text documents are used as the training set to train the classification model. Through the above methods, we achieve weak supervision. Although the accuracy of this method is only about 82%, it is still acceptable considering only relying on label names. We believe that if the relationship between sentences can be taken into account in the process of filtering out training set, a higher quality data set may be obtained. This work may make the final result better.

References

1. Zhu, X., Huang, J., Zhou, Z., Han, Y.: Chinese article classification oriented to social network based on convolutional neural Networks. In: 2016 IEEE First International Conference on Data Science in Cyberspace (DSC), pp. 33–36 (2016)
2. Xiao, J., Zhou, Z.: Research progress of RNN language model. In: 2020 IEEE International Conference on Artificial Intelligence and Computer Applications (ICAICA), pp. 1285–1288 (2020)
3. Vaswani, A., et al.: Attention is All you Need **1706**, 03762 (2017)
4. Devlin, J., Chang, M.W., Lee, K., et al.: Bert: Pre-training of deep bidirectional transformers for language understanding **1810,** 04805 (2018)
5. Ohashi, S., Takayama, J., Kajiwara, T., et al.: Text classification with negative supervision. In: Proceedings of the 58th Annual Meeting of the Association for Computational Linguistics, pp. 351–357 (2020)
6. Lan, Z., Chen, M., Goodman, S., et al.: Albert: A lite bert for self-supervised learning of language.representations **1901**, 11942 (2019)
7. Dai, Z., Yang, Z., Yang, Y., et al.: Transformer-xl: Attentive language models beyond a fixed-length context **1901**, 02860 (2019)
8. Liu, Y., Ott, M., Goyal, N., et al.: Roberta: A robustly optimized bert pretraining approach **1907, 11692** (2019)
9. Yin, W., Hay, J., Roth, D.: Benchmarking zero-shot text classification: Datasets, evaluation and entailment approach. In: Proceedings of the 2019 Conference on Empirical Methods in Natural Language Processing and the 9th International Joint Conference on Natural Language Processing, pp. 3912–3921 (2019)
10. Li, B., Zhou, H., He, J., et al.: On the sentence embeddings from pre-trained language models **2011**, 05864 (2020)
11. Gabrilovich, E., Markovitch, S.: Computing semantic relatedness using wikipedia-based explicit semantic analysis. In: IJCAI (2007)
12. Mekala, D., Shang, J.: Contextualized Weak Supervision for Text Classification. In: ACL (2020)
13. Yu. M., Shen, J., Zhang, C., Han, J.: Weakly-supervised neural text classification. In: Proceedings of the 27th ACM International Conference on Information and Knowledge Management, pp. 983–992 (2018)
14. Meng, Y., Shen, J., Zhang, C., Han, J.: Weakly-supervised hierarchical text classification. In: Proceedings of the AAAI Conference on Artificial Intelligence, vol. 33, pp. 6829–6833 (2019)
15. Wang, Z., et al.: X-Class: Text Classification with Extremely Weak Supervision **2010**, 12794 (2021)
16. Meng, Y., et al.: Text classification using label names only: a language model self-training approach. In: EMNLP (2020)

Research on the Construction and Application of Knowledge Graph in the Field of Open Data Policy

Gao Lu[1], Xingli Liu[2(✉)] (iD), Jianghong Ou[3], and Dahua Fan[3]

[1] Harbin Institute of Information Technology, No.9, University Town, Binxi Technological Development Zone, Harbin 150431, Heilongjiang, China
[2] School of Computer Science and Technology, Science and Technology, University of Heilongjiang, Harbin 150027, Heilongjiang, China
liuxingli@usth.edu.cn
[3] Starway Communication, No. 31, Kefeng Road, Guangzhou Science City, 510663 Guangzhou, China

Abstract. In this paper, data open policy documents, laws and regulations are used as corpus sources, and the Bi-LSTM + CRF deep learning algorithm is selected to complete the training of the named entity recognition model constructed by the knowledge graph, and realize a collaborative relationship, data openness and data security concepts as the ontology. The knowledge map in the field of data openness policy is used to construct the model to complete the automatic identification and analysis of the collaborative situation of data openness policy text. The final simulation verification shows that the Bi-LSTM + CRF named entity recognition algorithm is more accurate than the CRF + + machine learning model training accuracy P value, recall rate R value and the harmonic average F value have been significantly improved, and the "Outline for Promoting Big Data Development", a typical data development policy text coordination situation analysis, has been objectively completed from the perspective of data openness and data security.

Keywords: Policy Text Analysis · Named Entity Recognition · Bi-LSTM + CRF · Knowledge Graph · Data Open Policy

1 Introduction

Today, countries around the world have continuously improved their awareness of the value of data. Developed countries in Europe and the United States have formulated a series of policies related to big data. The United States has issued the Federal Big Data Research and Development Strategic Plan [1], and the United Kingdom has issued the Industrial Strategy: Artificial Intelligence. "Domain Action" [2]. Subsequently, the

This research is financially supported by the National Social Science Foundation of China (GrantNo. 20ATQ004).

X. Jiang (Ed.): MLICOM 2022, LNICST 481, pp. 137–147, 2023.
https://doi.org/10.1007/978-3-031-30237-4_13

analysis of open government data policy has become a research hotspot. For example, Ma Haiqun [3] proposed a scientific method system based on policy, and conducted research on open government data policy collaboration from multi-dimensional perspectives such as policy elements, policy processes, and policy categories. In recent years, with the increase of policy texts and the rapid development of artificial intelligence technology, the application of automatic semantic extraction methods for policy texts in specific application scenarios has gradually become a hot and difficult point. The challenge lies in how to use information science, computer science, and literature information. A comprehensive research method is used to complete the process of policy text analysis of automatic human-computer interaction, so as to interpret the semantics of a core issue in the policy text through computer intelligence [4]. This non-intrusive and imprecise research method is the process of conducting natural language processing of policy texts in an objective and neutral position, and realizing the cognitive and intelligent recognition of policy texts by computers [5]. This paper takes the "data openness" policy text document data as the research object, applies the knowledge graph structured knowledge representation, adopts the Bi-LSTM + CRF named entity recognition deep learning algorithm to perform fine-grained custom entity object extraction training, and uses "Take the Outline for Promoting the Development of Big Data as an example to complete the application analysis of collaborative situation, and explore the feasibility of an intelligent automatic extraction method of data opening policy text".

2   Related Research

Reviewing the research results and literature of different policy text analysis, it is found that by completing the mining of policy text information and the analysis of external attribute characteristics through quantitative statistical tools, objective and verifiable research conclusions can be obtained [6]. This kind of policy literature measurement is a The current main policy analysis method is the organic integration of bibliometric analysis and content analysis [7, 8]. Aiming at the results of quantitative method research on data open policy, Chu Dejiang, with the help of Nvivo12 qualitative data analysis software, followed the steps of analysis framework construction, policy text coding, frequency statistical analysis, etc., from the two dimensions of policy instrumentality and synergy. 33 A quantitative text analysis was carried out on the policies closely related to rural green development [9]; Yang Zheng [10] and others applied policy bibliometric methods to analyze the significance of China's data openness and utilization policy system for promoting data governance and mining data value; Jiang Xin [11] Evaluated and analyzed the open and shared policies of scientific data issued by foreign funding agencies through qualitative text analysis and put forward suggestions; for the results of policy collaborative research, Hong Weida [12] et al. For government policy, policy quantification standards were designed from three dimensions of policy strength, policy objectives and policy tools, and the collected policy texts were quantified by grades, and a measurement model of policy effectiveness, policy objective synergy degree, and policy tool synergy degree was constructed. From the time dimension to analyze the policy synergy degree of China's open government data; Zhang Tao [13] analyzed the theme synergy degree of 446 policy texts based on the policy text calculation method, and used the LDA theme clustering method to obtain the policy text theme synergy degree value; Mao Zijun [14] et al. took 12 provinces and cities data opening related policies as research samples, analyzed from two dimensions of vertical policy coordination and horizontal policy coordination, and revealed the policy coordination between cities; Chen Xuelin [15] et al. From the perspective of scientific knowledge map, Based on co-word analysis, the research on hotspots of entrepreneurship and innovation policies in China combined with the results of co-word clustering analysis, using multi-dimensional scale analysis method, to draw a knowledge map of entrepreneurship and innovation policies, and explore the closeness of keywords in the hotspot areas of entrepreneurship and innovation policies and the hotspots. The relationship between fields, and finally found the internal structural relationship of China's mass entrepreneurship and innovation policy.

Based on the above analysis, it can be seen that the analysis methods at the textual level such as knowledge graph construction and related named entity recognition are feasible. Therefore, this paper takes the data opening policy text as the research object, determines the methods of ontology construction and entity extraction named entity recognition in the construction of knowledge graph, analyzes the synergy of policy text from the semantic analysis level, and completes the analysis of domain knowledge graph in data opening policy text.

3   Research Methods and Results

3.1   Overall Framework

According to the general policy text analysis process, according to the policy text acquisition (Acquire Documents), policy text processing (Process), policy text analysis (Analysis), construct the data opening policy text synergy analysis framework, as shown in Fig. 1.

① Acquire Documents. Policy text acquisition is the premise and foundation of policy text calculation. The policy text acquisition of this model needs to obtain data policy corpus through CNKI, policy documents, etc., and conduct corpus screening.

② Policy text processing (Process). The policy text processing process mainly includes the following: corpus collection, knowledge representation, policy text segmentation, part-of-speech tagging, domain dictionary construction, and using this dictionary to expand the Jieba vocabulary of the Chinese word segmentation tool, and segment the corpus to provide data input for model training. After superimposing and quality noise processing for the number of policy corpora, the qualified corpus is converted into data format, including BIO data format, Word2vec word vector processing, and divided into training set, development set and test set according to 7:2:1 and imported into the model, set the number of model iterations, and complete the Bi-LSTM + CRF named entity recognition model training process.

③ Policy text analysis (Analysis). First of all, it is necessary to encapsulate the named entity recognition algorithm based on knowledge graph through the visualization platform, select the data opening policy text that needs to be automatically parsed, and conduct calculation and supply policy managers for application analysis.

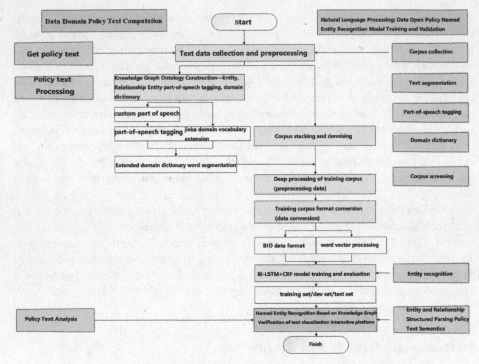

Fig. 1. Research framework of policy text analysis model

3.2 Ontology Construction of Policy Texts

According to the text analysis requirements of the data policy in this paper, a knowledge framework is constructed for the application scenarios: that is, according to the important principle of "opening while protecting" in the research hotspot of data development policy [16], the "open data" and "data open data" of the "data open" policy are customized. The two entity types of "safe" constitute a dictionary, and the entity types are set as: open and safe. The concepts of "open data" and "data security" based on the data open policy, and the knowledge graph ontology of the "collaboration" relationship are constructed, and the policy text is completed. Knowledge representation of corpus.

3.3 Data Collection and Preprocessing

This research selects text documents about data open policy in policy documents published by CNKI, government websites, and obtained on the Internet, and selects policy text corpus in the field of "data open" as a collection of policy text data, including policy text document corpus, government The website publishes the original text of the policy, the text of the policy interpretation in the network, the academic achievement literature on the policy interpretation of the research field in the CNKI literature knowledge base, and the self-built data open policy corpus as the data source [17], and completed 76 data open policy documents, There are 25 data security policy documents. After many manual extractions, 591 pairs of "data open" keywords and corpus sentences, and 295 pairs of "data security" keywords and corpus sentences are extracted. Complete the part-of-speech tagging of the data open in the data-safe topic dictionary, and expand the Jieba word segmentation vocabulary Opendata. The BIO tag category is indexed for the filtered corpus sentence, which is used as the training input of the model algorithm after the policy text corpus is processed.

3.4 Build Key Technologies

This paper uses the Bi-LSTM + CRF [18] named entity algorithm to complete the entity extraction task of the knowledge graph of the data opening policy text. Complete each word category label of an entity in a given sentence. The general idea is as follows: First, use Word2vec for the low-dimensional and dense word vector matrix of the dictionary corpus and the domain dictionary of the part-of-speech to supply Bi-LSTM + CRF, and load the training set After and the test set, use Bi-LSTM to automatically extract features from the context information of the word (character) vector sequence in the input policy text, and then provide the CRF model as a feature to process the dependency information between tags, and select the most suitable one. Predict the tag sequence to complete named entity recognition. Second, predict the results, that is, after training the model, reload the model, input new prediction text, and identify the named entity in the policy text. First load the character dictionary, then load the model, then preprocess the input text into a character sequence, and then the model predicts the output entity category at each moment. Add and import data, according to the trained word vector, find the corresponding word vector through Word2vec, build the Bi-LSTM + CRF model, calculate the loss function, optimize the loss function, update the model parameters, test the model function, and adjust the data format to suit the Model input, evaluate the training effect of the model.

According to the characteristics of the domain policy, this research designs the training system architecture of the named entity recognition model for policy text, as shown in Fig. 2. The architecture consists of 3 layers: look-up layer, bidirectional LSTM layer and CRF layer. The model uses the BIO annotation set in the Bakeoff-3 evaluation. It is completed in three steps: feature representation, model training, and model classification. It inputs a set of corpus (character) vectors about open data and open policy, and outputs a set of predicted tag sequences. The following According to the three aspects of policy text feature representation, model training and model classification, the key issues of the training process are described.

Feature Representation

Before the neural network model is executed, the words of the input data open policy corpus need to be converted into data. First, take the sentence as a unit, use one-hot coding to form the word embedding vector layer in each data open and data security field in each sentence of the data open corpus. In the first look-up layer, use the pre-The training or randomly initialized embedding matrix maps each word in the sentence from a one-hot vector to a low-dimensional dense word vector (character embedding), that is, designing and building a neural network model and representing the symbolic features of the text as distributed Feature information; Unlike traditional LSTM, Bi-LSTM considers both past features (extracted by forward process) and future features (extracted by backward process). The backward process is equivalent to inputting the original sequence into the LSTM in reverse. For example, the forward LSTM expresses the input sequence (x1, x2,…, xt,…, xn) as), and then uses the reverse LSTM to convert the input sequence (x1, x2,…, xt,…, xn) are expressed as (……,), and the concatenation of and is taken as xt as the final result.

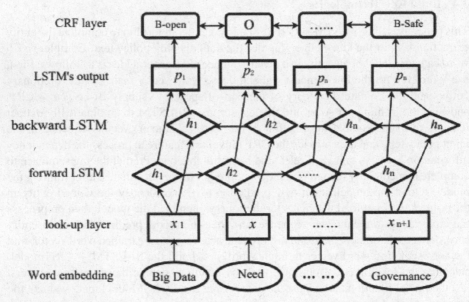

Fig. 2. Entity extraction model of data open policy text knowledge graph

Model Training

Use the splicing vector encoded by Bi-LSTM as the feature representation ht to perform softmax classification, obtain the label of each word, and splicing the K-dimensional vector (K is the number of labels) obtained from the representation of each word to obtain the input P, P is The n*k-dimensional matrix is uniformly input into the CRF model as a feature. The score of each sentence is shown in formula (1):

$$S(x, y) = \sum\nolimits_{i=0}^{n} A_{y_i, y_j,} + \sum\nolimits_{i=1}^{n} p_{i, y_j} \tag{1}$$

Among them, A is a transition matrix, which represents the probability of transition from one label to the next label in the label sequence. The parameters that need to be trained are: the parameters in Bi-LSTM and the transition probability matrix A in CRF, the supervised learning method is used in Bi-LSTM + CRF training, by maximizing the probability of predicting the real label sequence (take the logarithm of the probability and then take Negative, and then use gradient descent algorithm to optimize) to update the parameters in Bi-LSTM and the transition probability matrix A in CRF. At the beginning of training, "the real label sequence will not correspond to the maximum probability value", but through continuous iterative optimization of the samples, "the real label sequence should correspond to the maximum probability value" will eventually be realized; when Bi-LSTM + CRF is tested, directly according to the training The good parameters are used to obtain the scores corresponding to all possible prediction sequences, and finally the prediction sequence corresponding to the maximum score is taken as the final prediction result.

Model Classification

Use the trained neural network model to classify policy texts. First, use Bi-LSTM to represent the input text, and then input it into the CRF to classify the sentences of data openness, fine-grained data openness and data security in the policy, and the classification labels are entity type and BIO three kinds of label combinations, and finally output the classification result, that is, determine the boundary between the part of speech and the word, so as to complete the named entity recognition of the policy analysis.

Model Evaluation

①Evaluation indicators

The three important indicators in the neural network evaluation system include the accuracy rate, the recall rate, and the harmonic average F1. The specific formulas (2), (3), and (4) are as follows:

$$\text{Precision (Precison, referred to as P value)} \ P \ = \ TP/(TP + FP) \tag{2}$$

$$\text{Recall rate (Recall, referred to as R value)} \ R \ = \ TP/(TP + FN) \tag{3}$$

$$\text{Harmonic mean} \ F1 \ = 2 * P * R/(P + R) \tag{4}$$

Among them, TP represents the number of correctly recognized entities by the policy text model, FP represents the number of incorrectly recognized entities, FN represents the number of unrecognized entities, and TP + FP represents the total number of recognized entities, that is, FP + FN is the name of the class Total number of entities. P represents the ratio of the number of correctly identified entities in the prediction results to all identified entities, and R represents the proportion of entities that are correctly identified. F1 represents the harmonic mean of the precision rate P and the recall rate R. When both P and R are high at the same time, a higher F1 value can be obtained.

②Evaluation effect

According to the training log information of train.log, the experimental results of policy text entity recognition are displayed, as shown in Table 1. Without adding artificial features, the deep learning model iterates 46 times, and the model in the dev set is saved. Its accuracy P value, recall rate R value and the corresponding evaluation index of the CRF + + machine learning algorithm in the F1 control experiment The comprehensive index and the average index are significant promote.

Table 1. Experimental results of entity recognition model in policy text

Algorithm	P value	R value	F1 value
Bi-LSTM + CRFmodel	82.76%	92.31%	87.27
CRF + + model	66.54%	75.00%	70.52

4　Application of Knowledge Graph in the Field of Policy Text

4.1　Visual Application Interaction Platform

In this study, the combination of Flask + Uwsgi is used to request the API data interface of the NRE (Bi-LSTM + CRF) model from the web application server to complete the policy text analysis application request. Vue2.0 + Echarts + elementUI realizes the interactive front-end display of the visual platform. This paper selects the data opening policy text of the "Outline of Action for Promoting the Development of Big Data" issued by the State Council in 2015 [19], as shown in Fig. 3.

Fig. 3. Data opening policy text input interface

Obviously, the visual interactive verification platform provides an intuitive and visible analysis basis for the application of policy analysis and exploration. As shown in Fig. 4, the direct result of entity identification of the policy text of the "Outline of Action for Promoting Big Data Development" identified 433 "data open" entity objects and 77 "data security" entity objects. It can be seen that after applying the knowledge graph knowledge table method and customizing the knowledge ontology modeling of the relationship between "data openness", "data security" and "synergy", the data opening policy text for the "Outline of Action for Promoting the Development of Big Data" can be completed. Automatic calculation.

Further, the distribution of entities and relationships in the graph is used to more clearly show the situational distribution of the collaborative relationship between "data openness" and "data security" in the data openness policy text of the "Outline of Action for Promoting the Development of Big Data", as shown in Fig. 5.

识别结果

大数据是以容量大、类型多、存取速度快、应用价值高为主要特征的数据集合，正快速发展为对数量巨大、来源分散、格式多样的数据进行采集、存储和关联分析，从中发现新知识、创造新价值、提升新能力的新一代信息技术和服务业态。信息技术与经济社会的交汇融合引发了数据迅猛增长，数据已成为国家基础性战略资源，大数据正日益对全球生产、流通、分配、消费活动以及经济运行机制、社会生活方式和国家治理能力产生重要影响。目前，我国在大数据发展和应用方面已具备一定基础，拥有市场优势和发展潜力，但也存在政府数据开放共享不足、产业基础薄弱、缺乏顶层设计和统筹规划、法律法规建设滞后、创新应用领域不广等问题，亟待解决。为贯彻落实党中央、国务院决策部署，全面推进我国大数据发展和应用，加快建设数据强国，特制定本行动纲要。一、发展形势和重要意义全球范围内，运用大数据推动经济发展、完善社会治理、提升政府服务和监管能力正成为趋势，有关发达国家相继制定实施大数据战略性文件，大力推动大数据发展和应用。目前，我国互联网、移动互联网用户规模居全球第一，拥有丰富的数据资源和应用市场优势，大数据部分关键技术研发取得突破，涌现出一批互联网创新企业和创新应用，一些地方政府已启动大数据相关工作。坚持创新驱动发展，加快大数据部署，深化大数据应用，已成为稳增长、促改革、调结构、惠民生和推动政府治理能力现代化的内在需要和必然选择。（一）大数据成为推动经济转型发展的新动力。以数据流引领技术流、物质流、资金流、人才流，将深刻影响社会分工协作的组织模式，促进生产组织方式的集约和创新。大数据推动社会生产要素的网络化共享、集约化整合、协作化开发和高效利用，改变了

Fig. 4. Entity recognition results for data opening policy text

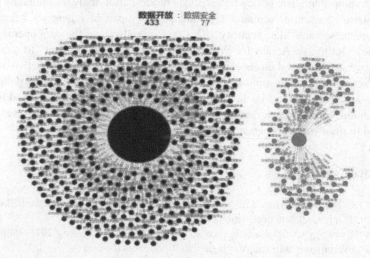

Fig. 5. Distribution of collaborative situation between data openness and data security

4.2 Collaborative Situation Analysis of Data Policy Texts

According to the analysis of the data opening policy in the "Outline of Action for Promoting the Development of Big Data", combined with the results of the visual map of the synergistic relationship between "data opening" and "data security", the analysis shows that: First, this document emphasizes the openness and sharing of big data while at the same time., to a certain extent, taking into account data security issues, and following the principle of "opening and sharing while paying attention to data protection". Second, from the analysis of the semantic ratio of "data" openness and "data security", as well as the degree of their synergistic relationship, it is clear that data openness and data security show an uneven distribution. The guiding significance of open data sharing. The formulation and implementation process of various local data opening policies can combine different regional characteristics, application field characteristics, and implementation object characteristics to strengthen data security.

5   Conclusion

This paper applies the natural language processing technology of computer science and linguistics, takes the semantic intelligent analysis of data development policy texts as the research goal, and takes the "cooperative problem of opening while protecting" under the demand of data opening as the research application scenario. The graph represents the framework of policy collaboration knowledge in the field of data development. According to the ontology definition of the concepts of "data openness" and "data security" defined in the application scenario, the synergistic relationship between the two is used as the relationship definition, and the Bi-LSTM + CRF algorithm is selected for training data development. The policy text analysis model, after analyzing the data opening policy, obtains an accurate semantic layer analysis of a pair of synergistic relationships of "data openness" and "data security". This research also uses the data opening policy text of the "Outline of Action for Promoting Big Data Development" to analyze the collaborative situation of data development policy texts. From the perspective of knowledge extraction, this paper aims at the semantic analysis of data opening policy texts. There are still some limitations in the exploratory application of the method based on model training. Further exploration and research on knowledge relationship extraction concerned in policy texts is needed.

References

1. ACM DL.The federal big data research and development strategic plan[EB/OL]. (11 Aug 2021).https://dl.acm.org/citation.cfm?id=3027595
2. Industrial strategy:artificial intelligence sector deal[EB/OL]. (11 Aug 2021). https://www.gov.uk/government/publications/artificial-intelligence-sector-deal
3. Ma, H., Hong, W.: Pilot research on policy coordination of open government data in my country. Library Construction 4, 61–68 (2018)
4. Li. J., Liu, Y., Huang, C., et al.: Reshaping policy text data analysis with bibliometric research: the origin, migration and method innovation of policy bibliometrics. J. Public Administration (2) (2015)
5. Pei, L., Sun, J., Zhou, Z.: Policy text calculation: a new way of interpreting policy text. Books Inf. 6, 47–55 (2016)
6. Peng, Z., Gao, F.: Quantitative research on china's mineral resources security policy texts from the perspective of policy tools. J. Central South Univ. (Soc. Sci. Ed.) 27(05), 11–24 (2021)
7. Huang, C., Ren, T., Li, J., et al.: Responsibilities and interests: a study on the evolution of intergovernmental cooperation in China's science and technology innovation policy based on quantitative analysis of policy literature. Manage. World 12, 68–81 (2015)
8. Tian, J., Yang, Z.: Homogeneity and difference: a bibliometric analysis of the implementation policy of provincial government power list system. J. Intelligence 36(5), 75–81 (2017)

9. Chu, D.: An analysis of rural green development policy texts: based on the dimensions of instrumentality and synergy. J. Zhengzhou Univ. (Philos, Soc. Sci. Edition), **54**(02), 14–21+126 (2021)
10. Yang, Z., Tian, J.: Policy bibliometric research on open utilization of government data: a three-dimensional analysis perspective. J. Intell. **37**(12), 175–181 (2018)
11. Jiang, X.: Research on open and sharing policy of scientific data of foreign funding institutions——analysis of policy text based on NVivo 12. Mod. Intell, **40**(08), 144–155 (2020)
12. Hong, W., Ma, H.: Research on the evolution and synergy of my country's open government data policy: Based on the analysis of policy texts from 2012 to 2020. J. Intell. **40**(10), 139 (2021)
13. Zhang, T., Ma, H.: Collaborative research on open data and data security policy based on policy text computing. Intell. Theory Practice, **43**(06), 149–155+141 (2020)
14. Mao. Z., Zheng, F., Huang, Y.: Research on government data opening from the perspective of policy coordination. Electronic Government Affairs, (9), 14–23 (2018)
15. Chen, X., Li, R.: Research on the hot Spots concerning my country's mass innovation and entrepreneurship policy based on Co-word analysis. Univ. Electron. Sci. Technol. China (Soc. Sci. Ed.) **21**(02), 9–17 (2019)
16. Catelli, R., Casola, V., Pietro, G.D., et al.: Combining contextualized word representation and sub-document level analysis through Bi-LSTM+CRF architecture for clinical de-identification. Knowl.-Based Syst. **213**(1), 106649 (2021)
17. Ma, H., Pu, P.: Analysis of the research status of open data policy at home and abroad and judgment of research trends in my country. J. Chin. Library **41**(5), 76–86 (2015)
18. Ma, H., Zhang, T.: Research on the construction of corpus for wisdom service from the perspective of literature information Inf. Theory Practice **6**, 124–130 (2019)
19. State Council of the People's Republic of China: Action Outline for Promoting the Development of Big Data. Group Technol. Moder. Production **32**(3), 8 (2015)

Comparative Study on the Methods of Atmospheric Early Warning Based on Machine Learning

Guanghua Yu[1,2(✉)], Jianghong Ou[3], and Dahua Fan[3]

[1] Heihe University, Heilongjiang, Heihe, China
Ygh2862@163.com
[2] School of Computer and Information Engineering College, HeiHe University, Heihe, China
[3] Starway Communication, No. 31, Kefeng Road, Guangzhou Science City, Guangzhou 510663, China

Abstract. This paper takes Beijing Meteorological environment data as the analysis object, and uses six eigenvalues to analyze PM2.5. Normal equation, gradient descent, ridge regression and xgboost are used to predict and analyze and compare the results. The mean square error of xgboost algorithm is 0.322. It is significantly lower than the other three algorithms, and its effect is far better than the other three algorithms, which is suitable for the prediction of this data.

Keywords: Atmospheric environment · Data forecast · Machine learning

1 Preface

Artificial intelligence is widely used in data prediction. These have greatly facilitated our lives. If we can predict the future environment and climate, we can make people better manage and prevent the problem of atmospheric change. Therefore, it is necessary to analyze and predict meteorological data based on Python machine learning.

2 Data Preprocessing

The meteorological monitoring data used are the results of Beijing meteorological condition detection, which from the kaggle platform. The data includes 18 meteorological characteristic information of different samples such as temperature and PM2.5, with a total of 52584 pieces (2010–2015).

The forecast process is divided into four parts:

First, the meteorological environment detection data should be preprocessed, including selecting the required features and standardizing the data.

Foundation item: School-level topics (KJZ202102); School-level topics (XJGY201923). Project of Heilongjiang Provincial Department of Education (2019-KYYWF-0462).

X. Jiang (Ed.): MLICOM 2022, LNICST 481, pp. 148–157, 2023.
https://doi.org/10.1007/978-3-031-30237-4_14

Second, Analyze the obtained data, exclude the characteristic value with large or small correlation coefficient, and compare the results to obtain a series of required characteristics.

Third, using the obtained environmental meteorological data, different algorithms are used to establish the model, and the optimal results of each algorithm are obtained by adjusting the parameters.

Fourth, Compare and analyze the data results and select the best method.

The process is shown in Fig. 1:

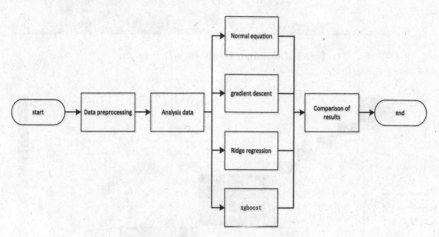

Fig. 1. Overall design flow chart

2.1 Target Value Processing

After the missing value processing, the target value with large mean square error in the data set and the data distribution not meeting the Gaussian distribution is processed. Use NP. Log() in numpy to logarithmically convert the target value, and the result is shown in Fig. 2.

2.2 Correlation Analysis

Not all data in the data set can be used as a training set, and the features with minimal correlation between the target values can be discarded, or the correlation between the two features is great, which will make the predicted value offset and is not conducive to the result prediction. Use the Seaborn module in Python to draw a thermal map, and use the thermal map to observe the relationship between features. The thermodynamic diagram is shown in Fig. 3.

It can be concluded from the thermal map that the correlation between the data label and the year is very strong, but the two characteristics have little impact on the target value, so it is not necessary to use them as characteristics. Prec and Iprec have a strong correlation, and one feature should be removed. However, the data in these two groups of

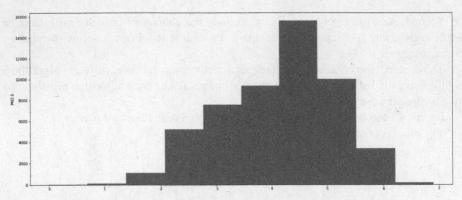

Fig. 2. Logarithm Transformation diagram

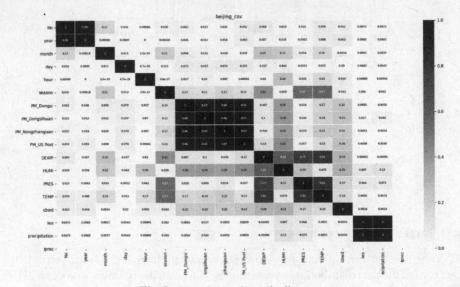

Fig. 3. Data thermodynamic diagram

data are almost zero, and the impact on the results is very weak, so they are not selected. The correlation between temperature and pressure (temp and PRES) also reached 0.82, and the correlation was quite high. Therefore, the temperature characteristic is discarded and only the pressure characteristic is retained. The four characteristics in the middle are the observation data of PM2.5 in Beijing from four different countries, which are highly relevant. In the forecast, select the data of the United States as the target value.

2.3 Labeling Treatment

Standardized algorithms were used for data processing. The principle of standardization is to convert the average value of feature data into 0 and the standard deviation into 1.

The standardized formula is shown in (1).

$$z = x - \upsilon/\partial \tag{1}$$

where υ and ∂ are the mean and standard deviation of the column where x is located. The values obtained after data normalization are shown in Fig. 4.

2	0.246991
3	0.246991
4	0.149542
5	0.052092
6	0.052092
7	0.052092
8	0.052092
9	0.052092
10	0.052092
11	0.052092
12	-0.142806
13	-0.142806
14	-0.240256

Fig. 4. Data standardization

3 Normal Equation Algorithm Prediction

The prediction of normal equation algorithm is divided into four steps: incoming data, data set segmentation, model training and model evaluation. The system flow chart is shown in Fig. 5.

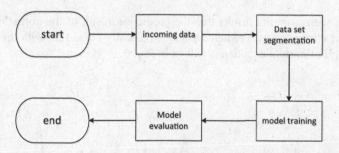

Fig. 5. Forecast flow chart

3.1 Incoming Data

Through the above process, six sets of eigenvalues PM_Dongsi, DEWP, Iw, Cbwd, HUMI, and PRES were selected as training data sets and PM_ Us post as the value of the objective function.

3.2 Data Set Segmentation

The data set is divided into two parts. The first part is the training set of the data. The selected six feature values are used to train the data. The second part is the verification set, which is used to verify the advantages and disadvantages of the model, that is the target value. The function of dividing data sets uses train_ test_ Split function, which in the Sklearn library. The training set of data accounted for 75%, and the validation set accounted for 25%.

3.3 Model Evaluation

The mean square error was used to compare the real value and the predicted value.
    The mean square error formula is:

$$MSE = 1/n \sum_{t=1}^{n} (x - x^*)^2 \tag{2}$$

where x is the real value and X * is the predicted value.

3.4 Normal Equation Prediction and Result Analysis

The predicted value and mean square error of the model are shown in Table 1.

Table 1. Mean square error of normal equation

Mean square error of normal equation	Time spent
0.534	0.14

It can be seen from the results that the prediction result of the normal equation is ideal, and the change of the predicted value is basically consistent with the real value. The line graph of normal equation is shown in Fig. 6.

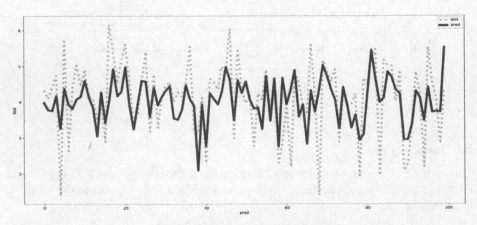

Fig. 6. Ridge regression line chart

4   Prediction of Gradient Descent Weather Algorithm

First, we need to determine the learning rate α, that is, the size of the learning pace.

Second, any given initial value.

Third, use the previously determined steps to advance and update the determined direction θ Value.

Fourth, if it is lower than the defined value ε, we can stop solving.

The algorithm formula is:

$$\theta_i = \theta_i - \alpha(h_\theta(x) - y)x \tag{3}$$

where α is the learning rate and $(h_\theta(x) - y)x$ is the step taken. If the value of α is set too small, the operation will take a long time. However, if a is set too large, it will lose its minimum value and cause gradient explosion.

4.1   Gradient Descent Prediction and Result Analysis

The predicted value and mean square error of the model can be obtained through the above process, as shown in Table 2.

Table 2. Gradient descent mean square error

Gradient descent mean square error	Time spent
1.766	0.06

The mean square error of the normal equation is 1.766, and the training model often uses 0.06 s. The line chart of the first 100 data of the predicted value and the target value is as follows: Fig. 7, Fig. 8 and Fig. 9.

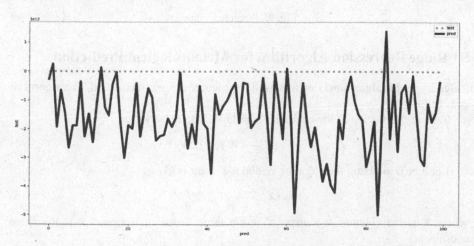

Fig. 7. Gradient descent line chart

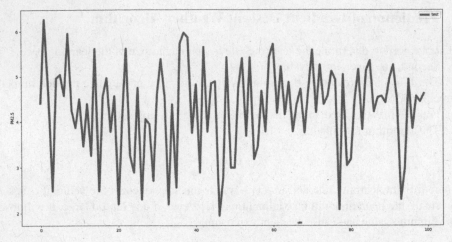

Fig. 8. True value

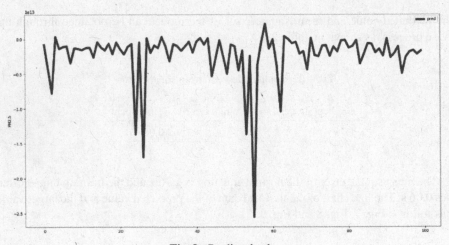

Fig. 9. Predicted value

5 Ridge Regression Algorithm for Meteorological Prediction

Ridge regression algorithm is an improved least square estimation method. The algorithm is as follows:

Take the derivative of the original formula W, The result is:

$$2X^T(Y - XW) - 2\lambda W \tag{4}$$

Let it be 0 to obtain the value of W and the result is (5)

$$\omega = (X^TX + \lambda I)^{-1}X^TY \tag{5}$$

where X is the eigenvalue matrix, Y is the target value matrix, and λ is the ridge coefficient.

5.1 Ridge Regression Prediction and Result Analysis

The predicted value and mean square error of the model are shown in Table 3.

Table 3. Mean square error of ridge regression

Ridge regression mean square error	Time spent
0.529	0.15

It can be seen that the mean square error of the normal equation is 0.529, and the training model often uses 0.15 s. The first 100 data figures of predicted value and target value are as follows in the Fig. 10:

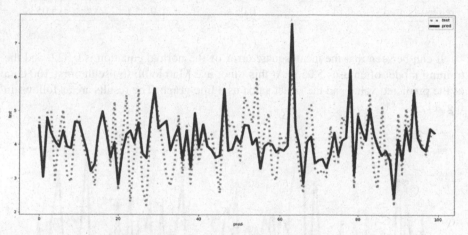

Fig. 10. Ridge regression line chart

6 Xgboost Algorithm for Meteorological Prediction

Xgboost is also called extreme gradient lifting tree, which is an implementation of boosting algorithm. For classification or regression problems, the effect is very good. The formula for evaluating the segmentation candidate set is:

$$L = \frac{1}{2}[\frac{G_L^2}{H_L + \lambda} + \frac{G_R^2}{H_R + \lambda} - \frac{(G_L + G_R)^2}{H_L + H_R + \lambda}] - \gamma \qquad (6)$$

Where $\frac{G_L^2}{H_L+\lambda}$ represents the effect obtained by the left subtree, $\frac{G_R^2}{H_R+\lambda}$ represents the effect obtained by the right subtree, $\frac{(G_L+G_R)^2}{H_L+H_R+\lambda}$ represents the effect produced by the tree before the partition, and represents the cost of complexity caused by adding new nodes.

6.1 Xgboost Prediction and Result Analysis

The predicted value and mean square error are shown in Table 4.

Table 4. Xgboost mean square error

xgboost mean square error	所用时间
0.322	5.05

Table 5. Comparison of prediction results

	Normal equation	gradient descent	Ridge regression	xgboost
Mean square error	0.534	1.766	0.529	0.322
Frequently used	0.14 s	0.06 s	0.15 s	5.05 s

It can be seen that the mean square error of the normal equation is 0.322, and the training model often uses 5.05 s. At this time, use Matplotlib to use the first 100 data of the predicted value and the target value as a line graph. The results are as follows in Fig. 11:

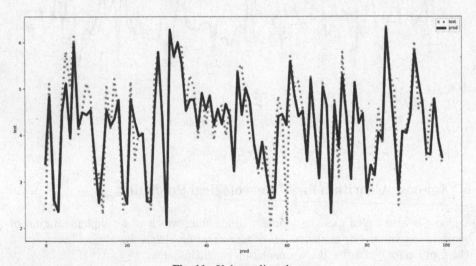

Fig. 11. Xgboost line chart

7 Conclusion

According to the mean square error analysis and the comprehensive analysis of the scatter chart and line chart, although the time of xgboost model is longer than that of other algorithms, its mean square error is 0.322, which is far lower than the values of 0.534, 1.766 and 0.529 of the other three algorithms. The parameter adjusted by xgboost this time is max_ depth = 5, learning_ rate = 0.1, n_ estimators = 160. It has a strong practical significance in atmospheric prediction and can achieve a relatively ideal effect.

References

1. Hanyang, L.Y., Pan, Y., Zhou, Q., Yang, A.: A comparative study of SVM, BP neural network and linear regression. J. North China Univ. Sci. Technol. (Nat. Sci. Ed.) (02) (2017)
2. Wang, C.: Research on new stock prediction and strategy application based on machine learning classification algorithm. Zhejiang University (2018)

Image Segmentation Based on Fuzzy Method

Yan Li[1($\boxtimes$)], Decheng Yang[1], Baojin Zhang[2], Zhuo Zhai[3], and Zhixu Luo[4]

[1] Heihe University, Heihe 164300, Heilongjiang, China
495287146@qq.com
[2] Internet of Things Engineering Class 1, 2020762061, Heihe University, Heihe 164300,
Heilongjiang, China
[3] Internet of Things Engineering Class 2, 2020762026, Heihe University, Heihe 164300,
Heilongjiang, China
[4] Communication Engineering Class 1, 2020752057, Heihe University, Heihe 164300,
Heilongjiang, China

Abstract. Image is an important means for human to cognize the world, and image processing technology is also a key research direction in machine learning. In image processing technology, image segmentation is a very critical part of the current academic research hotspot. At present, the fuzzy C-means clustering (FCM) algorithm of image segmentation algorithm uses iterative method to classify samples, which needs less storage space and time. However, FCM algorithm also has many shortcomings, how to use clustering algorithm for real-time, automatic, high-quality image segmentation, has been a problem to be solved. In order to solve the massive data of color image, this paper uses the SLIC method to calculate the super-pixel image over-segmentation. Direct processing of the huge amount of information contained in a color image will degrade the performance of the algorithm. Therefore, image preprocessing is very important.

Keywords: Fuzzy Clustering · Image Segmentation · Super Pixel

1 Introduction

FCM algorithm information technology gradually penetrates into daily life, leading the Hth Industrial Revolution to develop rapidly, the impact is growing. In the 21st century, with the rapid development of computer and microelectronics, the sensor system using W to collect and transmit data has gradually become the most competitive means of production. Image segmentation is an important technique of image engineering, which is used to extract interesting objects from images. Imaging engineering is a new subject, which involves all aspects of imaging. Image engineering can be divided into three interrelated parts [1]: the essence of image segmentation is to classify the pixels of the image, extract the pixel categories we need, and discard the unnecessary categories, which is the fundamental goal of image segmentation. But without prior knowledge, computer can only segment image by texture, edge, space characteristic and interaction of pixels. The difference between computer and human brain makes the distinction between image and background more complex.

© ICST Institute for Computer Sciences, Social Informatics and Telecommunications Engineering 2023
Published by Springer Nature Switzerland AG 2023. All Rights Reserved
X. Jiang (Ed.): MLICOM 2022, LNICST 481, pp. 158–163, 2023.
https://doi.org/10.1007/978-3-031-30237-4_15

2 Image Segmentation and Clustering Algorithm

In reality, image segmentation often lacks prior knowledge, and there is no segmented image for W. Because the method is based on the information contained in the segmented image itself, the segmentation can be effectively realized by clustering the pixels.

The aim of image segmentation is to replace part of human visual discriminant function with computer and analyze image attributes quantitatively with relevant tools. W can be used to solve the problem of image segmentation because W has two bases: first, the natural image itself has the characteristics of non-uniformity and relationship blur, which is embodied in the pixels of different regions. Therefore, fuzzy clustering is an effective analysis tool for image segmentation and its related fields.

3 Traditional Fuzzy Clustering Algorithm

The traditional FCM method mainly determines the range of each data point according to the size of membership degree, and its advantage is that it can deal with the normally distributed data clusters. This method has better convergence, so the fuzzy membership matrix obtained by this method has better consistency, but its disadvantage is that it can not cluster effectively if the data contains noise. This method is strongly dependent on the initial clustering center, and it is based on the whole situation. It is time-consuming and inefficient under large amount of data.

To solve these problems, this paper proposes several improved fuzzy clustering algorithms. PCM is an exhaustive search algorithm which uses membership constraints to improve clustering performance. However, PCM algorithm must have a good partition to ensure the correct classification. But the complexity of AFCM is also increased, because the clustering algorithm, which changes the scale of data, becomes very sensitive and easy to produce poor clustering effect, so its application range is not large. From the above results, we can see that the improved fuzzy clustering method has its own advantages, but also has its limitations, and needs to be further improved.

4 Algorithms

The use of SLIC is easy to understand. By default, the only parameter of this algorithm is k, meaning those super pixels that are almost the same size. In the classification of CIELAB color images, initialization is carried out at first. Here k initial centers are written into the images, and regular grids with S-pixels are sampled. To generate a superpixel of roughly the same size, the grid spacing is used here. Move the center to the minimum gradient corresponding to the region adjacent to 3×3. This is to avoid placing superpixels on edges and to reduce the possibility of receiving superpixels using noise pixels.

Next, in the assignment phase, each pixel i is associated with the nearest cluster center, which overlaps with the cluster center, as shown in Figs. 1, 2. This is important to speed up our algorithm because the limited search range significantly reduces the number of distance calculations, and each pixel must be compared to the full cluster compared to the traditional kmeans cluster. Only as described in section III-B can D be

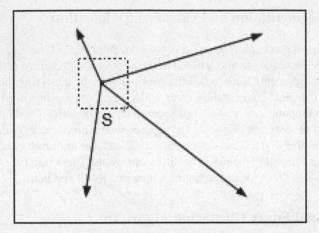

Fig. 1. The entire image is searched with stand k-means.

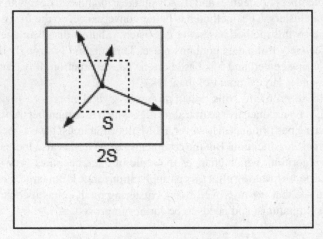

Fig. 2. Slic looks for a confined area.

determined by measuring the distance of the nearest cluster center of each pixel. Because the expected spatial range of superpixels is about the area of S * S, similar pixels are searched within 2Sx2S around the superpixel center.

Figure 2 Narrowing the Superpixel Search Area. When the traditional k- average algorithm is O (kNI), the complexity of SLIC is linear in O (N), where I is the number of repetitions. This provides a search space for each cluster center during the assignment phase. (a) In the traditional k-averaging algorithm, the distance from each cluster center to each pixel in the image. (b) SLIC calculates only the distance of pixels in the cluster center to the 2Sx2S region. Note that the required hyperpixel size is only S * S, represented in smaller squares. The algorithm can not only shorten the distance operation, but also make the complexity of SLIC independent of the number of superpixels.

Once each pixel is related to the nearest cluster center, the update step adjusts the cluster center to the average vector of all pixels belonging to the cluster here to write the image description [lab xy] T. By using L2 norm, the residual error E is calculated for the new cluster center position and the former one. It is possible to assign and update iteratively until the error converges, but we have found 10 iterations that are sufficient for most images. Finally, in the post-processing stage, the disjoint pixels are reassigned to adjacent hyperpixels to realize the connection. This algorithm summarizes the whole algorithm.

Algorithm SLIC super pixel segmentation
/* Initialize */
Initialize Ck = [lkakbk xk yk] with step s sampling pixels.
The cluster center is moved to the minimum gradient of 3×3.
Set flag l (i) = −1 for each pixel i.
Set distance d (i) = ∞ per pixel.
Repetition.
/* Allocation */
For each cluster center Cr.
For each pixel i in the 2S * 2S region around a Ck.
Calculate distance between Ck and i.
IfD < d (i) then.
Set up d (i) = D.
Set up l (i) = k.

SLIC super pixels correspond to clusters on the labxy color image plane. This raises the problem of defining distance measurement D, which is not immediately obvious. In algorithm 1, the distance between pixel i and cluster center Ck is calculated. In the CIELAB color space [ab] ^{T}, the colors of pixels are indicated with a known range of values. On the other hand, the value range of pixel [x, y] ^{T} changes as the image size changes. If D is simply expressed as a five-dimensional Euclidean distance, the clustering behavior of different superpixel sizes will be inconsistent. For large pixels, their spatial distance is greater than the affinity of color, and their relative importance is greater than color. This creates a compact superpixel that does not adhere well to the edges of the image. If it's smaller, the opposite happens.

To combine these two distances into a single measurement, you must use their maximum distance N and N. Used to standardize color proximity and spatial proximity. Write D as.

$$dc = [(Lk − Li)^2 + (ak − ai)^2 + (bk − bi)^2]0.5$$
$$ds = [(Xi − Xk)^2 + (Yk − Yi)^2]0.5 \qquad (1)$$
$$d = d\_lab + (m/S) * d\_xy$$

The expected maximum spacing in a given cluster should correspond to the sampling interval, $N_s = S = \sqrt{N/k}$. It is not easy to determine the maximum color distance for N_c because of the apparent difference in color distance from cluster to cluster and from image to image. Fixing nc to a constant m solves this problem, 1 becomes

$$D = \sqrt{d_c^2 + \left(\frac{d_s}{s}\right)^2 m^2} \tag{2}$$

This simplifies the distance measurement we use in practice

$$D' = \sqrt{\left(\frac{d_c}{m}\right)^2 + \left(\frac{d_s}{s}\right)^2} \tag{3}$$

By defining D in this way, m also allows us to measure the relationship between color similarity and spatial proximity. When m is larger, the higher the spatial proximity, the denser the resulting superpixel (that is, its area to perimeter ratio is smaller).

Within m hours, the resulting superpixels are more likely to stick to the edges of the image, but smaller in size and shape.

If the CIELAB color space is used, the range of m is [1, 40]. Equation 3 sets dc = to dc = suitable for grayscale images. The method can also be extended to deal with 3D supervoxels, for example, in Fig. 3, where the Eq. 3 contains depth dimensions to spatial proximity terms.

$$d_8 = \sqrt{(x_i - x_j)^2 + (y_i - y_j) + (z_i - z_j)^2} \tag{4}$$

5   Experimental Results and Analysis

SLIC, like other superpixel algorithms, is not required. At the end of the cluster processing, some "isolated" pixels may be retained that are not their cluster centers. To correct this, the nearest cluster center tag is assigned to these pixels using the join composition algorithm.

SLIC avoids thousands of redundant distance operations by locating clusters. Actually, the pixel value is below zero. Near the g cluster centers, SuIc is O (N) complex. In contrast, the conventional k-means algorithm has an upper bound of O (kN), while the actual time complexity is O (kNI), and 1 is an iterative number requiring convergence. At present, there are some schemes, i. e., prime sampling, random sampling, local clustering exchange, and lower and upper bounds, to reduce k mean complexity. SLIC is designed for superpixel clustering. Finally, compared with most of the superpixel algorithms and the K-average algorithm mentioned above, the complexity of SLIC is linear in terms of the number of pixels and independent of k.

6   Concluding Remarks

Superpixels are a very useful tool, and this article introduces you to the features of modern superpixel technology. Five current optimal super pixel algorithms are compared. In addition, a new clustering algorithm based on kmeans is introduced, which is better than the existing super pixel algorithm in every aspect.

The image is segmented by generalized fuzzy clustering method and compared with the traditional fuzzy clustering method. By reducing the initialization requirement, the operation speed is improved and the good segmentation effect of clustering algorithm is ensured, which proves the effectiveness of this method.

References

1. Zhang, L., Yang, S., Li, M., et al.: Application of automatic random walk algorithm based on fast FCM clustering in infrared image segmentation. Electronic World. **10**, 3 (2020)
2. Shai, A., Ariel, S.: Seam carving for content-aware image resizing. ACM Trans. Graph. (SIGGRAPH), **26**(3), 2007
3. Yang, Y., Hallman, S., Ramanan, D., Fawlkes, C.: Layered Object DetectionforMulti-ClassSegmentation. In: Computer Visionand Pattern Recognition (CVPR) (2010)
4. Lucchi, A., Smith, K., Achanta, R., Lepetit, V., Fua, P.: A fully automated approach to segmentation of irregularly shaped cellular structures in em images. In: International Conference on Medical Image Computing and Computer Assisted Intervention (2010)
5. Chen, J., Xu, X., Lei, T., et al., Image segmentation algorithm based on generalized type II fuzzy clustering. J. Shaanxi Univ. Sci. Technol. **38**(1), 10 (2020)
6. Zhu, Z., Liu, Y.: Image segmentation algorithm integrating chaos optimization and improved fuzzy clustering. J. Electron. **48**(5), 10 (2020)

Design and Analysis
on U-VLC-CC-CDMA Systems

Yang Qiu[1], Yu-juan Si[1], Xiao-yu Yu[2(✉)], Yue-xin Chen[3], Zai-xin Lin[1],
Jing-yi Li[1], and Shu-ming Gu[1]

[1] Zhuhai College of Science and Technology, Zhuhai 519041, China
qiuy@zcst.edu.cn, siyj@jlu.edu.cn, SakuraTear@stu.zcst.edu.cn
[2] SUN YAT-SEN UNIVERSITY, Zhuhai 519082, China
yuxy69@mail.sysu.edu.cn
[3] Jilin University, Changchun 130012, China
cyx21@mails.jlu.edu.cn

Abstract. Visible light communication (VLC) has dual functions of communication and lighting, and is widely used in the next generation wireless communication field. A suitable multiple access method is needed in the multi-user scenario of visible light communication to eliminate interference. This paper designs a VLC code division multiple access (VLC-CDMA) using complementary codes (CCs). CCs have ideal autocorrelation and cross-correlation properties, which can be used to distinguish different users. The issues on periodicity and correlation of CCs in VLC-CDMA systems are discussed as preliminaries. The transmitter uses LEDs of different wavelengths to separate different sub-codes in the CCs. The compensation circuit is used to synthesize white light and realize equal gain combination of the received signals. The receiver uses a filter with different central wavelength to separate signals transmitted by different sub-codes and convert them into electrical signals. B/U and U/B modules at transmitter and receiver are designed to complete the conversion between unipolar signals and bipolar signals. The anti-interference performance and a theoretical analysis on BER are conducted to verify the effectiveness. In addition, we compare the performance of VLC-CDMA systems using CC, Walsh sequences and Gold sequences, which shows that VLC-CDMA system using CCs can eliminate multi-user and multi-path interference.

Keywords: Visible light communication · CDMA · Complementary code

The work presented in this article was sponsored in part by the 2022 Featured Innovation Projects of General Colleges and Universities of Guangdong Province, the 2022 Enhancement of Key Construction Discipline Research Ability Project of Guangdong Province, the Natural Science Foundation of Guangdong Province, the 2022 Education Science Planning Project of Guangdong Province (Nos. 2022KTSCX189, 2022ZDJS140, 2023A1515011302, 2022GXJK087) and the Doctoral Promotion Program of Zhuhai College of Science and Technology.

X. Jiang (Ed.): MLICOM 2022, LNICST 481, pp. 164–180, 2023.
https://doi.org/10.1007/978-3-031-30237-4_16

1 Introduction

Visible light communication (VLC) adopts indoor basic lighting facilities, which has dual functions of lighting and communication [1–3]. Visible light communication has many advantages, but we also need to pay attention to the challenges. In multi-user scenarios, such as shopping malls and supermarkets, a suitable multiple access method is needed to meet the requirements of multi-user communication [4,5].

Code division multiple access (CDMA) technology has the function of satisfying the simultaneous access of multiple users to the network [6–8]. Therefore, we use CDMA technologies to achieve multiple access in VLC, which is named as VLC-CDMA. However, indoor optical signal transmission belongs to scattering link, and multipath transmission will cause multipath interference to visible light CDMA system [9]. Therefore, it is necessary to adopt appropriate methods to eliminate or suppress multipath and multiuser interferences. VLC-CDMA technology inherits the advantages of CDMA technology in conventional CDMA wireless communications [10].

The performance of a communication system using CDMA technology is greatly affected by correlations of signature codes. The resistance to multipath interference for the system is determined by the autocorrelation characteristics of the signature codes. The cross-correlation characteristics of the two signature codes reflect the multiple access interference (MAI) between two users in the system [11]. Therefore, the expectation of the correlation characteristics for signature codes in the communication system using CDMA technology is: 1) Ideal autocorrelation characteristics, that is, the correlation function of each signature code has only one impulse function when zero shift, and function values are all zero in other shifts; 2) The ideal cross-correlation characteristic, that is, the function value of any two signature codes is zero at any shifts.

In VLC systems, the signal transmitted by the LED is required to be positive and real, so a polarity conversion module needs to be added before the signal is loaded into the LED [12]. A common unipolar processing method is to add DC offset at the transmitter and remove it at the receiver [13]. In this paper, the method of code conversion is used to realize the polarity conversion of signals. Unipolar processing is performed on spread signal, which can guarantee the signal entering LED is positive and real. Based on previous researches [14,15], the design method of transmitter and receiver of U-VLC-CC-CDMA system is proposed in this paper.

The above discussion requires us to propose a suitable VLC-CDMA system design. The main contributions of this paper are as follows.

1) In this work, we introduce unipolar VLC-CDMA using complementary codes, which is named as U-VLC-CC-CDMA system.
2) We design the transmitters and receivers for the U-VLC-CC-CDMA systems. The transmitter uses LEDs of different wavelengths to separate different subcodes in the CCs. The compensation circuit is used to synthesize white light and realize equal gain combination of the received signals. The receiver uses

a filter with different central wavelength to distinguish signals transmitted by different sub-codes and convert them into electrical signals. B/U and U/B modules at transmitter and receiver are designed to complete the conversion between unipolar signals and bipolar signals.

3) We analyze the anti-interference capability and BER of the designed U-VLC-CC-CDMA system. The performance of U-VLC-CDMA system with CCs, Walsh sequences and Gold sequences are compared in simulation results.

2   System Model

In this section, we analyze the preliminaries of CCs, which are used as the signature codes in the designed U-VLC-CC-CDMA system. Then, we introduce a VLC-CDMA system model, which includes transmitter, and receiver.

2.1   Preliminaries of CCs

Theorem 1. *The two sequences are* $\mathbf{a} = [a_1, a_2, \cdots, a_N]$ *and* $\mathbf{b} = [b_1, b_2, \cdots, b_N]$, *the length of the two sequences are both* N, *the aperiodic correlation function of two sequences can be expressed as [10]:*

$$\phi(\mathbf{a}, \mathbf{b}; \delta) = \begin{cases} \sum_{i=1}^{N-\delta} a_i b_{i+\delta}, & 0 \le \delta \le N-1 \\ \sum_{i=1}^{N+\delta} a_{i-\delta} b_i, & 1-N \le \delta < 0 \end{cases}. \tag{1}$$

Signature codes with aperiodic ideal correlation characteristics are more suitable for practical communication systems, which can eliminate multipath interference and multiple access interference in CDMA communication systems. Therefore, the aperiodic ideal correlation characteristics of signature codes play an important role in the performance of communication systems using CDMA technology [16].

Denote a family of complementary codes as $\mathcal{C}(K, M, N)$, where K is the number of complementary codes, M represents the number of sub-codes in each complementary code, and N is the length of sub-codes. The matrix $\mathbf{C}^{(k)}$ is used to represent the kth complementary code in a family of complementary codes, $k \in \{1, 2, \cdots, K\}$, namely:

$$\mathbf{C}^{(k)} = \begin{bmatrix} \mathbf{c}_1^{(k)} \\ \mathbf{c}_2^{(k)} \\ \vdots \\ \mathbf{c}_M^{(k)} \end{bmatrix} = \begin{bmatrix} c_{1,1}^{(k)} & c_{1,2}^{(k)} & \cdots & c_{1,N}^{(k)} \\ c_{2,1}^{(k)} & c_{2,2}^{(k)} & \cdots & c_{2,N}^{(k)} \\ \vdots & \vdots & \ddots & \vdots \\ c_{M,1}^{(k)} & c_{M,2}^{(k)} & \cdots & c_{M,N}^{(k)} \end{bmatrix}, \tag{2}$$

where $\mathbf{c}_m^{(k)}$ represents the mth sub-code in the complementary code, $m \in \{1, 2, \cdots, M\}$.

The autocorrelation function of the complementary code can be calculated through this group of sub-codes, thereby reflecting its ideal autocorrelation characteristics. Since the signal transmission in the actual communication system needs to adopt aperiodic form, it is necessary to express the correlation function $\rho(\mathbf{C}^{(k_1)}, \mathbf{C}^{(k_2)}; \delta)$ of the complementary codes $\mathbf{C}^{(k_1)}$ and $\mathbf{C}^{(k_2)}$ as the sum of the aperiodic correlation functions of M sub-codes in the two complementary codes, which is shown in (3), $k_1, k_2 \in \{1, 2, \cdots, K\}$. Many research works have proved that when the number of sub-codes M in a family of complementary codes $\mathcal{C}(K, M, N)$ is not less than the number of supported users K by the system, the complementary codes can be guaranteed to achieve aperiodic ideal correlation properties [10], namely :

$$\rho(\mathbf{C}^{(k_1)}, \mathbf{C}^{(k_2)}; \delta) = \sum_{m=1}^{M} \phi(\mathbf{c}_m^{(k_1)}, \mathbf{c}_m^{(k_2)}; \delta) = \begin{cases} MN, & \delta = 0, k_1 = k_2 \\ 0, & \text{elsewhere} \end{cases} . \quad (3)$$

Compared with the signature codes used in traditional wireless communication, the biggest feature of complementary codes is its multiple sub-codes structure. In an actual communication system, the information of each user will be transmitted using multiple sub-codes of a complementary code, and its ideal autocorrelation characteristics can be achieved through multiple sub-codes. The signature codes of multiple users also need to use corresponding multiple sub-codes for cross-correlation calculation, so as to achieve ideal cross-correlation characteristics.

2.2 Transmitter

The transmitters and modulation are LEDs and Binary Phase Shift Keying (BPSK) in the VLC-CDMA system. The system transmitter model is shown in Fig. 1. $b^{(k)}$ is the signal of the kth user after BPSK. Each user data is copied to M data streams, and $b_m^{(k)}$ is the mth data stream of the kth user, where $m \in \{1, 2, \cdots, M\}, k \in \{1, 2, \cdots, K\}$. A set of complementary codes $\mathcal{C}(K, M, N)$ are used as the signature codes for K users in the system. Assume that $\mathbf{C}^{(k)} = \{\mathbf{c}_m^{(k)}\}_{m=1}^{M}, k \in \{1, 2, \cdots, K\}$ is the signature code for user k, shown as (2).

Assume that there are K users in the system, and a CC is assigned for each user. M data streams of a user are multiplied by M sub-codes of a CC. Since LEDs in the VLC system use IM/DD modulation, there is no phase information. Therefore, there is no negative physical quantity, we need to do a polarization process of the signal before it is modulated to LED, as shown in Fig. 1. The B/U module converts bipolar signals into unipolar signals to adapt to the physical characteristics of the VLC system. Regarding the specific processing process of the B/U module, we will introduce it in the next section.

LEDs are used to transmit spread signal. $F_m, m \in \{1, 2, \cdots, M\}$ are the optical filter gain for the receiving end. $\gamma_m, m \in \{1, 2, \cdots, M\}$ are the PD response sensitivity. Therefore, we add compensator circuits for LEDs with the gains of $1/(F_m \times \gamma_m), m \in \{1, 2, \cdots, M\}$, which is power allocation of a single LED to include multi-chip LED. According to this, equal gain combination can be obtained at the receiver, which can achieve the ideal correlation characteristics of CCs.

A separate LED is assigned to each data stream for a user, which can guarantee LEDs work in the linear regions [6]. Different sub-codes for one user adopt LED with different wavelength, which can eliminate mutual interference between subcodes of the same user. The specific process is explained as follows.

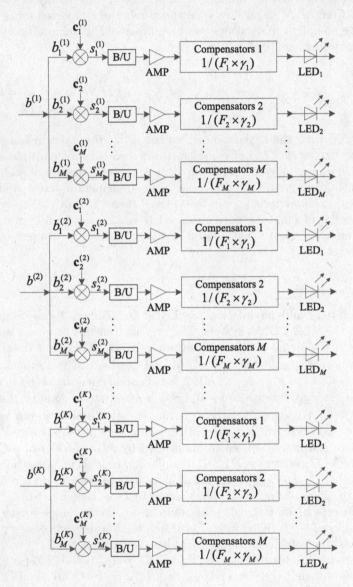

Fig. 1. Transmitters structure of the VLC-CC-CDMA system.

The spreading waveform of the mth sub-code for user k is

$$C_m^{(k)}(t) = \sum_{n=1}^{N} c_{m,n}^{(k)} q(t - nT_c + T_c), \qquad (4)$$

where $m \in \{1, 2, \cdots, M\}$, $n \in \{1, 2, \cdots, N\}$, $k \in \{1, 2, \cdots, K\}$, which are the same definitions in the rest of the paper. T_c is duration of one chip, $q(t)$ is chip pulse waveform with $q(t)$ being a rectangular pulse for simplicity, denoted as

$$q(t) = \begin{cases} \frac{1}{\sqrt{MNT_c}}, & 0 \leq t < T_c \\ 0, & \end{cases}. \qquad (5)$$

2.3 Receiver

We take the single user receiver structure as an example to analyze the system reception process, as shown in Fig. 2. The signal at the receiving end is the sum of all different LED signals. Bandpass filters are required to separate each data stream of different sub-code spread spectrum, which need to select filters with the same structure and different central wavelengths.

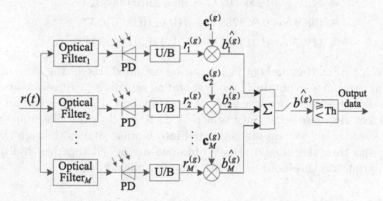

Fig. 2. Receivers structure of the VLC-CC-CDMA system with a single user.

The peak wavelengths of LEDs are: 400 nm, 450 nm, 507 nm, 545 nm, 600 nm, 650.2 nm, 700 nm and 750 nm, respectively. The FWHM are: 10 nm, 25 nm, 30 nm, 36 nm, 15 nm, 17.3 nm, 30 nm and 30 nm, respectively. Therefore, the bandpass filters at the receiver are assumed to be the model of Asahi Company [17], as shown in Table 1.

PDs are used to convert optical signals to electrical signals. For the chip of OSRAM Company, it is assumed that a silicon-based PIN photodetector BPX61 is used. On one hand, this chip is used in the experimental design literature, on the other hand, the photoelectric conversion efficiency value 0.53 A/W used in many literatures is consistent with this chip [1,7,18], and the chip has a high

Table 1. The chips and the parameters of the optical filters selected by receivers.

Optical filters	Center wavelength (nm)	FWHM (nm)	Transmission F (%)
ZBPA400	400±2	10±2	61.2262
ZBPB005	450±5	40±10	67.1512
ZBPB0026	500±5	40±10	67.5536
ZBPB050	550±5	40±10	74.0802
ZBPB090	600±5	20±10	78.6086
ZBPB124	650±5	40±10	77.2932
ZBPB146	700±5	60±10	84.1494
ZBPA750	750±3	12±3	87.0652

photoelectric conversion efficiency (maximum $0.62\,\mathrm{A/W}$) and a large viewing angle (110°). The response sensitivity values of different wavelengths can be obtained by the spectral sensitivity curve of the PDs, shown as,

$$
\begin{aligned}
\gamma(\lambda) = {} & -2031 - 2423\cos(0.003251\lambda) + 2449\sin(0.003251\lambda) \\
& + 47.08\cos(0.006502\lambda) + 1866\sin(0.006502\lambda) \\
& + 468.9\cos(0.009735\lambda) + 449\sin(0.009753\lambda) \\
& + 112.7\cos(0.013004\lambda) - 5.614\sin(0.013004\lambda).
\end{aligned} \tag{6}
$$

For chips from Hamamatsu [6, 19] can be assumed. Using the same method as BPX61, we can also obtain the corresponding sensitivity expression according to the response sensitivity curve given in the chip data. Therefore, we can obtain the different response sensitivity values at each wavelength. The unipolar signals received by the system are converted into bipolar signals through the U/B module, and then the bipolar signals obtained are added together and decided by an appropriate threshold to recover the transmitted data.

3   System Design and Analysis

In this section, we show the specific code conversion method through B/U and U/B for VLC-CC-CDMA system. Meanwhile, we give theoretical analysis on the ways to eliminate interference and derive BER.

3.1   U-VLC-CC-CDMA System

The main principle of polarity conversion of the U-VLC-CC-CDMA system is to remap the spread spectrum signal. If the spread signal "s" is positive, then map the signal to "$s0$, if the spread signal is negative, then map the signal to "$0|s|$, so as to ensure that the signal entering the LED is positive and real, which meets the requirements of the VLC system. Corresponding processes are performed at the receiver to restore it to a bipolar signal. The ideal correlation characteristics of the complementary code are used to restore the signal. This parallel method needs to use two times different wavelengths of LEDs, half of the LEDs are used to transmit the first one of each pair of data, and the other half of the LEDs are used to transmit the second one of each pair of data. The detailed processing procedure is as follows.

Transmitter: Assuming that the system uses the modulation method of BPSK, the modulated signal is bipolar after multiplying by the signature code. A code conversion process is required to meet the requirements of the VLC system, that is, the B/U module in Fig. 1. The signal becomes unipolar through the B/U module. The signal passing through the B/U module is represented by the symbol $s_{m_{\mathrm{PU}}}^{(k)}$, then the parallel signals $s_{m_{\mathrm{PU1}}}^{(k)}(t)$ and $s_{m_{\mathrm{PU2}}}^{(k)}(t)$ can be expressed as (7) and (8). Figure 3 shows a schematic diagram of a unipolar transformation.

$$s_{m_{\mathrm{PU1}}}^{(k)}(t) = \begin{cases} s_m^{(k)}(t), & s_m^{(k)}(t) > 0 \\ 0, & s_m^{(k)}(t) < 0 \end{cases}. \tag{7}$$

$$s_{m_{\mathrm{PU2}}}^{(k)}(t) = \begin{cases} 0, & s_m^{(k)}(t) > 0 \\ -s_m^{(k)}(t), & s_m^{(k)}(t) < 0 \end{cases}. \tag{8}$$

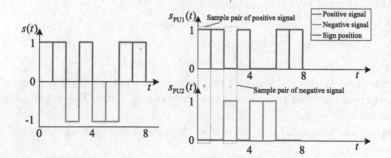

Fig. 3. The unipolar signals are changed from bipolar signals by parallel paired transform.

Therefore, the two parallel signals after the unipolar transformation are:

$$\begin{cases} s^{(k1)}(t) = \sum_{m=1}^{M} s_{m_{\mathrm{PU1}}}^{(k)}(t) S_{m1}(\lambda) \frac{1}{F_{m1}\gamma_{m1}} \\ s^{(k2)}(t) = \sum_{m=1}^{M} s_{m_{\mathrm{PU2}}}^{(k)}(t) S_{m2}(\lambda) \frac{1}{F_{m2}\gamma_{m2}} \end{cases}, \tag{9}$$

where $S_{m1}(\lambda)$ is the spectral expression of the first LED in the mth channel, and $S_{m2}(\lambda)$ is the spectral expression of the second LED in the mth channel [21]. $\lambda = ct$, c is the speed of light, F_{m1} and γ_{m1} are the gain of the first filter and photodetector in the mth path, F_{m2} and γ_{m2} are the gain of second filter and photodetector in the mth path.

Receiver: through optical filters and photodetectors and adding noise to the signal, the mth signal of the gth user is transmitted by two channels from the transmitter, $r_{m\text{PU}1}^{(g)}$ and $r_{m\text{PU}2}^{(g)}$ are shown as

$$\begin{cases} r_{m\text{PU}1}^{(g)}(t) = \sum_{k=1}^{K} h_m^{(k1)}(t) s_{m\text{PU}1}^{(k)}(t - \tau_k) + n_{m1}(t) \\ r_{m\text{PU}2}^{(g)}(t) = \sum_{k=1}^{K} h_m^{(k2)}(t) s_{m\text{PU}2}^{(k)}(t - \tau_k) + n_{m2}(t) \end{cases}, \qquad (10)$$

where τ_k is the delay of the mth data stream on user k.

It is necessary to use the inverse transformation of the code to convert the unipolar signal into a bipolar signal before despread, which is shown as the U/B module in Fig. 2. The paired detection signal recovery method of the U-VLC-CC-CDMA system is: subtract the second bit from the first bit of each pair of data, and the result obtained is the original signal. The processed signal $r_m^{(g)}$, shown as

$$r_m^{(g)}(t) = r_{m\text{PU}1}^{(g)}(t) - r_{m\text{PU}2}^{(g)}(t)$$

$$= \sum_{k=1}^{K} h_m^{(k1)}(t) s_{m\text{PU}1}^{(k)}(t - \tau_k) + n_{m1}(t) - \left[\sum_{k=1}^{K} h_m^{(k2)}(t) s_{m\text{PU}2}^{(k)}(t - \tau_k) + n_{m2}(t) \right]. \qquad (11)$$

Generally, it is assumed that the channel state information passed by the two LEDs in each channel are the same, that is, $h_m^{(k1)}(t) = h_m^{(k2)}(t) = h_m^{(k)}(t)$ [21–23]. Therefore, (11) can be expressed as:

$$r_m^{(g)}(t) = \sum_{k=1}^{K} h_m^{(k)}(t) s_m^{(k)}(t - \tau_k) + n_{m1}(t) - n_{m2}(t). \qquad (12)$$

At the end, M data streams of one user are added together and decided by an appropriate threshold to recover the transmitted data. The detail analysis is given as follows.

Step 1: The despread process of the jth data of the mth data stream for the gth user.

The electrical signals are converted from optical signals by PDs. The CC for user k is used to despread data streams of the use g. Assume that the receiver and signals of the user g can achieve ideal synchronization, and the despread results is

$$\widehat{b}_m^{(g)}(j) = \int_0^{NT_c} r_m^{(g)}(t + jT_b + \tau_g) C_m^{(g)}(t) \mathrm{d}t$$

$$= \sqrt{P_t} h_m^{(g)} b^{(g)}(j) + I_m^{(g)} + v_m, \qquad (13)$$

where τ_g is the delay of the mth data stream of user g. The simplification of (13) includes three terms. The first item shows the despread results of the jth data on the mth data stream of user g. The last term is the noise, which is still an additive Gaussian process. $I_m^{(g)}$ expresses the interference for the mth data stream of the user g from other users as

$$I_m^{(g)} = \sum_{k=1,k\neq g}^{K} \sqrt{P_t} h_m^{(k)} \left\{ \alpha_m^{(k)} b_m^{(k)}(j) + \beta_m^{(k)} b_m^{(k)} \left[j + \mathrm{sgn}(\delta_k) \right] \right\}, \qquad (14)$$

where sgn(x) is "1" when $x \geq 0$, and is "-1" when $x < 0$. δ_k is the relative delay of the mth data stream between the kth and the gth users, $\delta_k = (\tau_g - \tau_k)/T_c$. The values of $\alpha_m^{(k)}$ and $\beta_m^{(k)}$ are determined as

$$\begin{cases} \delta_k > 0: \alpha_m^{(k)} = \phi(\mathbf{c}_m^{(g)}, \mathbf{c}_m^{(k)}; \delta_k), & \beta_m^{(k)} = \phi(\mathbf{c}_m^{(k)}, \mathbf{c}_m^{(g)}, N - \delta_k) \\ \delta_k < 0: \alpha_m^{(k)} = \phi(\mathbf{c}_m^{(k)}, \mathbf{c}_m^{(g)}; -\delta_k), & \beta_m^{(k)} = \phi(\mathbf{c}_m^{(g)}, \mathbf{c}_m^{(k)}, N + \delta_k) \\ \delta_k = 0: \alpha_m^{(k)} = \phi(\mathbf{c}_m^{(g)}, \mathbf{c}_m^{(k)}; 0), & \beta_m^{(k)} = 0 \end{cases} \qquad (15)$$

where $\phi(\mathbf{a}, \mathbf{b}; \delta)$ is the non-periodic correlation function of $\mathbf{a}$ and $\mathbf{b}$, which is defined as (1).

Step 2: The combination of the M data streams. The M data streams of the gth user can achieve equal gain combination, which is shown as

$$\widehat{b}^{(g)}(j) = \sum_{m=1}^{M} \widehat{b}_m^{(g)}(j) = \sqrt{P_t} \sum_{m=1}^{M} h_m^{(g)} b_m^{(g)}(j) + I^{(g)} + V, \qquad (16)$$

where $I^{(g)}$ and V are the interference and noise terms, respectively. Based on this result, we present theoretical analysis on anti-interference characteristics and BER in Sect. 3.2.

Step 3: Data recovered with an appropriate threshold.

In this step, we usually set the appropriate threshold as 0 in simulations, so we can obtain jth data on the mth data stream and recover the M data streams for user g.

3.2   Theoretical Analysis on Elimination of Interference and BER

Assume that the system in the case of flat fading, that is, $h_1^{(g)} = h_2^{(g)} = \cdots = h_M^{(g)} = h^{(g)}$. From (13), the final decision threshold that can detect the ith data of user g is

$$\widehat{b}^{(g)}(i) = M\sqrt{P_t} h^{(g)} b^{(g)}(i) + I_U^{(g)} + V_U. \qquad (17)$$

Analysis on Elimination of Interference: Let us analyze the interference term $I_U^{(g)}$ in (17). We have

$$I_U^{(g)} = \sum_{m=1}^{M} I_m^{(g)}$$

$$= \sqrt{P_t} \sum_{m=1}^{M} \sum_{k=1,k\neq g}^{K} h_m^{(k)} \left\{ \alpha_m^{(k)} b_m^{(k)}(j) + \beta_m^{(k)} b_m^{(k)} \left[j + \mathrm{sgn}(\delta_k) \right] \right\}$$

$$= \sqrt{P_t} \sum_{k=1,k\neq g}^{K} \left\{ b^{(k)}(j)\Psi_1 + b^{(k)} \left[j + \mathrm{sgn}(\delta_k) \right] \Psi_2 \right\}, \qquad (18)$$

where $\Psi_1 = \sum_{m=1}^{M} h_m^{(k)} \alpha_m^{(k)}$ and $\Psi_2 = \sum_{m=1}^{M} h_m^{(k)} \beta_m^{(k)}$.

On the basis of VLC channel models in [21], we can see that the channels are flat and $h_1^{(k)} = h_2^{(k)} = \cdots = h_M^{(k)}$. Moreover, we have added compensator circuits in the transmitters. Therefore, the VLC-CC-CDMA system can realize an equal gain combining of all sub-codes through the correlation functions. Substitute (15) into Ψ_1 and Ψ_2. Comparing Ψ_1 and Ψ_2 with the correlation characteristics of CCs defined by (3), we can see that the $\Psi_1 = 0$ and $\Psi_2 = 0$. Thus, MAI can be eliminated completely using the above system assumption.

Derivation of BER: The third term in (13) is the noise term, $V = \sum_{m=1}^{M} v_m$. v_m is a statistical independent Gaussian random variable, whose sum is also a Gaussian random variable. Based on the previous analysis in [21], the expectation of noise is zero and its variance is

$$\text{var}[V] = \sigma_{\text{thermal}}^2 + \sigma_{\text{shot}}^2, \tag{19}$$

where $\sigma_{\text{thermal}}^2$ and σ_{shot}^2 are shown in (20) and (21), respectively.

$$\sigma_{\text{thermal}}^2 = \frac{8\pi k_B \mathcal{T}_\mathcal{K} \eta A_{\text{PD}} I_2 B^2}{\mathcal{G}} + \frac{16\pi^2 k_B \mathcal{T}_\mathcal{K} \varepsilon \eta^2 A_{\text{PD}}^2 I_3 B^3}{\mathfrak{g}}, \tag{20}$$

where k_B is Boltzmann constant, $\mathcal{T}_\mathcal{K}$ is absolute temperature, η is fixed capacitance per unit area of the PD, A_{PD} is the area of the PD, and I_2 is noise bandwidth factor. B is noise bandwidth equal to the value of data rate (R_b). $\mathcal{G}$ is open-loop voltage gain. ε is the channel noise factor of field effect transistor (FET), I_3 is noise bandwidth factor, and $\mathfrak{g}$ is the transconductance of the FET.

The variance of shot noise is usually $2e\gamma P_r B + 2e I_{bg} I_2 B$, where e is the electron charge, γ is the sensitivity of the PD, P_r is received optical power, and I_{bg} is background current [1,7]. However, in the proposed VLC-CC-CDMA system, the receivers have not only the sensitivity gains of PDs, but also the gains of the optical filters. We have added compensators with the gain of $1/F_m \gamma_m$ at the transmitters to compensate the gains of optical filters and PDs at the receiver. Therefore, we can not consider the gains of optical filters and PDs, and use P_r directly instead of γP_r. The variance of shot noise of each data stream can be modified as

$$\sigma_{\text{shot}}^2 = 2e P_r B + 2e I_{bg} I_2 B. \tag{21}$$

Let $P_t = \frac{E_b}{MNT_c}$. E_b is bit energy, and the system SINR can be obtained as

$$\text{SINR} = \frac{E_b}{\text{var}[I^{(g)}] + \text{var}[V]}. \tag{22}$$

As OOK modulation is used in the system, the bit error rate is

$$\text{BER}_{\text{OOK}} = Q\left(\sqrt{\frac{SINR}{2}}\right),$$

(23)

where, $Q(x)$ is expressed as

$$Q(x) = \frac{1}{2\pi}\int_x^\infty e^{\frac{-t^2}{2}}dt.$$

(24)

4 Simulation Details and Results

In this section, we show the simulation results of U-VLC-CDMA systems. We present and compare BER performances of U-VLC-CDMA systems with CC, Walsh sequences and Gold sequences.

4.1 Simulation Setup

The room model is assumed as $5 \times 5 \times 3$ m^3 and empty to eliminate intereference from other light sources. At the transmitter, four different LEDs can compose white light to achieve the duel function of lighting and communication. Optical signal is transmitted through indoor scattering link, and the channel model is discussed in [21]. The receiver is 2.15 m away from the transmitter and installed on a desktop with the height of 0.85 m. The data length is 10^6, the noise parameters are shown in Table 2.

We use $\mathcal{C}(4,8,4)$ as signature codes in the VLC-CC-CDMA system, i.e., the length of sub-codes (N) is 8, the number of sub-codes (M) is 4, and the number of users supported by each complementary code (K) is 4. We choose Walsh sequences and Gold sequences for a comparative experiment, which is widely used in CDMA systems. Specifically, the length of Walsh sequences (N) is 32, expressed as Walsh32. The length of Gold sequences (N) is 31, expressed as Gold31. Therefore, it is guaranteed that the processing gains MN of the three codes are the same. During system simulation, four user codes of Walsh32 and Gold31 are taken to ensure that they support the same number of users as the system using complementary codes.

According to the correlation function expression of (1), the correlation characteristics of $\mathcal{C}(4,8,4)$, Walsh32 and Gold31 used in the simulation are given. Figure 4 and Fig. 5 show their autocorrelation and cross-correlation function properties.

From Figs. 4 and 5, complementary codes have ideal autocorrelation and cross-correlation properties. The autocorrelation function of Gold31 is ideal and can resist multi-path interference. The cross-correlation function of Walsh32 has ideal characteristics and can resist multi-user interference. However, the even-periodic characteristics of signal propagation cannot be guaranteed, and a non-periodic scenario in general is usually assumed. Then, as shown in Figs. 4 and 5, neither Walsh sequences nor Gold sequences have ideal autocorrelation and cross-correlation properties at the same time. Therefore, the system using complementary codes has better resistance to multi-path and multi-user interference.

Table 2. Simulation Parameters.

Optical filters	Center wavelength (nm)
LEDs power	0.88 W
Semi-angle at half power ($\varphi_{1/2}$)	60°
Radiation angle (φ)	30°
FOV at a receiver	60°
Photodetector responsivity (γ_1, γ_2, γ_3, γ_4)	0.42, 0.25, 0.16, 0.35 A/W
Transmission of optical filter (F_1, F_2, F_3, F_4)	78.8%, 73.1%, 68.1,% 80.4%
Background light current (I_{bg})	5100 μA
Noise bandwidth factor 2 (I_2)	0.562
Noise bandwidth factor 3 (I_3)	0.0868
Detector area (A_{PD})	1 cm^2
Absolute temperature (T_K)	295 K
Boltzmann constant (k_B)	1.23×10^{-23} J/K
FET channel noise factor (ε)	1.5
Open-loop voltage gain ($\mathcal{G}$)	10
FET transconductance ($\mathfrak{g}$)	30 mS
Fixed capacitance (η)	112 pF/cm^2
Electron charge (e)	1.6×10^{-19} C

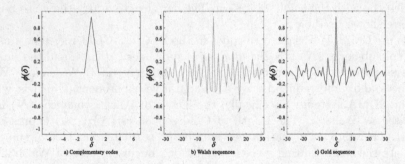

Fig. 4. Auto-correlation properties of $\mathcal{C}(4, 8, 4)$, Walsh32 and Gold31.

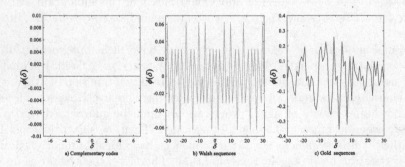

Fig. 5. Cross-correlation properties of $\mathcal{C}(4, 8, 4)$, Walsh32 and Gold31.

4.2   Simulation Results

In the simulation results of U-VLC-CC-CDMA system, the chip rate is 240 Mcps, and the data rates of systems using complementary codes, Walsh sequences and Gold sequences are 30 Mbps, 7.5 Mbps and 7.74 Mbps, respectively. The system adopts the parallel polarity conversion scheme, and the receiver adopts the method of subtracting the second bit from the first bit in each pair of values. The simulation results are shown in Figs. 6 and 7.

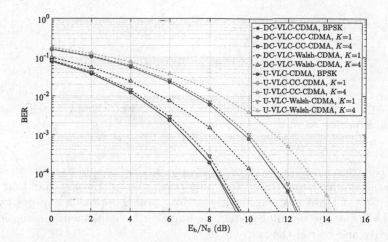

Fig. 6. BER performance of U-VLC-CDMA and DC-VLC-CDMA systems with CCs and Walsh sequences.

It can be seen from Figs. 6 and 7 that the system performance becomes better with the increase of the SNR. For obvious reasons, system performance can be improved by increasing the SNR. When the number of users $K=1$, the BER curves using complementary codes, Walsh sequences and Gold sequences are all coincident with the theoretical curves, which because there is no multi-user interference in the system. With the increase of the number of users, when $K = 4$, only the system BER using the complementary codes still basically coincides with the theoretical curves. The reason is that only the complementary codes can achieve the ideal autocorrelation and cross-correlation characteristics, which makes the system free from multi-path and multi-user interferences. However, the BER performance of Walsh sequences and Gold sequences will be deteriorated, which because the correlation characteristics of the two signature codes are not ideal, and they cannot resist multi-path and multi-user interferences. Since the chip rate is assumed to be the same in the simulation, the communication rate using the complementary codes is four times that of using the Walsh sequences and the Gold sequences.

In addition, in the U-VLC-CC-CDMA system, the parallel mode avoids the phenomenon of signal aliasing, therefore, the receiver can restore the original

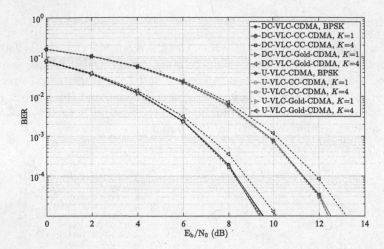

Fig. 7. BER performance of U-VLC-CDMA and DC-VLC-CDMA systems with CCs and Gold sequences.

signal. However, since the receiver adopts the method of subtracting two signals, the noise is doubled, and the system performance is 3 dB worse than that of the DC-VLC-CC-CDMA system. Moreover, this parallel approach requires twice as many LEDs as the original system assumption to implement, increasing the complexity and cost of the system.

It can be seen from the above analysis that the method of increasing the DC gain has the best system performance, but it needs to be assumed that the system delays an integer number of chips, and the same performance cannot be achieved in the system where multipath interference exists. It needs to be assumed that the LED still works in the linear operating region after increasing the DC bias, whose requirements for the system components are more stringent. The U-VLC-CC-CDMA system can avoid the phenomenon of signal aliasing at the receiver, but its noise amplification makes the system performance worse by half, and the demand for LEDs is doubled. Although this polarity conversion method can meet the requirements of the VLC system for signal polarity, its requirements are relatively strict. Therefore, it is expected that a more rationalized VLC-CDMA system can be further designed.

5   Conclusions

This paper mainly proposes a VLC-CDMA system using complementary codes, and studies its transmitter and receiver models. The transmitter with multiple sub-codes architecture is designed. The single-user receiver with multiple sub-codes structure despreading is presented.

Aiming at the requirement of non-negative signals in VLC systems, a polarity conversion module is added to the system to realize unipolar processing of signals. U-VLC-CC-CDMA system is proposed, and the parallel implementation of the system is studied. Theoretical analysis shows that the parallel method can restore the signal, but the performance is worse 3 dB than that of DC-VLC-CC-CDMA system due to noise amplification. The parallel method requires twice as many LEDs of different wavelengths, which increases the system overhead and the difficulty of LED device achievability. The system simulation shows that the simulation curves of the unipolar processing method using complementary codes coincide with the theoretical curves, while the unipolar processing method using the Walsh sequences and the Gold sequences cannot overlap the theoretical curves due to their imperfect correlation.

Acknowledgment. The work presented in this article was sponsored in part by the 2022 Featured Innovation Projects of General Colleges and Universities in Guangdong Province (Nos. 2022KTSCX189, ZLGC20220204) and the Doctoral Promotion Program of Zhuhai College of Science and Technology.

References

1. Komine, T., Nakagawa, M.: Fundamental analysis for visible-light communication system using LED lights. IEEE Trans. Consum. Electron. **50**(1), 100–107 (2004)
2. Memedi, A., Dressler, F.: Vehicular visible light communications: a survey. IEEE Commun. Surv. Tutorials **23**(1), 161–181 (2021)
3. Aboagye, S., Ngatched, T.M.N., Dobre, O.A.: Subchannel and power allocation in downlink VLC under different system configurations. IEEE Trans. Wireless Commun. **21**(5), 3179–3191 (2022)
4. Bariah, L., Elamassie, M., Muhaidat, S., et al.: Non-orthogonal multiple access-based underwater VLC systems in the presence of turbulence. IEEE Photonics J. **14**(1), 1–7 (2022)
5. Al Hammadi, A., Sofotasios, P.C., Muhaidat, S., et al.: Nonorthogonal multiple access for hybrid VLC-RF networks with imperfect channel state information. IEEE Trans. Veh. Technol. **70** (1), 398–411 (2021)
6. Qian, H., Dai, S.C., Zhao, S., Cai, S.Z., Zhang, H.: A robust CDMA VLC system against front-end nonlinearity. IEEE Photon. J. **7**(5), 7801809 (1–10) (2015)
7. Shoreh, M.H., Fallahpour, A., Salehi, J.A.: Design concepts and performance analysis of multicarrier CDMA for indoor visible light communications. J. Optical Commun. Netw. **7**(6), 554–562 (2015)
8. Chen, D., Wang, Q., Wang, J., et al.: Performance evaluation of ZCC and OZCZ code set in an integrated VLCP-CDMA system. IEEE Photonics Technol. Lett. **34**(16), 846–849 (2022)
9. Rahaim, M., Little, T.D.C.: Interference in IM/DD optical wireless communication networks. J. Optical Commun. Netw. **9**(9), D51–D63 (2017)
10. Chen Hsiao-Hwa: The Next Generation CDMA Technologies. 1st ed. John Wiley & Sons Ltd, (2007)
11. He, C., Yang, L.L., Xiao, P., Imran, M.A.: DS-CDMA assisted visible light communications systems. In: 20th IEEE International Workshop on Computer Aided Modeling and Design of Communication Links and Networks, pp. 27–32. IEEE, Guildford (2015)

12. Salvador, P., Valls, J., Corral, J.L., et al.: Linear response modeling of high luminous flux phosphor-coated white LEDs for VLC. J. Lightw. Technol. **40**(12), 3761–3767 (2022)

13. Salvador, P., Valls, J., Canet, M.J., et al.: On the performance and power consumption of bias-T based drivers for high speed VLC. J. Lightwave Technol. **40**(18), 6078–6086 (2022)

14. Tsonev, D., Sinanovic, Haas H: Novel unipolar orthogonal frequency division multiplexing (U-OFDM) for optical wireless. In: 75th IEEE Vehicular Technology Conference, pp. 1–5. IEEE, Yokohama (2012)

15. Wang, K., Liu, Y., Hong, Z., Zeng, Z.: Efficient timing offset estimation method tailored for ACO-OFDM VLC systems. J. Lightwave Technol. **40**(8), 2307–2320 (2022)

16. Mursley, P.: Performance evaluation for phase-coded spread-spectrum multiple-access communication cpart i: system analysis. IEEE Trans. Commun. **25**(8), 795–799 (1977)

17. Asahi Homepage. http://www.asahi-spectra.com/index.asp. Last accessed 20 Sept. 2022

18. Lausnay, S.D., Strycker, L.D., Goemaere, J.P., et al.: A test bench for a VLP system using CDMA as multiple access technology. In: 17th IEEE International Conference on Transparent Optical Networks, pp. 1–4. IEEE, Budapest (2015)

19. Cui, L., Tang, Y., Jia, H., et al.: Analysis of the multichannel WDM-VLC communication system. J. Lightwave Technol. **34**(24), 5627–5634 (2016)

20. Biagi, M., Pergoloni, S., Vegni, A.M.: LAST: A framework to localize, access, schedule, and transmit in indoor VLC systems. J. Lightwave Technol. **33**(9), 1872–1887 (2015)

21. Qiu, Y., Chen, H.-H., Li, J., Meng, W.: VLC-CDMA systems based on optical complementary codes. IEEE Wirel. Commun. **27**(1), 147–153 (2020)

22. Lee, K., Park, H., Barry, J.R.: Indoor channel characteristics for visible light communications. IEEE Commun. Lett. **15**(2), 217–219 (2011)

23. Komine, T., Lee, J.H., Haruyama, S., et al.: Adaptive equalization system for visible light wireless communication utilizing multiple white LED lighting equipment. IEEE Trans. Wireless Commun. **8**(6), 2892–2900 (2009)

Author Index

© ICST Institute for Computer Sciences, Social Informatics and Telecommunications Engineering 2023
Published by Springer Nature Switzerland AG 2023. All Rights Reserved
X. Jiang (Ed.): MLICOM 2022, LNICST 481, pp. 181–182, 2023.
https://doi.org/10.1007/978-3-031-30237-4

Printed in the United States
by Baker & Taylor Publisher Services